D0143248

Biodiversity and
Ecological Economics

DISCARD

Biodiversity and Ecological Economics

Participation, Values and Resource Management

Luca Tacconi

Earthscan Publications Ltd,
London and Sterling, VA

First published in the UK and USA in 2000
by Earthscan Publications Ltd

Copyright © Luca Tacconi, 2000

ISBN: 1 85383 676 1 paperback
      1 85383 675 3 hardback

Typesetting by PCS Mapping & DTP
Printed and bound in the UK by Creative Print and Design Wales, Ebbw Vale
Cover design by Susanne Harris

For a full list of publications please contact:

Earthscan Publications Ltd
120 Pentonville Road, London, N1 9JN, UK
Tel: +44 (0)20 7278 0433
Fax: +44 (0)20 7278 1142
Email: earthinfo@earthscan.co.uk
http://www.earthscan.co.uk

22883 Quicksilver Drive, Sterling, VA 20166-2012, USA

A catalogue record for this book is available from the British Library

Library of Congress Cataloging-in-Publication Data

Tacconi, Luca.
    Biodiversity and ecological economics: participatory approaches to resources
    management / Luca Tacconi.
        p. cm.
    Includes bibliographical references and index.
    ISBN 1-85383-675-3 (cloth) — ISBN 1-85383-676-1 (pbk.)
    1. Environmental economics. 2. Ecology—Economic aspects. 3. Conservation of
    natural resources—Economic aspects. 4. Biological diversity conservation. 5.
    Ecology—Economic aspects—case studies. 6. Biological diversity conservation—
    case studies. I. Title.

HC79.E5 T33 2000
333.7—dc21
                                                                        00-050405

Earthscan is an editorially independent subsidiary of Kogan Page Ltd and publishes in
association with WWF-UK and the International Institute for Environment and
Development

This book is printed on elemental chlorine-free paper

Contents

Part II Case Studies

List of Figures, Tables and Boxes

Figures

Tables

Boxes

The Contributors

Nancy Dahl-Tacconi is the scientific officer in the Marine Protected Areas section of Environment Australia (Federal Government Environment Agency) providing and coordinating scientific input to the design and management of marine protected areas. She has a background in marine biology and ecology, and some of her previous work includes commercial fishing in Alaskan waters, marine biological research at Shannon Point Marine Centre (Washington, USA), observer on domestic fishing vessels for the US National Marine Fisheries Service, and teaching science in Vanuatu. Email: nancy.dahl-tacconi@ea.government.au.

John Dargavel is a Visiting Fellow in the Research School of Social Sciences in The Australian National University and is President of the Australian Forest History Society. Email: john.dargavel@anu.edu.au.

Jim Davie is a Senior Lecturer in Tropical Forestry in the School of Natural and Rural Systems Management, University of Queensland. He has conducted research and also lived and worked in Indonesia for several years. Email: j.davie@mailbox.uq.edu.au.

Jon Erickson is assistant professor in the Economics Department at Rensselaer Polytechnic Institute in Troy, New York, where he is helping to build a PhD programme in Ecological Economics. His current research interests include land use sustainability, community quality of life, and international energy and greenhouse gas policy. Recent publications include papers in *Science*, *Ecological Economics*, *Land Economics*, *World Development*, and *Energy Policy*. He is currently the Vice President and President-Elect of the Adirondack Research Consortium. Email: erickj@rpi.edu.

Petrus Gunarso is a doctoral candidate in the School of Natural and Rural Systems Management, University of Queensland. He is on leave from the Indonesian Ministry of Forestry and Estate Crops, where he has worked for more than 10 years. Email: p.gunarso@mailbox.uq.edu.au.

Peter Kanowski is Professor and Head of the Department of Forestry at The Australian National University, and is Chair of the Forest Forum for the Southern region of New South Wales in the Regional Forest Agreement programme. Peter's research and teaching interests include forest policy and genetics. Email: peter.kanowski@anu.edu.au.

Sanghamitra Mahanty is a doctoral candidate in the Graduate Program in Environmental Management and Development, Australian National University. She has worked for over 5 years as a researcher and a practitioner on conservation and development programmes in the Asia-Pacific region, focusing on social assessment and participatory monitoring and evaluation. Her current research is based primarily in southern India, studying an Integrated Conservation and Development Project from an actor-oriented perspective. Email: s.mahanty@anu.edu.au.

Sabine O'Hara is Professor of Economics and Provost at Green Mountain College. Her work has been in ecological economics, environmental policy, social economics, and sustainable development both in the USA and abroad. Her recent research work has focused on the use of discursive stakeholder models for integrated economic and ecological valuation, and developing economic valuation concepts. Sabine has been active in developing innovative models for teaching economics to non-economists, and in developing multidisciplinary courses that focus on both theory and practical application. She has served on the committee on curriculum development of the International Society for Ecological Economics since 1995. Email: sohara@greenmtn.edu.

Wendy Proctor is a doctoral candidate in the Centre for Resource and Environmental Studies at The Australian National University, and is completing a thesis on multi-criteria analysis for natural resource decision-making. She has worked with the Australian Bureau of Agricultural and Resource Economics as a Senior Economist. Email: wendy@cres20.anu.edu.au.

Peter Taylor is the Director of the Commonwealth Marine Protected Areas Section of Environment Australia (The Australian Federal Government Environment Agency). Over the last 4 years he has established a team of multidisciplinary specialists who have built a programme for the declaration and management of multiple use marine protected areas. With a background in biology and in adult and continuing education, Peter has had a varied career which has included the initiation of a range of government reform agendas related to indigenous issues, rural and regional development, local area planning, protected area policy, and community education. Email: peter.taylor@ea.government.au.

Luca Tacconi is a Rural Development Adviser with the Australian Agency for International Development, where he works on a range of development and natural resource management issues. He has held research positions at the University of Queensland, University of New South Wales and the Australian National University. Email: luca_tacconi@ausaid.gov.au.

Michael Warner works in the fields of social development and environmental assessment/management. His experience lies in applying the tools of dispute management and consensus-building to multi-stakeholder negotiations between civil society, government and the private sector. He has been involved with community-based natural resource management over the last 10 years with the consultants Environmental Resources Management, with University College London, and as a Research Fellow with the Overseas Development Institute. He currently manages the Secretariat of the Natural Resources Cluster of Business Partners for Development, based at CARE International UK. Email: bpd@uk.care.org.

Disclaimer

The views expressed in this book are those of the authors and not necessarily those of the organizations they are affiliated with.

Acronyms and Abbreviations

APA	Adirondack Park Agency
ARC	Adirondack Research Consortium
BCN	Biodiversity Conservation Network
CBA	cost–benefit analysis
CBC	community-based conservation
CITES	Convention on International Trade in Endangered Species of Wild Fauna and Flora
EA	Environment Australia
ECE	ecological economics
EKPA	Erromango Kauri Protected Area
FAO	Food and Agriculture Organization of the United Nations
FPCD	Foundation for People and Community Development
GABMP	Great Australian Bight Marine Park
HBPT	Hutan Bakau Pantai Timur Strict Nature Reserve
HC	human capital
ICDP	Integrated Conservation and Development Project
IIED	International Institute for Environment and Development
IUCN	World Conservation Union
LDC	less-developed country
MC	manufactured capital
MOFEC	Ministry of Forestry and Estate Crops
MPAs	marine protected areas
NC	natural capital
NEE	neo-classical environmental economics
NGO	non-government organization
NNC	nonrenewable natural capital
NRSMPA	National Representative System of Marine Protected Areas
NTFPs	non-timber forest products
PA	protected area
PNG	Papua New Guinea
RNC	renewable natural capital
SMS	safe minimum standard
TEV	total economic value
UNCED	United Nations Conference on Environment and Development
UNEP	United Nations Environment Programme
USAID	United States Agency for International Development
WCMC	World Conservation Monitoring Center
WRI	World Resources Institute
WTP	willingness to pay

Part One

Methodology, Paradigms, Ethics and Participation

1

Introduction and Background

The tree which moves some to tears of joy
is in the eyes of others only a green thing
which stands in the way
(William Blake, written in 1799)

Introduction

The world-view we hold influences how we construe reality. Values shape our views and actions. They affect conceptions of nature, influence how people interact with other people and with the environment, impinge on the study of these interactions and the actions undertaken to address environmental issues. This book seeks to contribute to the conservation of biodiversity by developing an improved ecological economics framework – which takes into account present and future people's values, how they may be researched and addressed, and the problems encountered in doing this – and by presenting case studies that show how specific aspects of the theoretical framework are, or may be, put into practice, thus providing ideas for the improvement of biodiversity conservation activities.

Ecological economics is a relatively new field of study addressing the relationships between ecosystems and economic systems (Costanza et al, 1991) and has initially focused on bringing together the economics and ecology disciplines. Neo-classical economics, as noted by Hausman (1992), encounters many problems that of course can also affect ecological economics unless they are addressed:

> 'economics has not been very successful and has not made much empirical progress ... its empirical difficulties are legion, and, if the speculative thoughts of these pages are correct, it will never conquer them. So the case of economics might seem hopeless. But there are better ways forward ... I would urge economists to be more eclectic, more opportunistic ... and more willing to collaborate with other social scientists.' (Hausman, 1992, pp279–80)

Ecological economics needs to heed this message too, and increase the attention it pays to social (science) issues. As noted by Barry and Proops (1999), environmental policy-making involves three steps:

1   the identification of the problem;
2   the analysis of potentially effective policy responses to the problem; and
3   the implementation of these policies.

They stress that ecological economics has been rather good at the first two steps but the third has received relatively little attention in the literature. The processes involved in policy implementation receive detailed attention in the book, as well as step processes for the definition of problems and the analysis of policy responses. Social (science) issues are certainly important factors in all three steps. Because of the limited attention they have received in the past, greater consideration is devoted to social (science) issues – including research methodology and institutional aspects – than to economic instruments, which may be used to achieve biodiversity conservation. These instruments have been the focus of several studies (eg Barbier et al, 1994; Perrings et al, 1995).

This chapter sets the scene by providing background information about the physical and social nature of the problem. It begins with a description of the current understanding of the functions and status of biodiversity, and a brief sketch of the global situation in forest and marine ecosystems. The proximate and underlying causes of biodiversity loss are considered before addressing the functions of protected areas (PAs), and the problems associated with their establishment and management. The chapter concludes with an outline of the book.

Biodiversity: Its Functions and Status

The term biodiversity refers to the diversity of life at all levels and it embodies the linkages between these different levels of the biological hierarchy (Wilson, 1992a). This is the meaning of biodiversity adopted in the Convention on Biodiversity ratified in June 1992 at the United Nations Conference on Environment and Development (UNCED) in Rio de Janeiro (United Nations Environment Programme (UNEP), 1993). The term biodiversity has also been used with the all-encompassing meaning of the 'totality of biological resources' (eg McNeely et al, 1990). Problems may arise in analysing biodiversity issues if this dual meaning is not recognized (Chapter 4).

Biodiversity is commonly considered at the genetic, species and ecosystems levels.[1] *Genetic diversity* may be considered at different levels (eg population) and it provides the basis for speciation. The productivity and resilience of populations may be related to their genetic composition. *Species diversity* refers to the number of species within a specific area. The existence of populations of a species in geographically and environmentally distinct areas is considered important in order to maintain diversity in the gene pool and to protect the species as a whole against events such as isolated epidemics of disease and predators that could exterminate entire populations (Norton, 1987). *Ecosystem diversity* refers to the variety of biotic communities and habitats, and to the diversity within ecosystems. Ecosystem diversity is normally considered at the landscape and regional level. At the landscape level, diversity includes a variety of ecosystems and is important due to the biogeographical characteristics (eg patterns, juxtapositions and interconnectedness) that allow for the free movement of individuals and for the maintenance of the shifting patterns of ecosystems (Noss and Harris, 1986).

Ecological research has greatly furthered knowledge of the complex aspects of biodiversity, such as ecosystem changes, habitat patchiness, and the role of natural and human-induced disturbances on biota (eg Reid and Miller, 1989). However, many fundamental questions about several aspects regarding the specific levels – and their linkage – at which biodiversity may be considered remain unanswered. The impacts of habitat fragmentation on genetic diversity and how biodiversity influences the ability of ecosystems to withstand stress are poorly known; so are the impacts of landscape fragmentation on the functioning of ecosystems, population viability and the functions and activities of many individual species (Ehrlich and Daily, 1993; Meyer, 1993; Perrings et al, 1992; Solbrig, 1991).

Despite this lack of knowledge about various aspects of biodiversity, ecologists tend to stress that a major function of biodiversity is the maintenance of ecosystem resilience[2] (eg Jørgensen, 1990). Thus, a challenge for biodiversity conservation is the maintenance of those ecosystem functions that generate ecological services and make ecosystems resilient to change. These ecosystem functions and services support life on Earth and contribute to the betterment of human welfare.

Economic aspects of biodiversity will be considered in Chapter 4. Here, it is sufficient to remark that the maintenance of biodiversity provides important economic benefits such as the maintenance of genetic material used for pharmaceutical purposes and plant breeding.[3]

The approximate state of biodiversity at the biosphere level may be understood by considering the trends affecting species diversity. The number of existing species is thought to be between 5 and 100 million, with a suggested conservative estimate of 12.5 million (World Conservation Monitoring Center (WCMC), 1992). The human-induced extinction rate is thought to be between 100 to 1000 times the non-human-induced rate (Reid and Miller, 1989). If current trends in biodiversity loss continue, the resulting extinction rates have been estimated to range between 10 per cent and 50 per cent of all species over the next 50–100 years (Bawa et al, 1991; Panel of the Board on Science and Technology for International Development, 1992; Reid, 1992; UNEP, 1992).[4]

Forests

Forests may initially be divided into the two major groupings of temperate forests and tropical forests. The latter category may be subdivided into tropical moist forests[5] and tropical dry forests. Tropical moist forests are then further subdivided into rainforests, deciduous forests and mangroves; rainforests account for about 50 per cent of all tropical forests and are the most diverse (Collins et al, 1991; Sayer et al, 1992; Sharma et al, 1992; Vanclay, 1993). The Food and Agricultural Organization (FAO, 1995) reports that:

- the global area covered by forests in 1990 was estimated at about 3.4 billion hectares;
- tropical forests covered about 1.715 billion hectares;
- rainforests accounted for 656 million hectares;
- deciduous forests covered 626 million hectares;
- during the 1980s, tropical forests decreased at a rate of 16.9 million hectares per year – a rate of 0.9 per cent per year.

Forests have a variety of ecological functions and provide a multitude of materials and services to human beings. They harbour a large genetic pool, they have positive effects on hydrological cycles, and they contribute to the regulation of the climate (Brown, 1998). Forests are a source of timber and non-timber forest products (NTFPs).[6] They are objects with religious value, cultural value and aesthetic value. Forests are also a medium for research and education (Jacobs, 1988).

Tropical moist forests are particularly important from a biodiversity conservation point of view. They are thought to harbour 50–90 per cent of all existing species (Reid and Miller, 1989; Wilson, 1988). The role of forests in climate stabilization is evidenced by the fact that tropical forests store more than 50 per cent of the Earth's organic carbon stock (Rowe et al, 1992). They report that between 1–3 billion tonnes of carbon are released annually into the atmosphere as a result of tropical forest burning, compared to 5.6 billion tonnes released from the use of fossil fuels. The other important function of forests noted above has to do with the regulation of the hydrological cycle. Brooks et al (1992) note that forests in their natural state tend to yield the highest quality water of any ecosystem, produce the lowest erosion and sedimentation rates and generate a more uniform streamflow in a watershed than any other vegetation cover. Calder (1998) reviews several *myths* about land use (particularly forests) and hydrology. Among other issues, the study finds that plantations may increase soil erosion and that there is little scientific evidence that deforestation causes increased flooding.

Marine Systems

The sea covers about 71 per cent of the Earth's surface; about 51 per cent of the surface is covered by ocean deeper than 3000 metres (WCMC, 1992). From an ecological point of view, marine ecosystems may be classified as benthic and pelagic,[7] but from a management perspective they are more appropriately defined as coastal and oceanic (Thorne-Miller and Catena, 1991).

These authors provide the following summary of ecosystems.

Coastal ecosystems may be categorized as:

- coastal benthic ecosystems are found where the land meets the sea, and include rocky intertidal and subtidal shores, sandy shores and mud flats, estuaries and wetlands, coral reefs, subtidal coastal shelf;
- coastal pelagic ecosystems include coastal shelf waters with maximum depths of around 1000 metres;
- coastal basins are enclosed or semi-enclosed sea such as the Gulf of Mexico and the Mediterranean Sea.

Oceanic biomes are defined by depth and major permanent currents; they may be subdivided into deep-sea benthic (below 1000 metres), and open-ocean pelagic.

The following ecosystems were accorded high priority status for conservation in Agenda 21: coral reefs, estuaries, temperate and tropical wetlands including mangroves, seagrass beds and other spawning and nursery areas (Kelleher et al, 1995). They also note that two gradients of species diversity appear to exist. Diversity increases from the poles to the equators, and from the west side to the east side of the oceans. At the species level, terrestrial ecosystems appear to be more diverse, as some 80 per cent of known species are terrestrial (Thorne-Miller and Catena, 1991). But at higher taxonomic levels, marine ecosystems are more diverse, for example, 28 animal phyla are found in the marine environment and only 11 on land (Kelleher et al, 1995). An important difference between land and marine biodiversity is that terrestrial organisms, as a result of large environmental variability, have developed physical or physiological mechanisms to cope with short-term variability (Thorne-Miller and Catena, 1991). Therefore, they note, marine ecosystems may be more vulnerable than terrestrial ones to large-scale environmental changes such as pollution and climate change. A detailed analysis of goods and services provided by marine ecosystems is presented by Moberg and Folke (1999).

Having outlined the contribution of biodiversity, forests and marine ecosystems to life on Earth, it is necessary to highlight the factors causing their degradation and biodiversity loss. These causes may be classified into proximate and underlying ones. Proximate causes are those activities having a direct impact, for example on species over-exploitation and habitat modification. Underlying causes are the social, cultural and economic factors driving the proximate causes.

Causes of Biodiversity Loss

The major proximate causes affecting terrestrial and marine biodiversity include: habitat loss, alteration and fragmentation; pollution; species over-harvesting; invasion by exotic species; global climatic change; and the development of industrial agriculture, fisheries and forestry (Norse, 1993;

Perrings et al, 1992; World Resources Institute (WRI) et al, 1992). In particular, the loss and fragmentation of tropical moist forests is one of the most significant threats to the world's biodiversity (Sayer and Wegge, 1992), together with climatic change.

Knowledge of the multiple causes of biodiversity loss helps in identifying the specific causes pertinent to the particular case studied. In turn, this helps in devising appropriate conservation initiatives. The summary of the proximate and underlying causes of deforestation presented in Table 1.1 exemplifies the range of causes leading to biodiversity loss.[8] It has to be stressed that in the literature there is not a large degree of agreement about the most important causes of deforestation.[9] For instance, it has long been debated whether shifting cultivators are the main perpetrators of tropical deforestation. This lack of agreement is not surprising as the identification and analysis of the *problems* depends on the specific paradigm[10] adopted. Stonich (1989),Tisdell (1990) and Blaikie and Jeanrenaud (1997) consider some of the paradigms adopted in their analysis of environmental problems and conservation approaches.

Causes of, and solutions to, biodiversity loss will vary from case to case, depending on the specific ecological, cultural, political and economic conditions. It is useful to identify the possible impacts that a specific factor may have on biodiversity loss. However, it is not helpful to make broad generalizations about the overall causes. Each specific case should be analysed in its own right.

Underlying Causes of Biodiversity Loss

Conflicting views about the underlying causes of biodiversity loss may be found in the literature. An example, further discussed below, is that concerning poverty and affluence. Some authors claim that poverty is a major cause of ecosystem degradation, and suggest that economic growth is therefore required to counteract degradation. Others suggest instead that it is affluence that causes degradation. The view espoused here is that the causes of environmental degradation are normally multiple. Different causes may be operating at the same time, depending on the specific case. The objective of the following analysis is to depict the range of causes rather than identifying any single cause of environmental degradation.

Population Pressure

It is widely accepted that population pressure can lead to ecosystem degradation. However, the relationship between population pressure and the environment is complex (eg Clay et al, 1994; Mink, 1993).

Concerning the relationship between deforestation and population, statistical studies support the existence of a positive relationship between increase in population and biodiversity loss (Allen and Barnes, 1985; Barbier et al, 1994; Burgess, 1993; Norse, 1993). However, population pressure does not automatically lead to environmental degradation as implied by the neomalthusian paradigm (eg Eckholm, 1976). The impacts of population pressure

Table 1.1 *Some proximate and underlying causes of deforestation*

	Rowe et al (1992)	Vanclay (1993)
Proximate causes	Agricultural expansion (mainly shifting cultivation) Overgrazing Fuelwood gathering Commercial logging Infrastructure and industrial development	Shifting cultivation Industrial agriculture Logging practices
Underlying causes	Market failure Policy failure Population growth Poverty State of the economy	Greed Corruption Overpopulation Poverty International trade policies Imperialism Bureaucratic inefficiency Ignorance of best logging practices

on ecosystems are mediated by a number of factors, such as consumption patterns, institutional structures and technology. Therefore, the localized effects of population pressure cannot be assumed *a priori*. For example, it has been reported that a decrease in population, due to migration, has led to a weakening of indigenous institutions regulating resource use which, in turn, has caused land degradation (Garcia-Barrios and Garcia-Barrios, 1990). On the other hand, it has also been reported that an increase in population within a geographic area has had environmental benefits (Tiffen et al, 1994). Blaikie and Brookfield (1987) note that major cases of land degradation are to be found not only in areas of high population density but also in areas of low to medium density.

Poverty and Affluence

A review of sustainable development issues observes that although several factors of environmental degradation have been acknowledged, attention has concentrated on the *vicious circle* by which poverty causes environmental degradation and vice versa (Lele, 1991). The creation of this supposedly single track link between poverty and environmental degradation probably has its roots in the politics of international relations and development. Angelsen (1997) argues that when the Brundtland commission started its work, countries in the south feared an international community attempt at constraining their economic growth to protect the environment. This resulted in the need to link economic growth and the environment in a positive way. Thus, the thesis that poverty has negative effects on the environment, and that economic growth will have positive environmental outcomes by reducing poverty.

The problem of environmental degradation is, however, much more complex than a simple poverty–environment link. First, it has been stressed that affluence may induce consumption patterns that can cause environmental degradation (Durning, 1991; Duraiappah, 1998). Second, the links between poverty and the environment are affected by a multiplicity of factors (Reardon and Vosti, 1995).

Reardon and Vosti (1995) present a complex framework that highlights the importance of considering the different types of poverty – welfare poverty and investment poverty[11] – the asset categories held by the poor – natural, human, on-farm, and off-farm resources – the different types of environments – soil, water, biodiversity and air – and the factors that affect their behaviour[12] – markets and prices, infrastructure, technology and population pressure. Through theoretical arguments and examples drawn from different environmental and socio-economic situations, they show that the composition of the assets held by rural people and the type of environmental problem they face influence the strength and direction of the links between poverty and the environment, and can even invert them. Their analysis has several important implications, and among others: policy prescriptions will have to be site-specific; alleviation of poverty does not necessarily reduce environmental degradation when no alternatives to current practices and/or strategies are available; an enhancement of the resource base may reduce poverty (eg soil conservation that improves agricultural output), but poverty may also be increased by resource conservation which reduces the resources available to the poor (eg a forest reserve excluding human use).

On the relationship between poverty, affluence and deforestation, Thapa and Weber (1990) argue that, in the Asian countries they consider, the affluent élite have carried out deforestation on a large scale (both for logging and commercial agriculture) and have marginalized the poor. The latter, relegated to small land-holdings, have contributed to deforestation in order to satisfy their needs for food, fuelwood and fodder. Evidence on the process of marginalization of the poor and their role in deforestation is also presented by Witte (1992).

Institutional Failure

The market and government are the institutions most commonly considered in environmental analyses. However, they are only two of the institutions that influence the management of ecosystems. Other relevant institutions are community-based ones, such as churches and village councils.

Market failure is said to occur when the market does not achieve a socially efficient allocation of resources. Market failure may be caused by the existence of externalities, lack of information, uncertainty, irreversibility, market imperfections and non-defined property rights. Government failure arises when policy interventions are either not undertaken (eg to correct market failure) or create distortions that lead to socially sub-optimal outcomes.[13]

First, in the case of ecosystem management, the concept of the efficient allocation of resources presents severe problems in itself. In fact, the great

EVERGREEN
CARE CENTER

New Season,
New Upgrades!

Park Primary
Care

Introducing Klara:
Secure Messaging for Healthcare

Evergreen Care Center and *Park Primary Care* are excited
to announce the introduction of **Klara**, the fastest growing
healthcare communication platform in the US!

- *Klara* is a way for patients to **easily** get in touch with your **Evergreen and Park Team** by accessing a secure, HIPAA-compliant website or mobile app!
- *It is as easy as sending a traditional text message!*
- *Saves "phone tag" delays regarding test results, prescription questions, appointments and appointment reminders.*
- *Works on all devices.*
- *No more 'Waiting on Hold'*

TEXT
OUR
KLARA
#

(708) 866-0918

or call (708) 423-6209
www.EVERGREENCARECENTER.com

or call (708) 423-8150
www.PARKPRIMARYCARE.com

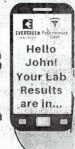

Hello
John!
Your Lab
Results
are in...

degree of uncertainty about ecosystem functions hinders the viability of determining the efficient allocation of resources (eg Cropper and Oates, 1992; Dietz and van der Straaten, 1992). Therefore, it is practically impossible to attempt to achieve efficient ecosystem use. Second, it should also be noted that for most ecosystem functions it is incorrect to speak of degradation due to market failure. It is rather a condition of *non-existent* markets (Bromley, 1991). It is unlikely that this situation will change substantially, because most ecosystem functions are not marketed and it is unlikely that they will ever be.[14] To face these conditions of non-existent markets and continuous market failure, the adoption of policies that tend to constrain the operation of market actors has been proposed. This issue is discussed in Chapter 4.

Government failure may originate from, and is often attributed to, ignorance and/or a lack of information. Government failure may also originate from rent-seeking behaviour (eg Bates, 1988). In order to stay in power, governments may implement policies that are economically inefficient but politically expedient. Several studies have pointed out that government failure, expressed in pricing distortions, causes accelerated biodiversity loss (Barbier et al 1994; Binswanger, 1991; Duraiappah, 1998; Repetto, 1988). Other studies show that extensive deforestation and biodiversity loss has resulted from policies designed to benefit government officials and the powerful élite (Dauvergne, 1993–94; Hecht, 1985; Thapa and Weber, 1990; Thompson, 1993). These latter studies suggest that deforestation originated mainly from the political process and that poverty and population pressure were only minor causes.

Of particular interest are property rights institutions that regulate access to and use of ecosystems. These systems have been classified into four categories: state property, private property, common property and open access (Bromley and Cernea, 1989). While the meaning of private property and state property is clear, it may be useful to clarify the meaning of common property and open access regimes. In an open access system there are no exclusive rights and resource use is available to everyone. In a common property regime the resources are owned and/or managed by a defined group. In this regime, specific rules detail the composition of the group and regulate the use of the resources. Common property differs from state property because in the former resources are owned and managed at a group level. There is evidence to suggest that private, state and common property regimes can all be viable systems for the management of ecosystems (Feeny et al, 1990; Shepherd, 1991). Although the establishment of private property rights is at times advocated as a solution to environmental problems, private property too may lead to irreversible environmental changes such as species extinction. It has been demonstrated that extinction may be efficient from an individual point of view (Farrow, 1995).

The role played by community-level institutions in resource management has often been disregarded. Government centralization of resource management has induced in some cases the breakdown of traditional management systems. This, coupled with a lack of government capacity to manage resources has virtually created a situation of open access regime and environmental degradation has followed (eg Bromley and Chapagain, 1984; Gadgil, 1992).

This realization has been one of the factors leading to an increased interest in decentralization (eg Lutz and Caldecott, 1996) and community-based resource management (eg Agrawal and Gibson, 1999).

International institutions also have an important role to play in the conservation of biodiversity (eg Barbier et al, 1994; Swanson, 1994). Biodiversity provides benefits of a global nature that go beyond those enjoyed by the individual host country. Therefore, national governments may not have an interest in conserving biodiversity to a degree that may be desirable from a global point of view. Institutions such as the Convention on International Trade in Endangered Species of Wild Fauna and Flora (CITES) and the Global Environment Facility are part of the international effort aimed at providing an appropriate framework and incentives to national governments to conserve biodiversity beyond the level considered to be beneficial from a national perspective. Several schemes have been proposed (and in some cases implemented) in order to increase the amount of benefits from biodiversity conservation captured by the individual states, to transfer funds to states willing to conserve biodiversity, and to increase investment in biodiversity conservation. These include the reform of intellectual property rights regimes, reform of wildlife trade regimes, international franchise agreements, debt-for-nature swaps, bio-prospecting agreements and direct compensation payments (Barbier et al, 1994; McNeely and Weatherly, 1996; Swanson, 1994).

Environmental Degradation and the Market

Some authors have considered the impact of the rise of capitalism and the development of the global exchange market on ecological functions and biodiversity (Eckholm, 1982; Redclift, 1987, 1988). These authors have argued, from a dependency theory point of view, that the social relations of production and reproduction undergo a substantial change during the adjustment of the economy to the conditions of the global market. This leads to increased demands on the environment which in turn result in degradation. This approach has been criticized on several grounds, especially because it does not consider the role played by institutions and individuals in the Third World. These actors may mitigate the demands of the core nations, with the consequent variability of social, economic and environmental outcomes (Stonich, 1989). Claims that indigenous societies have always managed their resources sustainably (eg Redclift, 1988) are not supported by other evidence (Edgerton, 1992; UNEP, 1995). Even if many examples of sustainable management by pre-capitalist societies can be found, the contrary is also true. Northern China, the Mediterranean region, Mesopotamia, and Mesoamerica all experienced deforestation and soil erosion induced by indigenous societies (Ponting, 1991).

It is not the market in itself that leads to environmental problems but the dynamics that entail the economic process. These include governance processes, such as corruption in the logging industry that allows very few people to benefit from the wealth of the forests (eg Redclift, 1988), changes in values, including loss of respect for the environment and decreased social cohesion of communities (Dasmann, 1975/76), demands arising from economic growth – such as increased demand in the north and in the south – the technologies used to satisfy these demands – for example drift-net fishing which results in large by-catch – and specialization – such as the case of mono-cropping cultures which reduce the diversity of crops and supporting species (Norgaard, 1988).

Protected Areas: Functions and Problems

The Functions of Protected Areas

The World Conservation Union (IUCN) recognizes six categories of protected areas (PAs) (IUCN, 1994).[15] These categories relate to the degree of human use allowed within the area. For example, in Strict Nature Reserves human use is not allowed, with the exception of research activities. Managed Resource Protected Areas are managed mainly for sustainable use of natural ecosystems. In 1996, PAs covered about 6.29 per cent of the Earth's land area (WCMC, 1999).

Several functions of PAs have been recognized (McNeely et al, 1990; IUCN, 1993). They:

1   contribute to the maintenance of ecological processes, species diversity, and the genetic variation within species;
2   safeguard ecosystems and specific species' habitats;
3   facilitate scientific research, education, and training;
4   maintain or enhance the productive capacity of the ecosystems and their use for recreational and tourism purposes;
5   contribute to the maintenance of the ecological functions of adjoining ecosystems;
6   may help to maintain the cultural capital of the local people.

PAs usually have multiple conservation objectives, such as the conservation of genetic resources, the control of erosion and sedimentation, the maintenance of indigenous use, and the provision of recreation and tourism services. They may be established in relatively unmodified habitats or in areas highly influenced by human intervention such as the protected landscapes found in Europe.

In the past, the conservation of biodiversity was an objective of minor importance in the establishment of PAs. The choice of PA sites was *ad hoc* and was often based on their recreational and tourism potential, or because they could not accommodate other land uses (Hall, 1989; Leader-Williams et al, 1990; Pressey and Tully, 1994). However, biodiversity conservation has become an increasingly important goal in the establishment of PAs (Braatz et al, 1992; Nilsson and Götmark, 1992; House of Representatives Standing Committee on Environment, Recreation and the Arts, 1993).

The *Global Biodiversity Strategy* (WRI et al, 1992) was developed through a world-wide consultation process with experts, governments and non-government organizations. This document provides the broad spectrum approach needed for the conservation of biodiversity, the majority of which is found in landscapes managed by local people (Miller, 1996; Pimentel et al, 1992). The *Global Biodiversity Strategy* details, both at the national and the international level, the institutional requirements, the policy changes and the funds needed to conserve biodiversity. PAs are an integral component of this strategy, because they are recognized as being among the essential means for saving biodiversity (WRI et al, 1992; Commission on Sustainable Development, 1999). However, PAs can only complement the other actions required to conserve biodiversity (eg changes in legislation, changes in ecosystem use, *ex situ* conservation) rather than substitute for them. In fact, PAs can help in conserving only a portion of all existing species. For instance, Reid and Miller (1989) have attempted to estimate the contribution of PAs to species conservation in tropical forests. In the scenario that all tropical forests were cleared with the exception of those in legally established PAs, the following percentage of species would survive: Africa 37–65 per cent; Asia and Pacific 44–71 per cent; and Latin America 28–58 per cent.

It has been noted that the land surface covered by PAs in categories I–V and category VI will probably never exceed 10 and 20 per cent respectively of the Earth's total land area (Reid and Miller, 1989). However, these are only suggested figures. There is limited knowledge about the extent to which existing PAs satisfy the criteria set forth in the design of national PA systems.[16] Because of this knowledge gap, it is currently impossible to determine exactly the amount of land that should be dedicated to PAs. Individual countries have different conservation needs determined by their specific environmental and socio-economic conditions. However, whilst the notion that a target percentage area (eg 10 per cent of the land area of a country) should be set aside for biodiversity conservation may be inappropriate, notional targets need to be set in order to assess the environmental, social and economic implications of alternative designs of PA systems.

Problematic Issues

Conservation initiatives have been criticized because of their narrow focus on genes, species and ecosystems and their consequent disregard of the interactions between the human population and the natural environment. The implementation of a biologically focused approach to conservation, and the existence of pressures from politically powerful vested-interest groups, have contributed to the cultural and socio-economic marginalization of many people living within or close to PAs.[17] These resource use conflicts are widespread and span most of the continents (Abel and Blaikie, 1986; Gadgil, 1992; Ghimire, 1994; Gurung, 1992; Hough and Sherpa, 1989; Sharma, 1990; Utting, 1994; Ghimire and Pimbert, 1997; Stevens, 1997).

As a result of resource use conflicts, and the fact that PAs have often encroached on local people (who were living in the area well before the declaration of the PA), many PAs around the world suffer from *encroachment* by local people. This problem persists even when there has been an attempt to devise projects that provide local people with alternative sources of income

(Ghimire, 1994; Ghimire and Pimbert, 1997). The existence of these problems is however increasingly acknowledged. The need to maintain the culture and the livelihood of the people living within, or close to, proposed and existing PAs has been recognized. It has featured as a main theme at international meetings, such as the IVth World Congress on National Parks and Protected Areas held in Caracas, Venezuela, in 1992. The recognition of people's rights to control and manage their resources is currently considered a fundamental requirement for the maintenance of their culture and livelihood.[18] As a result, more funds appear to be devoted to the establishment of PAs with the participation of local people at all stages of the process (eg Reti, 1993; Stevens, 1997). Certainly, there is no easy way out of resource distribution problems. However, given the positive attitudes towards conservation often registered among local people (Hackel, 1990; Newmark et al, 1993; Stevens, 1997), in some quarters it is argued that increased attention to their needs and problems may increase the likelihood of success for conservation and development initiatives. To respond to local development demands, the Integrated Conservation and Development Project (ICDP) approach emerged in the 1980s and has been implemented throughout the 1990s. This approach may present some opportunities for conservation; however, it also faces several problems, such as the complexities of implementing integrated projects (as became clear through the implementation of integrated rural development projects), the high cost of projects, and the uncertain environmental outcomes.[19]

A significant problem faced by a large but unspecified number of PAs is the lack of actual management of these areas according to their conservation objectives. Many PAs do not have management plans, and when they do, either they are not implemented or they are not respected. These areas are thus protected only on paper (IUCN, 1997). There are many examples of areas that are supposed to be protected but that are actually exploited. In Indonesia, for example, the politics of forest management allows logging companies to log in PAs without being prosecuted (Barber et al, 1994). Clearly, if management plans are not prepared and implemented, the contribution of PAs to conservation will be very limited (Paine, 1997).

A further issue to be considered is whether the development of PA systems will significantly constrain food availability. At a global level this is unlikely. First, about 36 per cent of the Earth's land area is dedicated to agricultural and pastoral uses (World Bank, 1992). The percentage of productive lands that will be included in PAs cannot be quantified at this stage, but it is likely to be only a fraction of the agricultural-pastoral land currently used. In fact, assuming that PAs will cover 10 per cent of the Earth's land area, a large fraction of this area will cover land of low agronomic potential. Second, food availability is not simply a question of productive capacity. It is well documented that social, political and economic factors are all causes of food scarcity problems (Drèze and Sen, 1989). Third, because of the low agricultural productivity of many tropical forest areas, agricultural output could often receive a greater boost from land redistribution policies and conservation measures applied to existing agricultural land, rather than from expansion onto forest land included in PAs.[20] The impacts that will occur at the local level will depend, however, on the specific management arrangements regulating each PA. Although PAs are increasingly being designed in ways that allow the local people to use food and other resources found within the area, there are still many cases, as noted above, in which PAs have negative effects on local livelihoods.

A further weakness of PAs is their susceptibility to damage caused by pollution and exotic species infestation. However, these problems endanger not only PAs but also, for example, agricultural production. They have to be addressed at the national and international levels through the development of responses such as the *Global Biodiversity Strategy*.

Finally, the current approach to the protection of biodiversity in PAs has been criticized by Noss and Harris (1986) because, among other reasons, it does not deal effectively with biotic change. Rather, it focuses on single PAs instead of whole landscapes and it concentrates on species and populations instead of ecosystems and landscapes in which they interact. It is on this basis that the concept of bioregional management has been proposed for the conservation of biodiversity. The bioregion should be sufficiently large to ensure the viability of ecosystems, the maintenance of ecological functions and to contain human communities; the consideration of biodiversity at the bioregional level allows the integration of PAs with the surrounding landscapes (WRI et al, 1992; Miller, 1996).

Outline of the Book

Part I presents the theoretical framework. The definition of a problem and the development of theory and policies aimed at addressing it, as well as their application, depend on the specific methodological paradigm adopted. Methodological issues are therefore discussed in the following two chapters. Chapter 2 considers the question of whether a rigorous research programme can be developed while ensuring that the research carried out is both relevant and able to have an impact on the decision-making process. A positivist philosophy of science, its influence on economics and its shortcomings are outlined. Then, a proposal for ecological economics to become a post-normal science is critically considered. Finally, a constructivist philosophy of science is discussed. The chapter provides a positive answer to the question outlined above, and concludes by noting that there are potentially fruitful complementarities between post-normal science and the constructivist philosophy of science that need to be further explored.

Chapter 3 examines the features of the ecological economics and the environmental economics paradigms, and their implications for decision-making processes concerning the use of ecosystems. Ecological economics is characterized by its focus on the sustainable use of ecosystems, their distribution among stakeholders, and their allocation to different uses. The concern regarding the efficient allocation of resources is shared with environmental economics. The conception of human behaviour that one holds is important in determining the preferred decision-making process. Therefore, the neoclassical model of human behaviour is considered, and an expansion of the model proposed. This extended model stresses that preferences and ends may change, individuals and institutions may show behaviour ranging from selfish to other-regarding, and from rational to normative. Individuals influence institutions and vice versa. Therefore, the focus of the analysis should not only be on the individuals and goods, as suggested by neoclassical economics, but also on institutions. Institutions provide the framework within which ecosystem use decisions are made. The existence of appropriate institutions has particular importance in determining whether ecosystem use patterns may be sustainable, equitable and efficient. The decision-making process should enable individuals and institutions to update their goals, to express their selfish to other-regarding views and to facilitate logical decision-making processes.

Chapter 3 also considers some of the weaknesses of cost–benefit analysis. They are further addressed in the subsequent two chapters with particular attention to the valuation of biodiversity and PAs. The shortcomings of neoclassical environmental economics point towards the need for the consideration of tools to complement, or replace where appropriate, cost–benefit analysis.

In Chapter 4, some economic aspects of biodiversity are reviewed first. Biodiversity is an important attribute of natural capital. Thus, the implications for biodiversity conservation policies of seeking to achieve intergenerational equity are analysed by addressing the wider issue of natural capital use. The concepts of the precautionary principle and the safe minimum standard are discussed, then contractarian ethics and its application to intergenerational equity questions are considered. Three degrees of intergenerational equity – extensive, intermediate and minimal – are derived. Minimal intergenerational equity requires the maintenance of critical renewable natural capital that provides life support functions. Efforts by countries to protect ecosystems and species in PA systems contribute to the conservation of *part* of their critical renewable natural capital. Therefore, this would comply only partially with the requirement for the achievement of minimal intergenerational equity.

Chapter 5 concludes the first part of the volume by considering processes and tools applied to the distribution and allocation of natural resources, with particular attention to their practical applicability, intragenerational equity, sustainability and policy implications. Practical problems encountered in the application of cost–benefit analysis to resource valuation and intragenerational equity are discussed first. Environmental economics faces several theoretical and practical problems in dealing with biodiversity conservation, and it is suggested that the adoption of a land use planning approach is required. Reviews of land use planning practices and current planning and conservation approaches highlight the importance of stakeholder participation. The concept of participation is discussed and the several meanings that it may take are noted. Among other issues, it is proposed that participation can address some of the concerns raised in Chapter Four about the limitations of the neoclassical economic framework in accounting for stakeholders' views and interests. It is stressed that participation is important but simple bottom-up approaches are not the answer. There is a need to reconcile top-down and bottom-up planning processes, especially in order to account for the political aspect involved in resource planning and use. A very relevant issue is that no matter how detailed and participatory the initial planning process is, unless the findings are carried through to implementation, the planning process is irrelevant.

Part II presents the case studies, which illustrate specific aspects of the framework presented in Part I, and which also provide self-contained analysis of issues affecting biodiversity conservation.

Chapter 6 opens Part II by analysing the Regional Forest Agreement programme. It is the most ambitious, comprehensive, and expensive environmental and resource planning programme ever undertaken in Australia. It is aimed at allocating ecosystems to production or conservation. The origin of this programme partly rests on the earlier conflicts between conservationists on one side, and the industry and state forest services on the other. The programme is studied in terms of its historical and political circumstances, its scientific and forestry traditions and its industrial structures and public expectations. Some preliminary lessons are drawn. These include the findings that the establishment of a structured process for dealing with complex issues is a major achievement, conflicts appear to be under control, at least temporarily, and stakeholder participation has taken place non-uniformly across the different states – ranging from information distribution to consultation – and has been affected by some stakeholders' ability to advance their interests more effectively through the political process.

Chapter 7 provides a government's perspective on some of the benefits of cooperative arrangements, such as informal collaborations and formal partnerships. It does this by outlining some of the Australian Commonwealth Government's policies and programmes associated with integrated management and protection of the Australian marine environment. Australia has one of the most diverse marine environments in the world, and one of the most advanced marine resource management systems. The chapter discusses some of the challenges associated with the development of Australia's National Representative System of Marine Protected Areas. In relation to participation, the difficulty of reconciling the interests of opposing stakeholders is noted, and the strategies that have been recognized as central to the success of marine protected areas include the need for:

- clear understanding of all socio-economic issues relating to individual positions;
- mechanisms to identify and acknowledge common goals throughout consultation processes so that conflicts can be addressed without jeopardizing established agreements;
- commitment to addressing conflicts as they arise in order to minimize speculation, rumour and uncertainty;

- promotion of the principle that all stakeholders have a responsibility to protect and manage marine biological diversity;
- provision of opportunities to allow stakeholders to make tangible contributions to the design, planning and ultimately the ongoing management and monitoring of marine protected areas.

Chapter 8 exemplifies policy and political issues facing biodiversity conservation. The applied analysis considers the case of Indonesia, one of the most biologically diverse countries. The focus is on the effects that policy and politics are having on decentralization, community resource use and participation, and the continued existence of PAs. It reviews Indonesia's achievements in biodiversity conservation and some of the most pressing issues challenging its capacity to deliver on international expectations. This analysis includes an assessment of national and local level issues, using the case of the Hutan Bakau Pantai Timur Nature Reserve as an example. Then, it examines the obstacles created by the government's policy to reconciliation between local communities and the government itself. Finally, the potential for devolved power in conservation management is considered, as it could assist local level governments and communities to exercise control over the alarming rate of degradation of forests and PAs.

Chapter 9 summarizes the significance of the Adirondack Park experience, a unique combination of protected state and privately owned land regulated by zoning laws. This combination of ownership models has made the Adirondack Park a unique application of land use planning compatible with large-scale biodiversity protection. However, gains in environmental protection were achieved at the expense of the individual liberties of private landowners and local communities. This has led to repeated tensions between public agencies and representatives, and local stakeholders and citizens. One reason for these tensions is that today's Park has evolved from a rather top-down planning process that considered little input from local communities. The chapter offers a historical overview of the decision-making process responsible for today's patchwork quilt of the public and private lands within the Park. It discusses recent developments in research and decision innovation that seek to bridge the knowledge gaps between various stakeholder groups, decision-makers, and those most affected by land use decisions. Four current examples of this bridge-building process are discussed to illustrate the potential that community-based research and policy-making offers for improving sustainable development efforts within the Adirondacks.

Chapter 10 discusses the approach adopted in reconciling the national agenda for biodiversity conservation with local needs for development and conservation in Vanuatu (South Pacific). The application of a constructivist methodology is examined before considering policy and institutional issues. Vanuatu is an interesting case because, unlike many tropical areas, the land is not owned by the state but by the indigenous people. People's views about forest management, conservation, and future generations are assessed, and it is found that although they appear to be interested in conservation and the interests of future generations, they are also concerned about presently deriving benefits from their forest resources. These views influenced the approach adopted for the evaluation and establishment of one of the protected areas considered. The case studies highlight several issues involved in developing participatory approaches to research and decision-making, including the use of economic analysis. A discussion of issues relevant to integrated conservation and development projects and national conservation policy concludes the chapter.

Chapter 11 examines the complex relationships from the international to the local scale, between actors, landscape, and formal and informal institutions that conservation initiatives must negotiate. It does this by looking at the case of the Rajiv Gandhi National Park in Karnataka, a park receiving assistance in the form of an integrated conservation and development project under the India Ecodevelopment Project. The chapter considers how the interactions noted above shape the evolution of an intervention, its likely outcomes, and the broader implications for conservation programmes. To do this, it develops an analytical framework, rooted in constructivist methodology, focusing on the actors in relation to their landscape and their institutional context. This analytical framework highlights previously unquestioned assumptions about actors, landscape and institutions in integrated conservation and development projects. Among other findings, it is noted that integrated conservation and development projects attempt to manipulate relations between actors and landscape to a prespecified end. An actor-oriented framework questions the capacity of any such intervention to ever meet their prespecified objectives. In the case study, the intervention has been obviously overtaken by negotiations and politics between actors; this process may be paralleled in less obvious ways elsewhere. This finding points to the need for a more open ended, process-oriented and site-specific approach than is embodied in most existing integrated conservation and development projects and community-based conservation programmes.

Finally, the theoretical framework and several of the case studies have pointed out, directly or indirectly, the importance of conflict in natural resource management. Therefore, Chapter 12 specifically addresses conflict management. It is concerned with the problem of non-violent conflicts and disputes as constraints to the sustainability of natural resource management at the community level. First, it provides some background to the role of conflict in natural resource management. Then it presents a methodology designed to contribute to the removal of conflict as an obstacle to sustainability. The methodology was developed to guide a programme of conflict management within NGO-sponsored community-based natural resource projects in the South Pacific. Examples of the outputs of the methodology are described, drawing from conflict management activities undertaken in the Lakekamu Basin ICDP, Papua New Guinea. The overall benefits of conflict management in community-based natural resource projects are discussed in relation to building social capital and sustaining livelihood security.

Notes

1　Norse et al (1986) were probably the first ones to describe biodiversity at three levels; Soulé (1991) describes five levels (genetic and ecosystem biodiversity are subdivided into two levels each). Functional diversity is an additional way of categorizing biodiversity; this refers to the variety of biological processes characteristic of an ecosystem and reflects its complexity (Thorn-Miller and Catena, 1991).

2　Resilience is defined by Holling (1986) as the capacity of an ecosystem to withstand perturbations and shocks.

3　World Conservation Monitoring Centre (WCMC) (1992) and World Resource Institute (WRI) et al (1992) provide a wide range of examples of the economic values of biodiversity.

4　See Barbier et al (1994) for a summary of studies concerned with the prediction of rates of extinction based on tropical deforestation.

5　Myers (1980) provides a detailed definition of tropical moist forests.

6　NTFPs are all biological materials other than timber which are obtained from natural forests (de Beer and McDermott, 1989). Forest areas may be under some form of management in order to maintain the natural production of NTFPs, but these products are not cultivated.

7　Benthic refers to marine assemblages associated with the bottom; pelagic refers to those species associated with water columns.

8　Norse (1993) describes in detail the proximate causes affecting marine biodiversity.

9　For extensive surveys and analyses of tropical deforestation see, for example, Palo and Mery (1996), Jepma (1995), Rock (1996) and Verolme and Moussa (1999).

10　The meaning of paradigm and its importance in conditioning research processes and outcomes is discussed in Chapter 3.

11　Welfare poverty refers to standard measures of poverty which consider, for example, the capacity to attain a minimum level of caloric intake. Investment poverty refers to the capacity to invest in relevant natural resources to maintain or enhance their quality. Welfare poor can be expected to be investment poor, but the converse does not necessarily apply (Reardon and Vosti, 1995).

12　For examples of studies about rural people's socio-economic strategies see Ellis (1998).

13　The concepts of efficiency and optimality are considered in Chapter 4. Here, it is useful to anticipate that both concepts (and particularly social optimality) present relevant theoretical and empirical problems.

14　Current attempts at developing a market for carbon emissions represent, however, a significant change. It can be assumed that there will be attempts to develop a biodiversity market. This faces considerable problems because of the multifaceted aspects of biodiversity.

15　The IUCN categories are: Category I, Strict Nature Reserve/Wilderness Area; Category II, National Park; Category III, Natural Monument; Category IV, Habitat/Species Management Area; Category V, Protected Landscape/Seascape; Category VI, Managed Resource Protected Area. The IUCN defines a PA as an area dedicated to the protection and maintenance of biodiversity, and of natural and associated cultural resources; the area needs to be managed through legal or other effective means.

16 Ecological criteria used to assess PAs include rarity and representativeness (Smith and Theberge, 1986), and more recently, comprehensiveness, adequacy and representativeness (Commonwealth of Australia, 1997).

17 It has been estimated that about 50% of the PAs worldwide, and as much as 80% in some regions (eg Latin America), have people living in them (Borrini-Feyerabend, 1996).

18 For a collection of papers addressing these issues see Kemf (1993), Western et al (1994) and Stevens (1997).

19 See for example Wells and Brandon (1992), Brown and Wyckoff-Baird (1992), Western et al (1994), Barber et al (1995), Barrett and Arcese (1995), Caldecott (1996), MacCallum and Sekhran (1997), Wainwright and Wehrmeyer (1998) and Wells et al (1998) for discussions about the dilemmas and opportunities presented by conservation and development projects. Further consideration to ICDPs is given in Chapters 8, 10 and 11.

20 See Fearnside (1993) for a detailed discussion of the issue of forest conservation and food availability.

2

Scientific Methodology[*]

Introduction

Can a rigorous research programme be developed while ensuring that the research carried out is both relevant and influential on the decision-making process? This is a question that is of fundamental importance to social science research in general, and to the development of ecological economics, which has been defined as an issue-driven discipline, concerned with the analysis and the achievement of sustainability (Costanza et al, 1991).

At times economists have expressed the view that methodology[1] is irrelevant to the practice of economics. However, Hoover (1995, p733) rightly stresses that those 'who believe themselves to be quite exempt from any methodological influences are usually slaves of some defunct methodologist'. In fact, Kuhn (1970) argues that the specific paradigm adopted by the researcher structures the research problem by providing implicit rules regarding what issues are relevant, how to proceed in the analysis and what analytical tools may be employed in addressing the research questions. The significance of considering methodological issues for an emerging discipline such as ecological economics was pointed out in the first volume of *Ecological Economics*.

> '*Most of the methodological intersects between ecology and economics are simply too narrow to generate interesting results ... In summary, ecological economics will more likely evolve into a useful discipline if it maintains the breadth of the methodological base of economics and ecology and reaches out to the methodologies of other disciplines as well.*' (Norgaard, 1989, pp51–3.)

Since Norgaard's article, the major contribution to the methodological development of ecological economics has been provided by Funtowicz and Ravetz (1991, 1993a, 1993b, 1994), who introduced the concept of post-normal science. This chapter explores and further develops the methodological base of ecological economics by considering post-normal science and constructivist methodologies. This analysis suggests that there are complementarities between these two methodologies; their eventual integration could be further considered by ecological economists in order to build a richer methodological base for the discipline. It should be pointed out that in ecological economics we are only at the beginning of a voyage of methodological exploration. Since the 1970s, methodological proposals alternative to positivism have flourished. Apart from post-normal science and constructivism, other alternatives are critical realism (Gandy, 1996), postmodernism (Harvey, 1989; Midmore, 1996) and soft system analysis (Checkland and Scholes, 1990). Given their recent origin there is a need to assess their strengths, weaknesses and complementarities. Apart from the present chapter, another example of the analysis that should be done is given in the paper by Woodhill and Röling (1998), who consider positivism, constructivism, post-normal science and soft system analysis.

Positivist philosophy has dominated scientific research throughout most of the twentieth century, but it has been discredited or rejected within the philosophy of science (eg Feyerabend, 1975; Kuhn, 1970; Suppe, 1974). Nevertheless, many, if not most, scientists view the world through positivist glasses and attempt to adopt – or subscribe to, at least in their rhetoric[2] – positivist prescriptions for scientific inquiry (Caldwell, 1982; Lincoln and Guba, 1985; McCloskey, 1985). Given that many researchers are not fully aware of the details of positivist methodology, the tenets of positivism, its major shortfalls and its influence on economics are outlined first.[3] This is followed by a discussion of post-normal science. Then, the application of constructivism to the study of economic-environmental issues is discussed.

Some readers may not be familiar with methodological issues and may ask how they influence applied analysis. For example, in discussing biodiversity policies, Norton and Ulanowicz (1992) note that while studying ecosystems, conservation biologists should be obligated to follow both a criterion of rigour and a criterion of relevance to policy development. In fact, there appears to be 'an inverse relationship between rigour and relevance in most social science work' (Uphoff, 1992, p295). Uphoff refers to that concept of rigour normally associated with quantitative hypothesis testing (the Scientific Method), and notes that social scientists have become trapped in what is considered to be the Scientific Method. Uphoff's team worked on water management in Sri Lanka. He notes that they could have followed the Scientific Method in their work by testing various hypotheses about the factors determining the hopeless situation of the water management system being considered. In that way, they could have easily predicted the demise of that water management system; however, they actually decided to influence the system and against the odds made the water management system viable. These examples highlight the importance of considering methodological issues for the study of environmental questions.

Before proceeding, it is useful to define the meaning of paradigm. Here, paradigm refers to a set of beliefs (or world-view) around which *reality* is organized (Berman, 1981; Kuhn, 1970; Lincoln and Guba, 1985). Any paradigm of inquiry may be categorized by detailing its ontology (or nature of reality that the paradigm postulates), its epistemology (the nature of the relationship between the knower and the known), and its methodology (the method of investigation to be followed).

Positivism and its Influence on Economics

Positivist Philosophy

Logical empiricism is the current version of positivism (Caldwell, 1982).[4]
Logical empiricists stress the primacy of empirical evidence and accept the
existence of theoretical statements in scientific theories. They do not require
that these statements be individually tested. It is the theory as a whole that has
to be confirmed by physical evidence. Logical empiricists hold that only testable
hypotheses are considered scientific. The introduction of the concept of falsification of hypotheses is due to Popper (1959). He points out that instances that
confirm a hypothesis are not difficult to encounter. However, a theory can never
be definitely shown to be correct. Instead, if an instance that disproves the
theory is found, the theory is proven to be incorrect. Therefore, Popper (1959)
recommends that scientists should carry out tests that seriously seek instances
that would falsify the theory being tested. According to Popper (1959), the
falsifiability principle is the demarcation criterion that should be adopted in
distinguishing between science and non-science. Scholarly endeavours that do
not produce falsifiable hypotheses do not constitute scientific activities.

There have been several interpretations of what positivism actually implies
(eg Bryant, 1985). It is important, therefore, to clearly detail what is implied
by positivism in the following analysis. The ontology, epistemology and
methodology of positivism as intended here are well summarized by Egon
Guba.

> 'Ontology: Realist: – *reality exists out there and is driven by
> immutable natural laws and mechanisms. Knowledge of these
> entities, laws and mechanisms is conventionally summarized in
> the form of time – and context free generalizations. Some of these
> latter generalizations take the form of cause–effect laws.*
> Epistemology: Dualist/objectivist – *it is both possible and essen-
> tial for the inquirer to adopt a distant, noninteractive posture.
> Values and other biasing and confounding factors are thereby
> automatically excluded from influencing the outcomes.*
> Methodology: Experimental/manipulative – *questions and/or
> hypotheses are stated in advance in propositional form and
> subjected to empirical tests (falsification) under carefully
> controlled conditions.'* (Guba, 1990, p20)

The Decline of Positivism

Philosophers and scientists in various fields have rejected the tenets of
positivism. The rejection of positivism by philosophers of science dates back
to the early 1970s (eg Suppe, 1974) but it has filtered very slowly through to
the natural and social sciences.

The view that there exists only *one reality* to observe has come across
serious criticisms. Two positions, alternative to that which postulates the

existence of an objective reality, may be distinguished. These have been termed the *constructed reality* position and the *created reality* position (Lincoln and Guba, 1985). The *constructed reality position* (eg Hesse, 1980) purports that reality is a construction of the minds of individuals. Therefore, there are multiple individually constructed realities rather than one objective reality. Objects are tangible entities but the meanings ascribed to them in order to make sense of them are constructed realities. The *created reality position* presents a more radical view of reality and may be identified with the work of physicists. This position advances the case that reality does not exist at all. Reality comes into existence when it is perceived. It may be said that in a certain way we contribute to its creation.[5] Physicists have noted that when studying subatomic particles they cannot determine both the momentum and the position of a particle (eg Wolf, 1981). Therefore, they have to choose which of the two properties they want to determine. By doing so, they effectively create the other property. As a result of the acknowledgment of the role played by the researcher in influencing the reality being studied, scientists are no longer referred to as observers – which has a connotation of neutral, objective entity – but as participators (Wolf, 1981; Zukav, 1979; Lincoln and Guba, 1985).

Positivist epistemology has also been the object of detailed critique. There cannot exist value-free and objective research as postulated by positivist philosophy. First, the development of theory depends on the specific researcher's values and interests. Second, observation is not independent of theory. Observation cannot be a neutral collection of facts; it involves selection and interpretation. These are guided by the theoretical construct developed, or subscribed to, by the researcher. Researchers not only see a specific reality; they may also influence this reality directly or indirectly. For example, if researchers attempt to not influence a situation by refraining from any action, events will take a different course from that which they would have followed otherwise. Several authors from a variety of disciplines have put forward these arguments (Beed, 1992; Easlea, 1973; Harre, 1972; Kuhn, 1970; Myrdal, 1957; Polanyi, 1969; Wright Mills, 1959; Wolf, 1981).[6]

In relation to methodology, the problems faced when applying falsificationism are considered in the following section with specific regard to economics. It is useful to make a few remarks in relation to the concept of hypothesis. Medawar (1974) notes that one of the weaknesses of the hypothetico-deductive model[7] rests in not being able to provide any explanation of how hypotheses are generated. He defines a hypothesis as 'an imaginative preconception of what might be true in the form of a declaration with verifiable deductive consequences' (Medawar, 1974, p279). He asserts that good hypotheses are felicitous strokes of creative scientists. Popper (1974) subscribes to this view and adds that luck is also needed to advance good hypotheses. Later in the paper, when presenting an alternative model to the hypothetico-deductive one, a different definition of hypothesis will be provided. An approach to the generation of hypotheses that appears to be more fruitful than that advanced by the two latter philosophers is also presented.

Positivism in Economics

Positivism has been regarded as a philosophy that could lead economics towards becoming a more objective and value-free discipline (Caldwell, 1982; Gee, 1991). The influence of positivist thought on many economists is exemplified by the subdivision of economics into *positive* economics and *normative* economics. Positive economics is supposed to describe and explain the functioning of the economic system. Given that it is supposed to describe and explain *facts*, it is said to be value-free and objective in a pure logical empiricist style. It may be noted that even within welfare economics, which is normally regarded as part of normative economics, economists have attempted to establish an objective foundation for analysis. For instance, Hennipman (1976) seeks to provide an objective interpretation of Pareto optimality. However, these assertions are untenable. It has been stressed in the previous section that observation cannot be value-free.

Two main implications of the arguments developed above are worthwhile noting. First, making a distinction between positive and normative economics may not be as useful as is often argued (Caldwell, 1982). Any research activity, which according to the established view is classified in the domain of positive economics, involves value-judgements and subjective factors. Second, akin to the previous point, some schools of economic thought have become separated from philosophy due to the attempt to establish a positive economic science (Sen, 1987).

Hypothesis testing in the form of falsificationism is considered to be the hallmark of positive scientific inquiry by many economists. Blaug (1992), a neoclassical economist, has stressed that economists appear to have endorsed falsificationism, at least in their rhetoric. However, he notes that the tenets of falsificationism have not been put into practice. Despite this failure in applying falsificationism thus far, he stresses that economists *should* strive to apply it. That is, they should attempt to produce theories that are testable and falsifiable. By taking this view, Blaug implies that falsificationism can actually be put into practice in economics.

The view that falsificationism may be successfully applied to economics has been called into serious doubt by Caldwell (1982), among others. In putting forward this argument he follows the same line adopted by other philosophers of science regarding the applicability of falsificationism to the natural sciences. He contends that disconfirming tests do not normally appear to be unambiguously interpretable in economics.[8]

The decline of positivist philosophy together with the limited applicability of falsificationism may appear to leave a methodological void. However, there are alternatives to positivist methodology, and post-normal science is an important one.

Post-Normal Science: A Methodology for the Study of Environmental Issues

The study of the paradigm of a discipline may address two distinct issues. First, it may attempt to detail those aspects that constitute the paradigm of the discipline as normally practised. Second, it may be prescriptive. That is, it may propose certain characteristics that should be part of the paradigm. Prescriptive issues for the study of environmental questions, with specific reference to ecological economics, have been considered particularly by Funtowicz and Ravetz (1991, 1993a, 1993b, 1994) – hereafter, these studies are referred to as F&R. The methodological issues raised by these authors are considered below.

Normal Science

F&R coin the neologism post-normal science to differentiate their conception of scientific activity from that of normal science, and to emphasize that the concept of post-normal science has evolved from that of normal science, first developed by Kuhn (1970). Let me first outline the concept of normal science.

Kuhn's analysis provides a sociological explanation of how science evolves, of how scientists operate. Kuhn's work not only describes how science evolves; it also advances a specific methodology that he believes should be endorsed by scientists.

Normal science is the kind of scientific inquiry that is normally undertaken by the vast majority of scientists. It is the hallmark of science. Normal science is research carried out within a specific paradigm. The values that underlie the paradigm are normally unspoken. A paradigm structures the research problem by providing implicit rules regarding which issues are relevant, how to proceed in the analysis and which analytical tools may be employed in addressing research questions. Normal scientific activity is a puzzle-solving activity. To qualify as a puzzle, a problem must have more than one assured solution. Also, there must be rules regulating the type of solutions that are acceptable and the procedure by which the solutions may be attained.

Kuhn praises normal scientific research for its essential contribution to the progress of science. By carrying out normal science, scientists are able to delve into problems with a detail and depth otherwise impossible. However, he also recognizes the limitations of normal science. Kuhn (1970) stresses that normal science:

> *'seems an attempt to force nature into the preformed and relatively inflexible box that the paradigm supplies. No part of the aim of normal science is to call forth new sorts of phenomena; indeed those that will not fit the box are often not seen at all.'* (Kuhn, 1970, p24)

And:

'To a great extent these are the only problems that the [scientific] community [subscribing to the specific paradigm] will admit as scientific or encourage its members to undertake. Other problems, including many that had previously been standard, are rejected as metaphysical, as the concern of another discipline, or sometimes as just too problematic to be worth the time. A paradigm can, for that matter, even insulate the community from those socially important problems *that are not reducible to the puzzle form, because they cannot be stated in terms of the conceptual and instrumental tools the paradigm supplies.*' (Kuhn, 1970, p37; emphasis added)

To summarize, Kuhn (1970) proposes that normal science is the hallmark of science. Scientists should undertake puzzle-solving activities because this contributes enormously to scientific development. He also acknowledges the limitations of normal science, and points out that when scientists encounter anomalies that cannot be dealt with within the existing paradigm, a crisis may arise and research becomes *extraordinary* rather than normal. In other words, it may lead to changes in the paradigm.

Kuhn's characterization of scientific development and his methodological proposal are not without critics. Reviewing criticisms of the former point is beyond the scope of this chapter. The latter point is dealt with indirectly by considering the position expressed by F&R.

Post-normal Science

F&R stress that post-normal and normal science are complementary. According to them there are, however, important differences between the two approaches to scientific work:

'*post-normal science is a development from and extension of traditional science, appropriate to the conditions of the present age. Its essential principal is that uncertainty and ignorance, even in practice based on science, can no longer be expected to be conquered; instead they must be managed for the common good.*' (Funtowicz and Ravetz, 1993b, p102)

'*We adopt the term "post-normal"' to mark the passing of an age when the norm for effective scientific practice could be a process of puzzle-solving in ignorance of the wider methodological, social, and ethical issues raised by the activity and its results. The scientific problems which are addressed can no longer be chosen on the basis of abstract scientific curiosity or industrial imperatives. Instead, scientists now tackle problems introduced through policy issues, where, typically,* facts are uncertain, values in dispute, stakes high, and decisions urgent.' (Funtowicz and Ravetz, 1991, p138, emphasis added)

F&R first provide a framework for defining the problems that pertain to normal science and those that should be classified as post-normal ones instead. Then, they proceed to explain their post-normal methodology that focuses on problem-solving strategies. These issues are considered in turn. Before doing this, however, it is useful to remark that F&R, according to my reading of their work, equate the concept of normal science with that of positive normal science. That is, normal scientific work carried out according to the tenets of positivist philosophy described above (eg scientific work is value-free).

The demarcation between a normal science problem and a post-normal science one is based on two aspects of the specific issue being considered: (a) the intensity of the uncertainty, and (b) the intensity of the decision stakes. F&R define three levels at which uncertainty may be managed. In order of increasing degree of uncertainty, these three successive levels are:

1   the technical level, where standard routines such as statistical methods may be used to deal with uncertainty;
2   the methodological level, at which values are disputed and personal judgements depending on higher-level skills are required;
3   the epistemological level, where irremediable uncertainty is involved, such as ignorance of ignorance.

The term 'decision stakes' refers to the 'costs, benefits, and commitments of any kind by the parties involved' (Funtowicz and Ravetz, 1991, p144). The meaning of these two concepts may be better understood with specific examples. Normal scientific research deals by definition with puzzle-solving problems that present low levels of uncertainty. This level of uncertainty may be managed technically by standard statistical techniques. In normal scientific research decision stakes are also low. This kind of research is curiosity-motivated, and a failure in addressing the problem will not have repercussions on the wider community.

When a problem presents a high degree of uncertainty and/or high decision stakes, it befits post-normal science. This kind of problem should be dealt with according to the methodology of post-normal science. Given that post-normal science concerns itself with issues that present diversity of perspectives (ie values held by the various stakeholders about the high stakes involved) and large uncertainties, its methodology aims at dealing with these specific issues. This methodology focuses on the management of both uncertainty and the quality assurance. These two issues are considered in turn.

Funtowicz and Ravetz (1994) note that in the mature quantitative sciences uncertainty is simply managed by the scientists on the basis of their inherited (presumably from other scientists?), unselfconscious craft skills. To improve on this state of affairs, that is to increase transparency and quality of information, F&R develop a system that provides guidelines for the presentation and management of information displaying a high degree of uncertainty. The notation system has five categories:

1 numeral;
2 unit of measurement;
3 spread (ie random error provides a measure of the degree of precision);
4 assessment (ie systematic error relates to the degree of accuracy);
5 pedigree (describes the degree of ignorance concerning highly uncertain information).

In relation to quality assurance, no better words than those of the authors themselves can summarize this concept.

> *'we speak of "quality assurance", which relates to the whole [research] process, and that in a reflective way (that is, quality assurance is more comprehensive than quality-control). Our first justification for the extended peer communities is in terms of quality assurance, as a total function ... For us, Quality is a replacement for [positivist] Truth in our methodology. We argue that this is quite enough for doing science, and that Truth is a category with symbolic importance, which itself is historically and culturally conditioned.'* (Jerry Ravetz, personal communication.)

F&R propose that the guiding principle for quality assurance should be that *the values* involved in post-normal scientific analyses should be made explicit. To do this, scientific argument should not be based on *formalized deduction* but on *interactive dialogue*. They stress that post-normal scientists should not claim ethical neutrality and push forward their arguments on the basis of the prestige of objective research, nor should they be indifferent to the consequences of their arguments toward policy.

To guarantee high quality assurance F&R advance three interlinked methodological recommendations. First, traditional peer review of the quality of scientific research is not sufficient any more in the presence of large uncertainties and high decision stakes. A wider debate of the issues investigated is warranted. This leads to the second methodological suggestion. The stakeholders with interest in the issue being investigated should take part in the process of quality assessment of information and, possibly, in the actual research process. The latter may take place through the process outlined in the third methodological suggestion: 'post-normal science may well include investigative journalism and related techniques' (Funtowicz and Ravetz, 1994, p205).

After having outlined the position of F&R, let me consider critically some methodological aspects of their discourse.

Comments on the Funtowicz and Ravetz Proposal

F&R importantly point out the relevance of stating values explicitly. This is not a novel contribution but an important reminder (see also Beed, 1992; Nelson, 1996; Norgaard, 1989; Tisdell, 1983). It has already been stated above that the critics of positivism have stressed that value-free science cannot exist. Reminders such as those of F&R will help in making this argument flow through to natural and social sciences.

They also point environmental and ecological economists in an important direction on the road to the improvement of their methodology. Researchers should not only attempt to include the views of the stakeholders in their research; proper social processes for the inclusion of the latter in the actual research should be devised. Some reasons to justify this statement will be provided in the next section.

A further important contribution made by F&R is to have stressed that the choice of a particular methodology employed in addressing an issue depends on the context specific to the issue. When high stakes are involved, a methodology different from that adopted when the stakes are low may be appropriate. Clearly, this is a departure from the unity of science view held by positivist philosophers and practitioners. In relation to quality assurance, some comments will be provided after the analysis of constructivism.

After recognizing the significant contribution made by F&R, it is now appropriate to consider a weakness of their proposal. This weakness relates to the methodological proposal of including the various stakeholders in post-normal science research. F&R suggest that the various stakeholders should be involved in the review of scientific information. Therefore, this process is extended beyond the traditional peer review. Stakeholders may also be involved in producing *extended facts* that may be collected, for example, through investigative journalism. This suggestion goes in the right direction of defining a research process extended to various parties. However, it falls short of satisfactorily outlining how this process may be carried out. By saying that the review of scientific research is extended to other stakeholders, and that other 'information that will not usually be in the traditional scientific form' (Funtowicz and Ravetz, 1991, p150) should be considered, they appear to:

1   define a policy process in which the views of the different stakeholders are taken account of;
2   state that not only traditional scientific information is valid.

They do not consider how a researcher may go about carrying out research incorporating the views of the stakeholders both in order to define the research problem and to make explicit the views and interests of the stakeholders. This aspect of F&R's methodology is due to the fact that their approach to research is rooted in the natural sciences. This is exemplified by F&R's examples being primarily concerned with computer applications and model building.[9]

F&R stress that a range of methodologies may be required in addressing environment-economy related issues. The methodology that they propose may be suited to those issues that require a research approach rooted in the methodology of natural science. When the issues being investigated are in the area of the social sciences, ecological economists may be in need of a methodology different from, or that may complement, that proposed by F&R.

Constructivism

Constructivism has evolved over the last three decades. It has its roots in the works of scholars from various disciplines such as education, psychology, sociology and human ecology (eg Geertz, 1973; Hannigan, 1995; Jackson, 1968; Lincoln and Guba, 1985; Maturana and Varela, 1992; Weber, 1968). A description of the evolution of the constructivist paradigm and of its different strands is provided by Schwandt (1990). Egon Guba, a significant contributor to the development of this paradigm, summarizes the constructivist paradigm as follows.

> 'Ontology: Relativist – *realities exist in the form of multiple mental constructions, socially and experimentally based, local and specific, dependent for their form and content on the persons who hold them.*
> Epistemology: Subjectivist – *inquirer and inquired into are fused into a single (monistic) entity. Findings are literally the creation of the process of interaction between the two.*
> Methodology: Hermeneutic, Dialectic – *individual constructions are elicited and refined hermeneutically, and compared and contrasted dialectically, with the aim of generating one (or a few) constructions on which there is substantial consensus.'* (Guba, 1990, p27)

It has already been suggested above that there are good reasons for adopting a relativist ontology. However, the ontological position presented by Guba (1990) is not fully endorsed here. The adoption of the constructivist paradigm is criticized by some ecological economists because it denies biophysical constraints on social life (Jacobs, 1996). Critical realists (eg Gandy, 1996; Pratt, 1995) suggest that the constructivist ontological position suffers from a shortcoming: in constructivist ontology being is determined by knowledge. Consider the Earth without human beings. A reality would exist but would not be socially constructed.

Therefore, a reality exists whether constructed or not by humans. Existing human beings see only particular aspects of *reality*. This leads to a reformulation of the relativist ontology presented above.

> There exists a physical reality subject to differing interpretations by human beings. Thus, there exist multiple socially constructed realities.

In terms of environmental studies, this definition implies that there may be biophysical limits to social life. However, these limits are interpreted differently by different actors. Thus, there are problems in defining and measuring sustainability.

Let me now present the epistemology and methodology of constructivism by closely following Lincoln and Guba (1985).

Constructivist epistemology recognizes that inquiry is value-bound. The research process is influenced, for instance, by the inquirer's values (eg they may determine the choice of the problem), and by the theory used to collect and analyse data and to interpret the findings. Constructivism also asserts that the inquiry cannot be an objective, detached process. Moreover, it also claims that the inquiry process *should not* be an objective and detached process in the positivist sense. Let us consider these two latter issues in turn.

Inquiry cannot be objective. The absence of one single reality clearly precludes *a priori* that inquiry may be objective. However, even if it can be agreed that there exists a reality, there are at least three factors that stand in the way of objective social research. These are reactivity, indeterminacy and interaction.

Reactivity refers to the respondents' knowledge of being investigated. Even if the respondents are well intentioned and cooperative, their behaviour may confound the data. In this case, research may be said to disturb the researched. *Indeterminacy* refers to the fact that what is observed is seen through the specific perspective derived from the methodology of investigation adopted. The situation being studied can only be seen by creating a disturbance through the use of the research methodology. In this case, research shapes the researched. *Interaction* relates to the bidirectional influences in the relationship between the inquirer and the subject of research. These mutual influences occur, for example, both in survey questionnaires or direct interviewing. What is meant here is that the researchers' conduct is influenced, for example, by their expectations about the respondents' attitudes and reactions, and vice versa in the case of the respondents.

Since interaction of the researcher with the researched cannot be eliminated, Lincoln and Guba (1985) argue that it should be actively used to improve the quality of research.

Inquiry should not be objective-detached. Several items tend to indicate the importance of research interactions. Three of these are highlighted below.

The unambiguous choice of a theory and the explanation of facts based on strictly technical processes such as falsification is not viable. It has already been stressed above that several theories may explain a set of facts, and a set of facts may support a variety of theories. Informed, sound judgement is required to provisionally accept a theory and to assess the degree to which a set of facts supports the theory. To pass this kind of judgement, an in-depth knowledge of the phenomenon being studied is required. This may only be achieved through interaction.

The process of change is continuous and inevitable. Social science research that attempts to understand change has to highlight the contradictions and conflicts that characterize the process of change. Dialectical social science research cannot be carried out without constant and sensitive interaction with the human beings under study. People always interact with each other and also with the investigator. The forced exclusion of these relationships from the research process would create distortion in the data and their meaning would be partly destroyed. If the people being researched do not understand and cooperate in the research process, findings of social science research may be vitiated.

Fundamentally, I agree with the current constructivist epistemological position; however, I propose a more moderate position than that advocated by Guba (1990). I suggest that *there is a distinction between inquirer and inquired into*. This separation, however, is far from being the totally detached state typical of positivism. This position is compatible with accepting that the findings of the research process are generated *to a certain degree* by the interaction of inquirer and inquired into. This view may be thus summarized.

> The inquirer and the researched are not two totally separate entities. Findings are strongly influenced by the process of interaction between the two.

In relation to methodological issues, positivist methodology is based on proposing laws (generalizations) that support theories. Hypotheses are derived and tested according to the hypothetico-deductive model. Constructivists reject this approach and propose an alternative approach: the working hypothesis (Cronbach, 1975).

There are always local and unique conditions that limit the usefulness of time, and context-free generalizations which are characteristic of the positivist methodology. However, researchers may derive time and context-specific generalizations, or working hypotheses, using their in-depth knowledge of the specific situation gained through the extended, interactive research process. Working hypotheses come late in the research process and are tentative both for the particular condition in which they are developed and for other contexts. Working hypotheses may be transferable to other situations. However, the degree to which this is possible depends on the similarity between the different contexts. This may be judged by comparing the conditions specific to the context in which the working hypothesis was developed – information that should be provided in the study reporting the hypothesis – with the conditions prevailing in the alternative context. This description of the specific conditions is referred to as a *thick description*.

The constructivist research process differs considerably from the conventional positivist one. Therefore, it is useful to outline the salient features of the former research process, as described by Lincoln and Guba (1985).

Research is carried out in its *natural setting*, that is the context of the entity being studied. This is because (a) realities cannot be understood in isolation of their context, and (b) knowledge of the specific context is determinant in deciding whether or not the findings may be extended to other situations.

- *Qualitative methods* are used to the same, if not greater, extent than quantitative methods because (a) they are more suited to dealing with multiple realities, and (b) they are more adaptable to the various influences and value patterns encountered in the field.

- *Inductive data analysis* is preferred to deductive data analysis because (a) it is better suited to fully describing the research context and to providing information about the transferability of the findings, and (b) to identify the mutually shaping influences present in the research context.
- *Grounded theory* is used. It is preferable to have the theory emerge from the data because (a) the realities that may be encountered cannot be fully described by *a priori* theory, and (b) *a priori* theory is based on generalizations that may poorly fit the specific context encountered. It should be obvious from the arguments presented above that some view of the world is required to go and find out more about the specific context. Therefore, I interpret grounded theory as updating one's view of the world, and possibly even totally changing it, if this need emerges from the research process. In turn, this implies that some theory (or considerations) have to be developed before going into the field.

The design of the research process, or *emergent design*, is allowed to unfold while research is carried out because (a) it is unlikely that enough could be known in advance in order to fully define the research design, and (b) the interactions between the researcher and the researched tend to influence the outcomes in ways that are not predictable.

The interpretation of the data is negotiated with the people from whom the data have been derived because (a) it is their views about the specific context that the inquirer seeks to describe, and (b) the working hypothesis that might apply to a specific context is best confirmed with the people who belong to the context in question. This process leads to what are termed *negotiated outcomes*. This does not imply that this necessarily brings about agreement (eg Chapters 6, 7 and 12).

Idiographic interpretation means that the data are interpreted in terms of the specific case (ie idiographically) rather than made into law-like statements. This is because (a) different realities may warrant different interpretations, and (b) the interpretations are determined to a large extent by the particulars of the specific context, such as the interactions between the researcher and the researched. As noted above when discussing the concept of working hypotheses, constructivists do not completely refrain from making generalizations. Certainly, they are more circumspect in doing so than positivists.

Action and Rigour in the Constructivist Paradigm

The constructivist paradigm is well suited to a research approach that is issue and policy driven and aims at implementing the research findings through the participation of the stakeholders. An important issue to be considered is how a rigorous research process may be maintained while adopting a constructivist research approach.

A constructivist research process may be used to conduct both curiosity-motivated research or action-oriented research. In the first case, researchers may aim at simply presenting the views of the different stakeholders or may also derive their own interpretations of the issues being researched. In the second case, where the implementation of the research findings is an important component of the process, the various stakeholders have to participate both in the research and implementation processes. The features of the constructivist research process that are particularly important in facilitating the participation of the stakeholders in this process – and the possible adoption of the findings – are the location of research in the natural setting, the adoption of qualitative methods, inductive data analysis, allowing the research design to emerge and the negotiation of outcomes. It is opportune to note that there are participatory research approaches that suit and complement the constructivist paradigm, such as participatory action research and participatory action and learning, which are aimed at modifying the situation being researched. Action research has been adopted in education, industry and agriculture (Kemmis and McTaggart, 1988; Whyte, 1991; Chambers, 1997).

A description of participatory research taking into account that research may be action or academically oriented is presented in Table 2.1. Academic research is not necessarily conventional; it can indeed adopt a participatory approach. Action oriented research, which is more likely to be oriented towards solving specific problems, needs to take into account that stakeholders other than researchers do have knowledge, but their knowledge and capacity to conduct research do have limits.

The rigour of the research process may be maintained by setting criteria aimed at guiding a *disciplined* inquiry process (Lincoln and Guba, 1985). A set of such criteria has been developed, discussed and revised in a series of studies (Lincoln and Guba, 1985, 1986; Lincoln, 1990; Marshall, 1990; Pretty, 1994; Smith, 1990). Nine major criteria are listed in Box 2.1.

Conclusion

The positivist view of scientific activities has had important implications for the work of natural and social scientists. Of particular relevance, first, positivism has led many social scientists to eschew inquiry into ethical questions in the name of value-free science. Second, it has directed many social scientists to attempt to undertake objective-detached research. In some situations this has meant that research has had little relevance to social entities and/or did not contribute to the improvement of problematic situations. Third, it has prompted the claim that research that does not attempt to apply falsificationism cannot be regarded as scientific work.

On the first point, in this chapter, it is stressed that the positivist stance that it is possible to conduct scientific work without making value judgements is untenable. Value judgements are always made at several stages of the inquiry process. Therefore, it is preferable to deal openly with these considerations. Any attempt at hiding the values implicit to any analysis is a misleading and dishonest[10] practice. Openly addressing the sets of values involved in any research problem can only improve the quality of the research output.

Table 2.1 *Two types of participatory research: action oriented and academic*

	Action oriented research	Academic research
What is the research for?	Understanding and action	Understanding with perhaps action later
Who is the research for?	Mainly for stakeholders, partly for institutional, personal and professional interest	Institutional, personal, professional interest, local people
Whose knowledge counts?	Stakeholders and researchers	Researchers and local people
Topic choice influenced by?	Local priorities	Funding priorities, institutional agendas, professional interests, local priorities
Methodology chosen for?	Empowerment, mutual learning	Disciplinary methodology, rigour, mutual learning
Who takes part in the stages of the research process?		
Problem identification	Stakeholders, researchers	Researchers, local people
Data collection	Stakeholders, researchers, enumerators	Researchers, enumerators, local people
Interpretation	Local concepts and frameworks, disciplinary concepts and frameworks	Disciplinary concepts and frameworks, partly local frameworks
Analysis	Stakeholders, researchers	Researchers; local people
Presentation of findings	Locally accessible and useful	In academic publications; also locally accessible publications
Action on findings	Integral to the process	Separate and may not happen
Who takes action?	Stakeholders, with/without external support	External agencies; local people
Who owns the results?	Shared	Shared
What is emphasized?	Process and outcomes	Outcomes; process to a lesser extent

Source: developed from the original framework presented by Cornwall and Jewkes (1995).

To turn to the second point, it seems nonviable to try to carry out objective-detached analysis. Attempting to do so may create two major shortcomings. First, research that attempts to present *one* objective reality actually presents the researcher's reality. The various stakeholders' realities are thus omitted. Second, when the research process considers policy issues, detached analysis may result in irrelevant analysis and/or policy inaction.

Box 2.1 Criteria guiding a constructivist research process

Prolonged and/or intense engagement. This is used by the researcher to understand the specific context, to build trust with the stakeholders, and to allow the stakeholders to assess whether their input into the process will be valued or not.

Persistent observation. It is used to understand the context and the issues being studied.

Triangulation. Multiple sources, methods and investigators are used and are involved in data collection and analysis.

Analysis of difference. A range of agents are involved in the research process in order to guarantee that the different realities are detailed.

Peer debriefing. This takes place during the research process. It helps in maintaining honesty in the research process and in guiding the emergence of the research design.

Member checks. The data, interpretations and conclusions are checked with the members of the stakeholders' groups that participated in the research process. This is the most fundamental test because the members have to recognize as their own the reconstructions provided by the researcher.

Reports with working hypotheses and thick description. This allows other researchers or interested people to judge the transferability of the research findings to other contexts.

Impact on stakeholders' capacity to know and act. A successful research process aimed at producing change should result in an enhanced understanding, on the stakeholders' side, of the different realities and how to act upon them.

Inquiry audit. This takes place at the end of the research process. It aims at assessing whether or not the conclusions drawn by the inquirers are supported by the data. It may take the form of conventional peer review of reports and/or may be carried out in a workshop (the latter should be the preferred means).

Finally, on the third point, because of the problems faced in the application of falsificationism, if this were the true demarcation line used to distinguish between science and non-science, then it would appear that there is no natural or social discipline that can be considered scientific. At best, falsificationism can provide guidelines for disciplined inquiry. However, the provision of these guidelines is not exclusively the precinct of falsificationism. Some criteria guiding research in a paradigm alternative to falsificationism have been summarized above. Research conducted within those criteria cannot be considered any less scientific than that which attempts to implement falsificationism. There are no objective criteria (or meta-criteria) that may be used in choosing between two research paradigms (Kuhn, 1970).

It is worthwhile pointing out that the research methodology espoused by the constructivist paradigm should not be considered as a substitute for the research process outlined by F&R. The constructivist approach provides instead detailed guidelines about the conduct of participatory research that are currently lacking in the F&R proposal.

It appears that there are complementary elements between the F&R proposal and constructivism in relation to the question of quality assurance. F&R stress explicitly the need to address the question of quality. The concept of quality has not been explicitly considered within the constructivist paradigm that, instead, refers to research rigour. It should be noted, however, that some of the suggestions made by F&R regarding high quality assurance closely parallel elements of constructivist research methodology. For example:

1 values should be made explicit;
2 scientific arguments should be based on interactive dialogue;
3 scientists should not advance their arguments on the basis of the prestige of objective research.

Given the arguments discussed here, there is scope for further considering how these two research approaches may enrich each other.

Finally, it is essential to remark that it is not implied here that *one and only one* research methodology should exist within ecological economics. This is the positivist view. The recognition that there are multiple realities appears to lead to the acceptance of the fact that multiple paradigms exist. The existence of multiple paradigms is important to the development of science. Therefore, this diversity should be maintained (Norgaard, 1985). Diversity of paradigms is to the development of knowledge as biodiversity is to the development of life on Earth.

Notes

*   This chapter is a slightly modified version of a paper published as Tacconi, L (1998) 'Scientific methodology for ecological economics', *Ecological Economics*, 27(1): 91–105. Elsevier Publications.

1   In a narrow sense, the term methodology has been used to refer to the study of the process through which theories are formed and justified (eg Blaug, 1992). In a broader meaning, methodology refers to the process of learning about the social and/or physical world (eg Hausman, 1992). A methodological study may assess how these processes *are* carried out or detail how they *should* be carried out.

2   This term is used here in its classical meaning of the art of arguing, rather than in the modern disparaging fashion.

3   There is certainly a need to look also at the influence of positivism on ecology, and some ecologists are aware of a methodological crisis within ecology (Peters, 1991).

4   The following summary of logical empiricism is derived from Caldwell (1982).

5   It has to be stressed that this position corresponds to a particular interpretation of quantum theory. Conflicting views among physicists exist.

6   Nelson (1996) recognizes the influence of values on scientific research and the problems inherent to the concept of objectivity as currently used by scientists. Rather than discarding the use of the word objectivity, she formulates the new concept of strong objectivity that is based on a dialectic approach to research. To avoid confusion, I prefer to do away with the concept of objectivity and consider instead that of rigour, as detailed below.

7   This model is composed of the following steps: (a) define the problem to be studied; (b) specify the hypothesis to be investigated; (c) identify the variables to be included; (d) note the expected relationships between variables; (e) outline the methodology of data collection and analysis; (f) test the hypothesis; (g) accept or reject the hypothesis.

8   In relation to the natural sciences, Kuhn (1970, p26) remarks: 'there are seldom many areas in which a scientific theory, particularly if it is cast in a predominantly mathematical form, can be directly compared with nature ... Furthermore, even in those areas where application is possible, it often demands theoretical and instrumental approximations that severely limit the agreement to be expected.'

9   For example: 'Science cannot always provide well-founded theories based on experiments for explanation and prediction, but can frequently only achieve at best mathematical models and computer simulations' (Funtowicz and Ravetz, 1991, p139).

10   At times scientists are not aware of the value judgements implied by their analyses; in those cases it may be more appropriate to speak of 'false consciousness within science' (J. Ravetz, personal communication). This refers to the positivist faith of being able to be objective.

3

Paradigms and Environmental Decision-Making

Introduction

While the previous chapter considered paradigmatic issues concerning the methodology of science, this chapter is concerned with paradigmatic aspects relating to environmental-economic issues. The tenets of ecological economics (ECE) are outlined first. It is noted that ECE is concerned with sustainability, scale, distribution and allocation issues. The focus on allocation is shared with neo-classical environmental economics (NEE) which is also concerned, although to a lesser extent than ECE, with distribution.

Because of the overlap between ECE and NEE, it is useful to consider in detail aspects of NEE. The latter is a more established discipline relative to ECE. A clear understanding of NEE, of its contradictions and shortcomings, provides useful background information for the development of an improved ECE framework.

In neo-classical economics, which underlies NEE, individuals are regarded as the only legitimate source of values. This chapter focuses, therefore, on the image of *Homo oeconomicus* assumed by neo-classical economics and its implications for the decision-making process envisaged by neo-classical economists. The neo-classical model provides important insights into human behaviour and it is useful in deriving implications regarding environmental management. It is argued, however, that the neo-classical approach presents several shortcomings. By integrating the image of *Homo oeconomicus* with the depiction of human behaviour presented in the writings of institutional economists and social economists, a description of what is termed here the human behavioural space is presented. This human behavioural space attempts to present a *fuller* image of the behaviour of *actual* individuals and of institutions, and of the factors that influence their behaviour. The implications for environmental decision-making of this expanded human behavioural model are then expounded.

Before proceeding, three issues deserve comment. First, the analysis will concentrate on the decision-making framework proper of NEE, rather than on what environmental economists – people whose work is *mainly* based on neo-classical economics – see as a useful or proper decision-making framework. The importance of making this distinction is better explained with an example. While NEE concerns itself with the efficient allocation of resources, there are environmental economists who consider relevant the issue of sustainability. NEE is a specific paradigm. Environmental economists work primarily within the environmental economics paradigm but may also draw on other paradigms.

Second, it is recognized that there are schools of thought which have their origins in neo-classical economics (eg new institutionalism and public choice theory) and may be applied to environmental decision-making. However, the following analysis focuses on neo-classical economics because it is the paradigmatic basis of environmental economics, currently the dominant approach within the academic world to economic decision-making in relation to environmental issues.

Third, the important contribution of NEE to a better understanding of, and solution of, environmental problems is recognized. The criticisms raised are aimed at improving our understanding of the issues at stake and at designing a more appropriate framework. It is not an attempt at claiming a territory for ECE; thus we seek to avoid the argument culture (Costanza, 1998).

Ecological Economics

Ecological economics is relatively new and its paradigmatic position is still evolving. ECE came into being in the 1980s, but it has deep roots in economics and ecology and, therefore, it has an evolutionary history of more than 200 years (Martinez-Alier, 1987; Costanza et al, 1997a). Costanza et al (1991, p3) describe ECE as:

> 'a new transdisciplinary *field of study that addresses the relationships between ecosystems and economic system in the broadest sense ... By* transdisciplinary *we mean that* ecological economics *goes beyond our normal conception of scientific disciplines and tries to integrate and synthesise many different disciplinary perspectives ... No discipline has intellectual precedence in an endeavour as important as achieving sustainability. While the intellectual tools we use in this quest are important, they are secondary to the goal of solving the critical problems of managing our use of the planet. ...* Ecological economics *will use the tools of conventional economics [neo-classical economics] and ecology as appropriate. The need for new intellectual tools and models may emerge where the coupling of economics and ecology is not possible with the existing tools.'*

It is clear that the analysis of sustainability and its achievement are the centrepieces of ECE. ECE is issue-driven. To better address the issues of interest, it maintains transdisciplinarity and attempts to avoid allowing the framing of problems to be dictated by the available tools. ECE may use the tools of neo-classical economics, but it recognizes that new approaches may also be needed. Other surveys of ECE have tended to emphasize the differences between ECE and NEE to a greater extent than Costanza et al (1991). This issue is considered below. However, before proceeding in the analysis, it is necessary to consider the concept of sustainability.

Sustainability

Many definitions of sustainability – and sustainable development – have been proposed.[1] Sustainability has been used in relation to the natural environment, to the economic system, and to the social system; furthermore, all these concepts have been analysed at different geographical levels. The concepts of environmental sustainability and sustainable development are clearly different. The former refers only to the natural environment whereas the latter relates not only to environmental systems but also to the social and economic systems. It has been noted that:

> '*positivists are inevitably frustrated and confused when faced with the notion of sustainability. In as much as they believe an independent reality exists, then so must it be possible precisely to define sustainability in value-free terms ... But no scientific method will ever be able to ask all the right questions about how we should manage resources for sustainable development, let alone find the answers.*' (Pretty, 1994, p38)

Because of its social content, sustainable development is a subjective concept and cannot be neatly measured. Instead, environmental sustainability is regarded by some as objectively measurable. Hueting and Reijnders (1998) argue that *admissible environmental burdens* (ie limits), which if exceeded lead to a loss of the environmental functions provided by ecosystems, can be established scientifically and, therefore, sustainability is an objective concept. They affirm that the subjective aspects enter the scene where discussions of how to stay within the admissible environmental burdens begin, which is the sustainable development sphere. While at an abstract level and for some basic cases (eg measurement of soil erosion) it may be possible to agree with this position, at an applied level and for more complex cases (eg measurement of forest ecosystem sustainability) it is difficult to concur with it. It is true that there appear to be thresholds beyond which species and ecosystems collapse. But it is uncertain what these thresholds are for complex ecosystems; furthermore, species and ecosystems change and evolve and so may their thresholds. Thus, the definition of these thresholds and their scientific assessment become to a certain degree a subjective issue (eg Norgaard, 1995). Thus, sustainability may be regarded as a general principle guiding resource management. However, one single, unifying definition of sustainability cannot be provided.

Tenets of Ecological Economics

NEE and ECE have been described as occupying niches that are in some respects complementary and in other respects competitive (Sahu and Nayak, 1994). These authors present a description of ECE and a classification of the similarities and differences between the ECE and NEE.

Major tenets of ECE and NEE are summarized in Table 3.1 (derived from Sahu and Nayak's Table 1).[2] It is clear from Table 3.1 that there are significant differences between NEE and ECE. This view is also put forward by Söderbaum (1992) and Opschor (1994). These authors, however, argue that ECE has roots in institutional economics, draws on biophysics and ecology, and borrows from modern evolutionary economics.[3] Due to its roots in institutional and evolutionary economics, ECE uses simulation models more than optimization models. These roots also imply that ECE considers 'institutionalized bounds to the domain of economic rationality and the scale of economic activity' (Opschor, 1994, p12).

Table 3.1 *Tenets of environmental economics and ecological economics*

Dimension	Environmental economics	Ecological economics
Main theory	Neo-classical economics	Biophysical plus physiocratic and classical economics
Approach	Allocation of resource use	Scale, distribution and allocation of resource use
World-view	Mechanistic-reductionist	Evolutionary-holistic
Knowledge-acquisition process	Positivist, supposedly value-free	Subjectivist, reflecting values and ideology
Character	Monodisciplinary	Multidisciplinary
Scarcity perception	Relative	Absolute
View of future	Technological optimism	Prudent pessimism
Problem-solving orientation	Based on market system	Based on laws of nature
Focus	Short-term	Long-term
Methods of (e)valuation	CBA[a]	EIS, positional analysis, carrying capacity analysis[b]
Dominant theme	Anthropocentric	Anthropocentric with attempts to include biocentric and ecocentric considerations

Notes: a CBA: cost–benefit analysis; CBA is used here to refer to the whole array of tools that employ both market and non-market information.
b EIS: environmental impact statements; positional analysis has been developed in Söderbaum's writings (1987; 1993; 1994).
Source: adapted from Sahu and Nayak (1994).

According to some ecological economists, scale is a particularly significant factor in distinguishing ECE from NEE. Scale refers to the physical throughput of the economy.[4] The concept of scale complements those of distribution and allocation according to Daly (1992), who suggests that the scale of an economy should be held within the carrying capacity of the environment. Daly suggests that sustainability is the criterion to be used in assessing the appropriateness of the scale, while equity and efficiency are, respectively, criteria for distribution and allocation. The concept of scale is a relatively new introduction, and its relevance and use are still subject to debate (eg Stewen, 1998). Daly (1992) argues that a logical sequence in policy-making would involve setting the scale of the economy, then distribution of resources, and finally the market would be left to allocate resources efficiently. While this is a logical argument in theory, its application is (currently) difficult, because there is a lack of knowledge of the carrying capacity of the environment. In other words, scale could be set at a level too high, resulting in an unsustainable system, or too low, with costs in terms of availability of resources to be distributed. For this reason, the application of the concept of scale may be reduced at present to the adoption of the precautionary principle and safe minimum standards, as discussed in the following chapter. A further issue concerning scale is that it is essentially a quantitative concept. Qualitative aspects are, however, important for the sustainable use of renewable resources, such as forests and marine environments, and the conservation of biodiversity. For example, to assess whether resource harvesting in a marine environment is sustainable, the quality of the process used to harvest them needs to be considered as well as the quantity (scale) of the resources extracted. Therefore, the concept of sustainability of renewable resources has a meaning broader than that of scale, and it is not simply a criterion to be used in assessing the appropriateness of the scale.

ECE searches for coevolutionary development (eg Norgaard, 1984). Swaney (1987a; 1987b) remarks that the concept of coevolutionary sustainability means development paths posing serious threats to continued compatible evolution of social and ecological systems should be avoided.

A characteristic that ECE has derived from institutional economics is that societal values are not just the sum of individual values. Institutional economics asserts that there is a hierarchy of values. For instance, in this hierarchy, values related to continuity of life or social reproduction are above the daily needs and wants of individuals (Swaney, 1987a). A practical reason explaining the deviation between individual values and societal values is the fact that society has a longer life expectancy than individuals (Opschor, 1994).

In relation to the classification of values, Ramstad (1989) notes that some institutionalists adhere to the instrumental value paradigm. Ramstad (1989) notes that instrumental value is construed as both a tool of analysis and a normative compass. Instrumental values are values that are good. Instrumental values are needs to be clarified through scientific inquiry (Tool, 1986). Ramstad (1989) stresses that the instrumental paradigm suffers several shortcomings. A most important one is that it seems difficult to reconcile the instrumental paradigm with a commitment to democracy.[5]

Two entries in Table 3.1 are of particular interest here. The entry 'Problem-solving orientation' describes ECE as 'based on laws of nature'. This is a rather generic definition which does not fully represent the problem-solving orientation of ECE and unduly accentuates the differentiation between ECE and NEE. In fact, the market system plays an important role not only in the problem-solving orientation of NEE but also of ECE. This has been stressed by Page (1991), who outlines the features of a two-tiered ecological economic approach. The first tier defines the circumstances under which the second tier operates. For example, the constitution of a country is part of the first tier. The second tier includes legislatures, courts and markets. The first tier should contain sustainability rules that would contribute to define the boundaries within which markets would operate. An important point is that the principle of non-interference should be adopted. 'The idea is that instruments implementing the conditions of the first tier should be broad, avoiding minute control in the day-to-day workings of markets and the ordinary second tier institutions' (Page, 1991, p70).

In respect to the 'Methods of (e)valuation' entry, two issues need to be raised. The first has to do with the distinction between *evaluation* and *valuation*. Valuation here refers to the application of CBA to resource allocation problems, whereas evaluation refers to a decision-making process that considers issues concerning scale, distribution and allocation. The tools adopted in this process may include CBA as well as other tools, such as those characteristically used in participatory analysis (eg participatory rural appraisal). The second point is that the sharp distinction between the tools employed within NEE and ECE, as implied by Sahu and Nayak (1994), is probably incorrect. For instance, CBA studies are being published by the journal *Ecological Economics*. This seems to show that CBA may be used in ecological economic analysis. This is because ECE seeks to remain a non-dogmatic discipline open to various contributions, and because allocative efficiency is accepted as an indicator to be used – together with scale and distribution – in environmental decision-making. Certainly, the ECE position that efficiency is *one of the factors* to be considered differs from NEE that takes efficiency as its guiding rule. It follows that CBA is only one of the possible tools to be employed in ECE. The specific role of CBA within ECE will be further discussed below.

To summarize the above discussion, the concepts of sustainability, scale, distribution and efficiency are all considered important factors to be addressed in the decision-making process relating to environmental-economic issues. This position is certainly based on the specific value judgements inherent to ECE. Value judgements are always important in influencing researchers' and practitioners' positions, for example an NEE scholar's view that only efficiency counts.

Neo-Classical Economics and the Environment

Neo-classical economics has been applied to ecosystem management in the two distinct fields of environmental economics and resource economics. Cropper and

Oates (1992) stress that the boundary between the two fields is fuzzy. However, they note that resource economics concerns itself mostly with the allocation of renewable and non-renewable natural resources (eg forests and minerals). NEE concerns itself with 'the regulation of polluting activities and the valuation of environmental amenities' (Cropper and Oates, 1992, p678). NEE has its roots in externality theory, public goods theory, general equilibrium theory and CBA (Kneese and Russell, 1987). Given the ubiquitous presence of externalities, some authors have noted that environmental economics studies the causes of and solutions to market failure (eg Common, 1988). NEE appears to be increasingly focusing on valuation issues (Vatn and Bromley, 1994).

A summary of the neo-classical paradigm facilitates the understanding of the paradigmatic position of NEE.

NEE relies on the market to achieve an efficient allocation of resources. However, given that several factors inhibit the achievement of an efficient allocation of resources (eg externalities), there is a necessary but not sufficient case for government intervention. The latter may occur through market mechanisms (eg taxes) or through direct intervention (eg establishment of protected areas). The merit of government intervention can be assessed with CBA in order to ascertain whether sufficient conditions for intervention exist (ie intervention is superior to non-intervention).

The neo-classical paradigm is summarized by the following ten points.[6]

1   The subject matter of economics is the study of the allocation of scarce means to given ends.
2   The economy may be reasonably described as being in competitive equilibrium.
3   Individuals (the sovereign consumers) are the decision-making units: neo-classical economics adopts methodological individualism.
4   Individuals repeatedly face the same, or similar, choice situations.
5   Individuals have stable preferences and thus may evaluate the outcomes of choices according to stable criteria.
6   Individuals seek to maximize their own utility.
7   Individuals act rationally.
8   Given repeated exposure, individuals can recognize and seize any available opportunity for improving outcomes.
9   It follows that there exists no equilibrium in which individuals fail to maximize their utility, subject to income constraints.
10 Positivism is adopted as the methodological basis.

It is worth noting that many neo-classical economists would probably subscribe to the view that *Homo oeconomicus* is not intended to describe actual human behaviour,[7] but it is a model useful for understanding and predicting human economic behaviour. This position is often justified by adopting Friedman's (1973) view that what matters in building a model is its predictive power rather than the realism of assumptions. This position has already been criticized in the previous chapter.

Implications for the Study of Environment–Economy Relationships and the Valuation of Ecosystems

The particular theoretical features of neo-classical economics described above determine how the problem to be studied is framed and how the study is carried out. In considering some of the implications for the study of environmental issues that these theoretical features hold, it is useful to list these implications under the specific theoretical assumption. However, more than one assumption (eg methodological individualism and positivism) may determine the specific feature under consideration.

Methodological Individualism

Methodological individualism makes no reference to objects and phenomena not definable in terms of human individuals, and it considers only laws of individual behaviour or laws that may be reducible to laws of individual behaviour (Mathien, 1988). Decisions made at the societal level are regarded as the sum of decisions made by atomistic individuals. The adoption of methodological individualism has four major implications.

First, there is no legitimate source of values apart from individuals. Thus, valuation studies attempt to ascertain only the values assigned to the environment by individuals. No consideration is given to the fact that other social entities may assign values to the environment that differ from the sum of the values held by the individual members of these entities.

Second, to assign values to the environment, the individual decision-making processes have to be assumed by the researcher. This creates a peculiar circular process. Many neo-classical economists regard the *Homo oeconomicus* construct as a fiction, useful in predicting economic behaviour. Usually, it is not thought that this model reflects actual behaviour. However, CBA studies adopt this model of the individual and tell what human economic behaviour towards the environment *should be* simply on the basis of this fictional model. Whilst it is recognized that at times this model may reflect actual behaviour, it cannot be assumed that this is always the case.

Third, the emphasis on the individual seems to result, at first glance, in an accent on individual rights, but this is misleading. For example, it has been remarked that the adoption of the potential Pareto improvement test implies the rejection of 'paternalism – the notion that the government, scientists, or any other élite group knows best what should be done to increase an individual's utility' (Mitchell and Carson, 1989, p22). However, this rhetoric is contradicted by practice. By using questionnaires, individuals are not allowed to express the full range of their values and concerns on a specific project. Also, it is well known that the adoption of the sum-ranking principle requires interference in individual affairs whenever total utility can be increased by doing so (Hahnel and Albert, 1990).

Fourth, no consideration is usually accorded to the inner working of decision-making processes that occur at aggregation levels higher than the individual (eg government, non-government organizations). Environmental issues are addressed in terms of allocation of scarce resources (eg air, water) among atomistic individuals (eg Tietenberg, 1988).

Preferences

The assumption of stable, unchanging preferences, together with the assumptions of maximizing behaviour and market equilibrium, form the heart of the neo-classical economic approach (Becker, 1976). It has been noted that the 'efficiency and Pareto optimality properties of general equilibrium models rest on the assumption of fixed tastes ... One of the reasons why economists did not very deeply discuss this question may be that that their present concepts of Pareto optimality and efficiency possibly are not flexible enough to cope with endogenously changing tastes' (Weizsäcker, 1971, p346). In fact, to predict economic behaviour and to apply valuation tools, such as CBA, that propose to replicate the individual's approach to choice, assumptions about the actual content of individual preferences have to be made.

In relation to environmental decision-making, if preferences were given, there would be no need to question whether an education campaign focusing on the issues to be assessed in a CBA study (eg impact of air pollution on health) could actually change individual preferences. If it were possible for preferences to be changed as a result of the campaign, the appropriateness of undertaking a questionnaire survey of individuals that have not had the opportunity to be exposed to specific education should be questioned.

However, contingent valuation studies have shown that the provision of information affects respondents' behaviour. In particular it appears to increase their willingness to pay. This raises the question of how much information should be provided. A further important issue relates to the form in which this information should be provided. For instance, the assumption of a rational individual would imply that any amount of information could be provided at once. The individual would be able to process it without any problem. This issue is further pursued below.

Utility and Pareto Optimality

Material welfare economists attempted to compare the well-being of social groups, but refrained from comparing the utility of individual persons. The latter was deemed not feasible (Cooter and Rappoport, 1984). Robbins (1952) remarked that utility could not be observed and therefore, under the influence of logical positivism, asserted that interpersonal comparisons of utility are outside science (Cooter and Rappoport, 1984). Following Robbins, other economists revised consumer theory, ridding it of any reference to concepts related to cardinality. The concept of marginal utility of goods was replaced by the marginal rate of substitution (Hicks and Allen, 1934). The concept of utility employed in contemporary microeconomics theory is based on the work of these economists and is referred to as ordinal utility. Utility does not have any reference to intensity of sensations.

It is claimed that the concept of cardinal utility is rejected in CBA studies and that contemporary microeconomics is the theoretical basis adopted

(Mitchell and Carson, 1989). However, contemporary microeconomics employs the concept of utility as a simple index of preferences. Any number attached to the utility ranking has a purely ordinal meaning.

Clearly, it is not viable to aggregate ordinal numbers but aggregation is required in CBA studies. Thus, in practice these studies are said to measure utility levels enjoyed by individuals (Mitchell and Carson, 1989). Changes in these utility levels are at times referred to as money-valued gains (or losses) (Randall and Peterson, 1984). Are these money-valued gains (losses) indices of preferences or actual monetary values? If money-valued gains (losses) arising from contingent market studies are taken as indices of preferences, they cannot be aggregated across individuals and, furthermore, they cannot be summed to values derived from actual markets.[8] However, if money-valued gains (losses) are interpreted as actual monetary values, they may be aggregated across individuals and summed to values arising from actual markets. This interpretation, however, is not consistent with the view of contemporary microeconomics that utility cannot be measured.[9] It is obvious from the above discussion that the resource allocation option that maximizes total utility cannot be pinpointed by CBA. CBA actually indicates the option that maximizes the net present value in monetary terms. In fact, the particular concept of efficiency adopted in CBA is the one in which 'resources are put to their most productive (high valued) use' (Mitchell and Carson, 1989, p21 fn. 9).[10]

CBA studies are applications of the potential Pareto improvement test[11] (Hicks, 1946). This test was developed to allow economists to make recommendations without recourse to interpersonal comparisons of utility. It has been stated that '[r]ecognition of this limited public role of BCA in no way undermines the importance of complete and accurate benefit cost analysis. While an empirical test for potential Pareto-improvements has a limited role, it is nevertheless essential that such a test be as complete, accurate, and faithful to the relevant economic theory as is feasible' (Randall, 1984, p70). However, in the descriptions of the economic theory underling CBA (eg Mitchell and Carson, 1989; Randall, 1984) no mention is made of the fact that the potential Pareto improvement test has been shown to be flawed (Samuelson, 1950). A question arises: is it essential to carry out a test that has been shown to be flawed? This issue is addressed later. However, a short note on this argument is worth considering.

The weaknesses of CBA have been noted not only by those who are against its use. There are also scholars who practise CBA (eg Randall, 1984) who argue that CBA should not be seen as providing the only (and final) decision rule to be adopted in public decision-making. Rather it should regarded as a useful information system providing an indication of the implications for the efficiency of alternative policies. The results of a CBA study would be only one component of the decision-making process. This view departs from the standard view of welfare economics that the potential Pareto improvement test should guide economic decision-making.[12] In relation to protected areas, for example, the view that efficiency (as measured by CBA) should be *the deciding rule* to be applied is suggested by Dixon and Sherman (1990). Finally, some scholars support the view that CBA should be used as an information system, but they do not clarify the place that efficiency should have in the decision-making process.

The adoption of efficiency as a sole guide has two implications relating to distribution and sustainability.

First, the attempt to maximize total monetary benefits may result in inequitable policies. In fact, CBA 'is indifferent as to whether the gainers are those already well off and the losers already badly off, or vice versa' (Randall, 1987, p42). Due to the discounting process adopted in CBA, long-term costs and benefits are accorded little weight in a CBA study. This may negatively affect future generations.

Second, an efficient allocation of resources may well be a pattern of resource use that is not sustainable (eg Bishop, 1993). Given that there are infinite efficient allocations of resources which depend on the specific distribution pattern, there is scope for seeking those patterns of resource use that are environmentally sustainable, acceptable from a distributive point of view and efficient.

Finally, it is worthwhile noting that other-regarding behaviour (see below) cannot be accounted for in CBA. There is, therefore, a need to establish decision-making processes – of which valuation studies are only one component – that enable eventual other-regarding behaviour to be expressed.

Rationality
Individuals are assumed to be fully rational and do not exhibit non-rational behaviour. Rationality as used in economics is defined by Simon (1986) as substantive rationality, since rational behaviour is seen in terms of the choices it produces. Simon remarks that three main aspects set apart neo-classical economics from other social sciences in relation to the treatment of rationality. Economics:

1   is silent about the content of goals and values;
2   postulates global consistency of behaviour;
3   postulates objectively rational behaviour in relation to the total environment (on the basis of the positivist philosophy which underlies neo-classical economics, it is possible to see the world as one, exactly specified reality).

Simon notes that other social sciences:

1   attempt to analyse values;
2   consider the processes that lead to the selection of specific aspects of *reality* and how these become the factual bases for reasoning about action;
3   seek to understand the computational strategies adopted in reasoning about complex realities under the constraint of the limited information processing capabilities of the human brain;

4 consider how non-rational processes, such as emotions and sensory stimuli, influence the definition of the factual bases used in the rational processes.

Because of the particular focus on the processes underlying rational behaviour, the conception of rationality adopted in psychology is defined as procedural rationality (Simon, 1986).

The neo-classical model requires the individual to be able to process an amount of information equal to that a central planner has to analyse (Arrow, 1986). The concept of global rationality that is at the basis of this model has been criticized by Simon (1982), who has put particular emphasis on the computational limitations of the human brain. Simon rejects the view that individuals are global maximizers and proposes an alternative model in which decisions are rational but bounded. Given the limited computational powers of the brain, the individual cannot deal with all the information required to attain a maximum. Simon (1957; 1982) proposes the alternative model of *satisficing*. The individual does not maximize, but attempts to reach acceptable minima. If Simon's criticism of rationality in economics is accepted, the whole neo-classical model is put into question (Hodgson, 1988).

The assumption that the human brain has unlimited computational powers holds significant implications. First, it implies that individuals can actually use all the available information to rank all the possible alternatives and make complex trade-offs when asked, for example, their willingness to pay for the conservation of an ecosystem. Thus, it seems possible to identify the option that maximizes social welfare. Second, this assumption denies that market failure could arise from information overload or from the lack of a capacity to process the information available. This suggests that the list of possible sources of market failure considered in neo-classical economics should be expanded.[13]

The assumption that the human brain has unlimited computational powers coupled with that of stable preference (and given ends) leads economists to attempt to carry out analyses of environmental issues in a *snapshot approach*. That is, the analysis is carried out at a certain point in time by, for example, submitting questionnaires that can be answered by globally rational individuals with set preferences. In contrast, if individuals are not assumed to have unlimited computational powers and stable preferences, a *process approach* to evaluation and decision-making should be preferred as it would improve the understanding of the problem being considered and, eventually, preference updating and modification of ends. This is further considered in Chapter 5.

From the assumptions that individuals are globally rational and that it is possible to describe the world objectively as it really is, it ensues that there is no difference between how the individuals perceive the *real* world and how this *really is* (Simon, 1986). Therefore, it is possible to predict the choices that a rational agent will make simply from our knowledge of the real world, once his or her utility function is known.[14] After having assumed the content of the utility function (which in CBA corresponds to the maximization of monetary benefits), the economist indicates the resource use option that is preferred by the individuals, without their direct involvement in the decision-making process. The use of CBA in a technocratic fashion has been widely reviewed, critiqued and criticized (McAllister, 1980; Self, 1975). Here, it suffices to note that once the objectivity of CBA is rejected (Tacconi and Tisdell, 1992; and Chapter 2), its use in a technocratic approach loses its remaining pillar.

Expanding the Human Behavioural Space

There are other dimensions to the human behavioural space (beyond those of neo-classical economics) that should be taken into account in the study of environmental questions. This expanded human behavioural space, which includes the one employed in neo-classical economics, is depicted in Figure 3.1.

Briefly, behaviour may range from self-interested to other-regarding. At the aggregation level, decision-making may occur from the individual level (the unit of analysis in neo-classical economics) to societal level. The types of decision-making processes adopted by individuals and institutions are grouped under the label behaviour mode. Rational behaviour, in Figure 3.1, corresponds to that adopted in neo-classical economics. At the other end of behaviour mode is normative behaviour. This category is defined by Etzioni (1988) as normative/affective behaviour. It refers to that behaviour that is guided by values (eg need for equality) rather than rational calculation.

The model presented in Figure 3.1 describes the different types of behaviour that individuals and institutions could adopt, and the factors influencing them. This model could also be used to chart the frequency and occasion of specific types of actual behaviour, considered at various aggregation levels (eg how often and when did individuals behave in normative and self-regarding behaviour?).

The human behavioural space of neo-classical economics is essentially confined to vertex B. The rational, self-interested individual is the decision-making unit. Models such as those of Margolis (1982), Andreoni (1990) and Common et al (1993)[15] may be located at intermediate points along the axis BC. Models within the NEE paradigm cannot be expanded beyond this space.

It is not argued that individuals act in other-regarding ways rather than in a self-interested way, or that specific institutions should be the focus of the analysis instead of the individual. Nor is it attempted in the identification of a point in Figure 3.1 that corresponds to actual human behaviour or that is the ideal focus of analysis. Rather, it is argued that each individual and institution may present irrational and rational behaviour, self-interested and other-regarding behaviour, and that there is a continuous interaction between the lower aggregation level (the individual) and higher aggregation levels. This interaction shapes and re-shapes rules, behaviour and goals. This variety of behaviour should be accounted for in the decision-making process, and in the design of tools employed in the analysis of environmental issues (see Chapter 11).

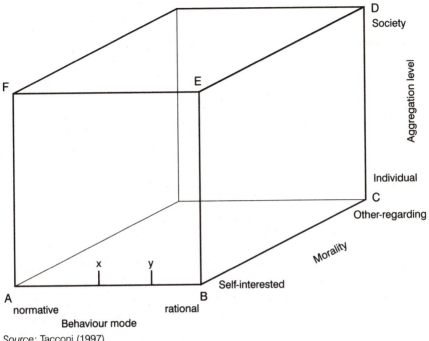

Figure 3.1 *Human behavioural space*

Behaviour Mode

Behaviour mode refers to the type of processes underlying the choice of goals and means made by individuals and institutions. Etzioni (1988) proposes a behaviour mode broader than that assumed in the neo-classical model (that is, global rationality in choosing means). He asserts that *normative* and *affective* values are the most important bases for the choice of ends and means. Normative values is a category that includes both moral values (eg do not kill, do not steal) and social values (eg freedom, justice). Affective values refer to emotions such as love, hate and stress. Affective values are particularistic (ie apply to a restricted personal basis), whereas normative values have wider claims that extend beyond the personal level.

Etzioni (1988) suggests that the behaviour mode may be considered as a continuum that may be divided into three different zones.

In the first zone, the *exclusion zone* (Ax, Figure 3.1), only normative and affective values determine choice. Rational calculation, or logical and empirical factors in Etzioni's terminology, are not used. In this zone, means that could be considered on a logical-empirical basis are excluded *a priori* on a normative and affective basis. The concept of committed behaviour proposed by Sen (1987) is germane to Etzioni's exclusion zone. Commitment reflects the desire to abide by certain rules, to follow a code even if this may be endangering one's own welfare.

In the second zone, the *infusion zone* (xy, Figure 3.1), normative and affective values are the main factors influencing choice; however, logical and empirical factors are also used. In this zone, normative and affective factors influence the decision-making process in two ways: by loading and intrusion. First, normative and affective factors load the interpretation of facts and the inferences made from them. Choices resulting from the subsequent logical and empirical calculations are therefore loaded by normative and affective values.[16] Second, intrusion is said to take place when normative and affective factors hinder the proper conclusion of the cycle of logical and empirical analysis (eg data collection, interpretation, derivation of inferences). For example, stress increases random behaviour and error rates.

In the third zone, the *indifference zone* (yB, Figure 3.1), logical and empirical calculation is deemed a suitable basis (according to the held normative and affective values) for decision-making. Normative and affective values do not influence choice in this zone; they demarcate it. Other factors affect logical and empirical calculation in this zone (and in the infusion zone). The consequences of the limited computational powers of the brain, pointed out in the work of Herbert Simon, are an important factor in limiting rational decision-making in this zone. Intra-cognitive limitations also affect rational decision-making. Their relevance has been stressed in the work of scholars such as Nisbett and Lee (1980) and Kahneman et al (1982). Several biases in decision-making under uncertainty have been reported. For example, people tend to over-estimate the frequency of events that they can remember more easily. They adopt a starting point to estimate a value but then fail to adjust their estimates as more information becomes available. They find it very difficult to assess low probability events. They see patterns that do not exist, and are affected by the form in which probabilities are expressed, instead of considering what these probabilities actually are.

Because of all the factors noted above, global rationality, if it exists at all, should therefore be regarded as the exception rather than the rule, according to Etzioni (1988), who takes sub-rational decision-making as the rule. He stresses that this position is also supported by the fact that rational decision-making is not effortless. Energy is required to carry out rational decision-making because of the several steps involved in this process.[17]

Morality

Morality refers to the range of behaviour that spans from self-interested to other-regarding behaviour. No ranking of behaviour from a moral point of view is implied (eg other-regarding behaviour is superior to self-interested behaviour).

Self-regarding behaviour may be distinguished from other-regarding behaviour (Hausman and McPherson, 1993). Self-regarding behaviour refers to those actions that the individual carries out to benefit other individuals, but he or she also derives benefits from doing so.[18] Other-regarding behaviour does not provide any benefit to the individual that carries out the action, and it may even be disadvantageous.

Neo-classical analysis of altruism has been confined to self-regarding behaviour in relation to the supply of public goods (eg Margolis, 1982; Andreoni, 1990). Margolis (1982) constructs a dual-utility function to include altruism in the form of *participation altruism* (the individual benefits from the act of giving resources away) and *goods altruism* (the individual benefits from an increase in the welfare of the individuals receiving the resources). Both categories imply self-regarding behaviour. Even the introduction of self-regarding behaviour in a neo-classical model concerned only with public goods creates certain problems.[19] The inclusion in the neo-classical model of other-regarding behaviour in the provision of public goods (and especially of private goods) would result in a neo-classical deductive model empty of predictive power (Etzioni, 1988; Lutz and Lux, 1988; Przeworski, 1985).

Sagoff (1988) proposes that individuals act not only as consumers (self-regarding behaviour) but also as citizens (other-regarding behaviour). The citizen is concerned with the public interest and judgement is based on historical, ideological, aesthetic, sentimental and moral values. The individual faces an internal conflict between the consumer-self and the citizen-self. However, according to Sagoff, people act as citizens when deliberating on social questions such as environmental problems. Sagoff appears not only to attempt to understand how people make decisions about the environment. In his writings there appears to be a rather strong emphasis on the fact that people *ought to* decide on environmental issues as citizens (Jacobs, 1994). Acceptance of the fact that people may act as citizens does not of course imply the endorsement of the *ought to* position.

That the individual has a dual self has also been advanced by Lutz and Lux (1988, p18), who state: 'Humanistic economics aims for a more complete image of the person. In addition to the self-interest side it posits a mutual interest side or, put it in other terms, in addition to advantage seeking it posits the existence of truth or fairness seeking.'

Other-regarding behaviour is also an important feature of market transactions (Etzioni, 1988). That is, other-regarding behaviour does not apply only to social issues as argued implicitly by Sagoff (1988). For example, firms' concern with fairness in market transactions has been documented by Kahneman et al (1986).

Aggregation Level

The individual is the only relevant unit of analysis in neo-classical economics. However, there are other units at higher aggregation levels that make decisions, which cannot be regarded as the simple sum of individual decisions.

In an all-encompassing view, an institution may be defined as 'a social organization which, through the operation of tradition, custom or legal constraint, tends to create durable and routinized patterns of behaviour' (Hodgson, 1988, p10). This definition, which emphasizes the factors that shape institutions, includes both immaterial institutions such as habits and rules of the game (eg property right system), and institutions intended as actual organizations. Several types of institutions, forming aggregation units higher than the individual, may be identified. For example, at an aggregational level, Uphoff (1986) identifies ten decision-making levels (individual, household, group, community, locality, sub-district, district, regional, national and international). Murphree (1994) adopts an actor-oriented approach (see Chapter 11 for a detailed discussion), which considers the political dimensions of environmental management, at the micro and macro level, and treats *the community* as an etherogeneous entity, rather than a homogeneous one as often assumed in conservation and also development activities (this is considered in more detail in Chapter 5). Murphree (1994) identifies a range of institutional actors, ranging from the traditional authority structures and self-interest organizations, to government political actors (eg regional administrations, line ministries) and non-governmental actors (eg national NGOs, private sector entrepreneurs).

Institutions have several functions, some of which are of specific interest here. They contribute to the formation of the conceptual framework employed by agents in the interpretation of *reality* (Hodgson, 1988), and influence the perception of what constitutes the agent's self-interest (Etzioni, 1988; Hodgson, 1988). Institutions, by establishing routine behaviour, provide information to agents, thus reducing uncertainty, and reduce the demands on the limited capacity of the human brain (Hodgson, 1988; Runge, 1984; Sjöstrand, 1992). Those institutions that make decisions (such as the corporation and the clan) have larger cognitive powers than the individual, and may be able to carry out decision-making processes of a higher rational degree than the individual (Etzioni, 1988). Of course, this does not exclude the fact that organizations may make decisions according to normative factors, or that they do not face limitations in carrying out rational decision-making processes. Finally, institutions can advance the particular interest of its members (actors).

The analysis carried out in this section and in the previous ones has highlighted several issues that have influence on the decision-making framework regarding biodiversity conservation. It is now time to draw these issues together, and consider their implications.

Implications for Decision-Making

Sustainability, distribution and efficiency. There may be efficient allocations that are not compatible with the sustainable use of ecosystems and may be inequitable. The standpoint adopted here is that resource use patterns should be chosen according to their sustainability and distributional aspects together with the efficiency aspects. This would not appear to conflict with the neo-classical view that resource allocations should be efficient. The two positions would only be in conflict if the particular neo-classical view were held that the resource use option that provides the highest monetary benefits should be chosen.

Distribution. The positivist view that it is possible to carry out value-free science has resulted in the progressive separation of economics from ethics, as was noted in the previous chapter. Neo-classical economists have tended to shy away from openly addressing ethical issues. This has resulted, of course, in taking ethical positions by default. By not addressing the question of resource distribution, the implicit ethical position is that equity issues are irrelevant. Distribution may refer to the distribution of resources between generations or within a generation. Both aspects are of particular interest to environmental management policies. Intergenerational distribution will be considered in the next chapter.[20] Aspects of distributional issues with respect to the current generation will be considered in Chapter 5.

Decision-making process. It was argued above that preferences and ends may change. Individuals and institutions may show behaviour ranging from selfish to other-regarding, and from rational to normative. Individuals influence institutions and vice versa. All these elements have important implications.

First, the focus of the analysis should not only be on the individuals and goods but also on institutions. Institutions provide the framework within which ecosystem use decisions are made. The existence of appropriate institutions has particular importance in determining whether ecosystem use patterns may be sustainable, equitable and efficient.

Second, the decision-making process should enable individuals and institutions to update their goals, to express their selfish to other-regarding views, and to facilitate the logical decision-making process. A participatory approach to decision-making (considered in Chapter 5) may go a certain way towards better addressing the above points compared to a *snapshot* approach to decision-making. This has particular influence for the role of the researchers and practitioners, as already noted in the previous chapter.

Vatn and Bromley (1994, p145) affirm that 'the most fundamental environmental choices will continue to be made without prices – and without apologies.' The standing questions are: How can these choices be made? What is the role of economics in the environmental decision-making process? What alternatives to the standard economic approach are available? The next two chapters delve deeper into these questions, with specific focus on future generations, people, biodiversity and protected areas.

Notes

1   Pearce et al (1989) provide an early collection of definitions. Lele (1991) and Auty and Brown (1997) review the concept of sustainable development and (the latter) present case studies, while Goodland (1995) reviews the concept of environmental sustainability.

2   Table 3.1 presents only some of the points considered by Sahu and Nayak. These are the points that are considered as the salient ones.

3   Opschor (1994) describes modern evolutionary economics as a hybrid of neo-classical economics and neo-Austrian economics. Then, according to this definition of modern evolutionary economics, it follows that ECE must also draw to some extent on neo-classical economics.

4   The throughput is defined as the flow of raw materials (low entropy matter and energy) from the environment to the economic system, and back to the environment as waste with high entropy (Costanza et al, 1997a).

5   Ramstad (1989) points out that Tool appears to rely on the élite with *reliable knowledge* to decide what the instrumental values are.

6   Etzioni (1988), Gee (1991), North (1990) and Winter (1986) have been especially useful in deriving this summary.

7   There are economists who regard *Homo oeconomicus* as a correct description of real people (eg Phelps, 1985).

8   A full CBA study may require the assessment of the total economic value (TEV) that may be composed by use values (UV) and by non-use values (NUV): TEV = UV + NUV. Market information is often available to assess UV, but to estimate NUV (that includes existence values, option values and quasi-option values) hypothetical markets are designed.

9   It is claimed that CBA studies measure changes in welfare. This claim must be based on the assumption that monetary values are a good proxy for welfare. This is clearly disputable.

10 This definition is germane to that of 'efficient depletion' of resources, interpreted as that pattern of resource use which results in the maximization of the present value of net benefits from resources (Fisher, 1981).

11 A state A is a potential Pareto improvement over B, if those who gain (in moving from B to A) could compensate the loser and have something left for themselves.

12 See, for example, Feldman (1980) for a review of welfare economics. In welfare economics decisions should be made according to social utility functions. However, given that these present notorious problems, efficiency is the issue normally being considered.

13 It was noted in Chapter 2 that market failure may originate from lack of information. This category is different from that advanced here that market failure may originate from information overload.

14 The assumption of rational behaviour would have limited implications were it not coupled with the further assumption of broad homogeneity of utility functions across individuals (Arrow, 1986).

15 These authors consider some implications for contingent valuation studies of adopting the view, borrowed from Sagoff (1988), that individuals may respond as citizens rather than *consumers* in valuation studies.

16 Neo-classical economics 'makes no distinction between sense data, information, and knowledge, and assumes that information or knowledge are provided from experience independently of beliefs, concepts or theories of the observer' (Hodgson, 1988, p83).

17 Some of the steps are: (a) wide-ranging assessment of alternatives; (b) analysis of the range of objectives; (c) assessment of consequences; (d) search for new information (Janis and Mann, 1977; cited in Etzioni, 1988).

18 This differs from self-interested behaviour, which is concerned solely with one's own welfare.

19 It is difficult to explain which ranking of the different choices will take place in which situations (Hausman and McPherson, 1993).

20 The lack of consideration of intergenerational issues by neo-classical economists is also partly due to two widely held views: (a) technical progress will take care of natural resource shortages; (b) current markets reflect future as well as current demands through the actions of speculators.

4

Economics, Intergenerational Equity and Biodiversity Conservation

Introduction

Biodiversity contributes to the maintenance of ecosystem functions that support life and contribute to human well-being. All generations stand to benefit from ecosystems services. If it is recognized that future generations have rights, then consideration should be given to these rights and the implications for ecosystem management. This chapter explores these issues, and in particular the question of what may constitute intergenerational equity in natural resources use. The implications for the economic analysis of biodiversity and PAs are considered.

We take as given that future generations have rights. This acknowledges the principles stated in the Rio Declaration on Environment and Development, ratified at the United Nations Conference on Environment and Development in June 1992. The objectives of the declaration are the conservation of biodiversity, its sustainable use for the benefit of both current and future generations, and the equitable sharing between countries of the products derived from genestocks. Three principles adopted in the final declaration of the conference make explicit the preferred underlying approach to biodiversity policies. These principles state that:

1 the right to development should be achieved by equitably meeting the developmental and environmental needs of the current and future generations;
2 environmental protection shall constitute an integral part of the development process so that sustainability may be achieved;
3 the precautionary approach should be widely adopted to protect the environment.

The chapter reviews some economic aspects of biodiversity. Biodiversity is an important attribute of natural capital (NC). Thus, the implications for biodiversity conservation policies of seeking to achieve intergenerational equity are analysed by addressing the wider issue of the use of NC. Then the contractarian theory developed by Rawls (1972) is discussed, and the implications of intergenerational equity for biodiversity conservation policies and for the economic analysis of PAs are considered.

The Economics of Biodiversity

Irreversibility and uncertainty relating to ecological processes characterize the study of biodiversity. These are considered before addressing the economic assessment of biodiversity, the precautionary principle, and the safe minimum standard (SMS) of conservation.

Irreversibility and Uncertainty

Irreversibility is typical of biodiversity loss as once a species has become extinct it cannot be restored. Similarly, an ecosystem may collapse with irreversible effects when its ecological functions fall below a threshold level. Ciriacy-Wantrup (1963) refers to this kind of irreversibility as a *technical* one. He also stresses the importance of *economic* irreversibility. This occurs when the cost of restoring an ecosystem, with the aim of resuming the previous land use, is higher than the benefits of such an action.

Ciriacy-Wantrup (1963) is concerned about irreversibility because of the implications it may have for society. An irreversibility may cause immoderate losses which, in the worst case scenario, may threaten the continuity of a social group. Irreversible processes may have significant implications for evolution:

> '*irreversibility ... limits opportunities of adaptation and narrows the potential development of a society. Both the biological and social sciences have come to the conclusion that such a limiting and narrowing force directs development towards specialization rather than diversification. Such a direction has been held responsible for retarded and abortive growth ... stagnation, and death of species and civilizations.*' (Ciriacy-Wantrup, 1963, p252)

If the point at which a process becomes irreversible is known, appropriate management rules could be devised. The fact is that threshold levels are often unknown. The presence of uncertainty renders the management problem more complex.

Uncertainty may be first categorized into social and natural uncertainty (Ciriacy-Wantrup, 1963; Bishop, 1978). Uncertainty refers to the lack of knowledge about future income levels, technologies, institutions, needs and wants of current and future generations that will influence society's development patterns and pressures on the environment. Natural uncertainty refers to the lack of knowledge about ecological processes.

A classification of uncertainty which applies to social and natural uncertainty is provided by Wynne (1992).[1]

- risk, the probability distribution of the event is known;
- Knightian uncertainty (Knight, 1921), the probability distribution is unknown;
- ignorance, the relevant facets of the issue are not known;
- indeterminacy, questionable appropriateness and sufficiency of scientific knowledge.

The formulation of biodiversity policies is particularly problematic because biodiversity is characterized by irreversibilities and, mainly, by indeterminacy and ignorance. The presence of uncertainty and irreversibility points to the conclusion that the conservation of biodiversity cannot be left to the market alone. When a market does exist, uncertainty and irreversibility may cause market failure. Uncertainty and irreversibility also create serious problems for the application of valuation techniques.

The Economic Value of Biodiversity

What is the value of biodiversity? This is a question economists have considered in relation to biodiversity policies. To date, it appears that no satisfactory answer has been provided.

Some authors have recommended the use of CBA (cost–benefit analysis) for the valuation of biodiversity (eg Randall, 1988; Pearce and Moran, 1994). While some theoretical shortcomings of CBA have been considered in the previous chapter, here it is useful to consider some of the limitations of CBA in regard to biodiversity valuation. First, even advocates of the CBA approach have recognized that CBA is ill suited to decision-making that involves intergenerational issues: when 'considering events that may greatly restrict the opportunities of future generations, it seems that discounting theories based on the logic of ordinary investment are simply out of their depth' (Randall, 1987, p240). Second, CBA cannot deal satisfactorily with uncertainty. This is treated as if it were risk. Bishop (1978) notes that it is at times suggested that the problems of irreversibility and uncertainty may be solved by assessing option values. However, he remarks, when there are significant natural and social uncertainties, option values cannot be known beyond one or two decades. We might add that the inclusion of option values does nothing to solve problems of ignorance and indeterminacy. Third, specific techniques such as contingent valuation are deemed suitable to value goods that are familiar to the consumer (Mitchell and Carson, 1989). This does not seem to apply to biodiversity, because even scientists have limited knowledge of many aspects of biodiversity. The final, and probably most crucial, problem facing any attempt to measure the value of biodiversity in a CBA framework is the lack of knowledge about the functions of biodiversity and about the implications for ecosystem services of modifications in these functions.

Biodiversity refers to the diversity of life at all levels, and it also comprises the linkages between these different levels of the biological hierarchy. The *diversity* of genes, species and ecosystems cannot be equated to the actual *biological resources*.

It is the value of biological resources that CBA studies have assessed, rather than the value of biodiversity. This is due to two main reasons. Earlier economic studies confused biological diversity with biological resources. This is not surprising given that studies such as McNeely et al (1990) used the term biodiversity in the encompassing meaning of totality of biological resources. Later studies have continued to use biological resources as a proxy for the value of biodiversity because it was found impossible to value the latter. This is exemplified by a book titled *The Economic Value of Biodiversity* (Pearce and Moran, 1994). These authors speak of the value of biodiversity. However, all the references they cite, and the calculations they make – for example in relation to the value of medicinal plants and carbon absorption functions – consider (for their own admission) values of biological resources.

Finally, another exploratory attempt aimed at assessing the value of ecosystem services provided by natural capital (Costanza et al, 1997b) has been shown to present several theoretical and applied shortcomings.[2]

In conclusion, economic valuation currently does not appear capable of providing estimates of the benefits of biodiversity. It may provide estimates of (a) the benefits derived from biological resources, (b) the costs of implementation of biodiversity conservation initiatives, and (c) the forgone benefits of alternative uses of areas to be conserved. Some problems involved in specific applications of CBA will be highlighted in the next chapter.

Due to the problems faced by standard economic valuation techniques, it has been suggested that the precautionary principle and the SMS of conservation should be adopted for the management of both biodiversity and biological resources.

The Precautionary Principle

The precautionary principle emerged in Germany in the 1980s (Boehmer-Christiansen, 1994). Since then, it has been included in several international treaties, including the Rio Declaration adopted at the Conference on Environment and Development (Cameron, 1994). As adopted in Germany, the precautionary principle results in government activism because authorities are responsible for the protection of the environment, for the benefit of the present and future generations; because of the need to adopt precaution, action can take place without the requirement to determine damage scientifically and to cost it accurately (Boehmer-Christiansen, 1994). Boehmer-Christiansen also stresses that the main aim of the precautionary principle is to overcome the opposition of vested interest to public policies, and it does not provide specific guidance about the instruments to be adopted. It is a general guiding principle. Myers (1993) states that:

> *'the precautionary principle asserts that there is a premium on a cautious and conservative approach to human interventions in environmental sectors that are: (a) unusually short on scientific understanding, and (b) unusually susceptible to significant injury, especially irreversible injury.'* (Myers, 1993, p74)

International treaties, such as those signed at the World Climate Conference (Geneva, 1990) and at the United Nation Conference on Environment and Development (Rio de Janeiro, 1992) have stated that when these two conditions apply, lack of full scientific knowledge should not be used as a reason for postponing cost-effective measures to prevent environmental degradation.

In relation to biodiversity policies, Myers (1993) interprets the precautionary principle as shifting the burden of proof from the conservationist party onto the potential developer. As will be noted below, this interpretation is similar to that given to the SMS of conservation. In forest management, for example, without the precautionary principle the conservationists have to prove that the exploitation of a specific ecosystem has negative environmental implications. The introduction of the precautionary principle would shift the burden of proof onto the loggers. They would have to prove that their actions do not cause environmental degradation. The precautionary principle could be applied by introducing a bonding system (Costanza and Perrings, 1990). The loggers would pay a bond equal to the value of the largest estimated environmental damage that could be caused by their activities. The bond would be refunded if damage did not take place. In case of limited damage, the loggers would either repair it or part of the bond would be forfeited in order to compensate for the damage.

However, for biodiversity conservation purposes, the adoption of a bonding system presents two shortcomings. First, it has been noted above that the value of biodiversity has yet to be successfully assessed. Thus, the potential environmental damage could be estimated with a reasonable degree of accuracy. Second, when irreversible damage occurs, compensation of current and future generations could only take place if the services provided by the irreversibly damaged ecosystems could be substituted, for example, by human-made capital (Barbier et al, 1994). However, substitution is not always possible.

The precautionary principle may be used as a general principle in biodiversity conservation (Chapter 7) and specific rules and tools are needed for policy development and implementation. The SMS of conservation is considered for this purpose.

The Safe Minimum Standard of Conservation

From a dynamic, evolutionary standpoint, the assessment of allocative efficiency is not the main focus of the analysis, contrary to the case of studies concerned with the valuation of biodiversity. 'In a world of uncertainty, no one knows the correct answer to the problems we confront ... The society that permits the maximum generation of trials will be most likely to solve problems through time' (North, 1990, p81). Two relevant matters are contained in this passage. First, in an environment characterized by uncertainty, flexibility may be maintained by keeping open a wide range of options. This enhances the probability that a system is sustained in the event of failure of one or more of its components (be they ecological or social). Second, diversity leads to different patterns of experimentation. These may result in a further increase in diversity and new ways of solving problems. This is of particular relevance to the economic process. Marshall (1910; cited in Carlsson and Stankiewicz, 1991) recognized that the tendency of individuals to variation is a major source of progress. The opportunity to innovate is supported by a high degree of diversity in the natural resources available. This can lead to the diversification of the goods and services produced, which is a major cause of economic change (Carlsson and Stankiewicz, 1991).

Biodiversity not only contributes to the maintenance of life support functions. It is also a prerequisite for economic adaptability and provides a diversity of options for economic development. A decrease in biodiversity may cause a technical as well as an economic irreversibility. On these propositions, it may be argued that the economic analysis of biodiversity should not underestimate the fact that the diversity of natural resources per se contributes to the evolution of economic systems over time.

The concept of an SMS of conservation was introduced by Ciriacy-Wantrup (1963) with the explicit purpose of dealing with problems of uncertainty and irreversibility. Ciriacy-Wantrup regarded the SMS of conservation as an approach that would help in maintaining flexibility with respect to the options for the economic use of ecosystems, and avoiding the occurrence of immoderate losses resulting from irreversibility. He stressed that the SMS could be defined for animals, plants and ecosystems. The SMS may be achieved by avoiding the resource's critical zone, a threshold that delimits the reversibility of the process.

The SMS approach was first reviewed and modified by Bishop (1978; 1979). Among other problems, he noted that the characterization of the SMS in a game theoretic framework assumes that the probabilities of the outcomes are unknown, but the outcomes and their values can be foreseen. This is not a realistic assumption given the existence of uncertainty. Thus, he proposed that the adoption of the SMS could not be based on unknown gains and losses. Rather, the SMS should be adopted unless the social costs are unacceptably large. The definition of what are unacceptably large costs, Bishop (1978) remarked, should include considerations relating to intergenerational equity. However, he deemed economics ill-suited to deal with the definition of unacceptable costs.

After a period of relative neglect, the need to address the issues of uncertainty and irreversibility inherent in biodiversity policies has revived interest in the SMS. In fact, Perrings et al (1992) remark that SMSs might be essential elements in a biodiversity conservation strategy.

Randall (1991) considers how to value species or ecosystems in situations of conflict between conservation and modification of the environment. The valuation framework suggested is based on the application of CBA to account for individuals' willingness to pay (WTP) for conservation, integrated with the SMS of conservation. This approach is aimed at avoiding outcomes that could be regretted. On the assumption that the value of conservation is given by the sum of individual WTP, the policy alternative chosen is the one that yields the maximum net present value. Choices are, however, constrained by the adoption of the SMS. It is recognized that individual preferences may be myopic, and might lead to ecological irreversibilities. The introduction of the SMS is seen as necessary in order to supplement the inability of CBA to deal with uncertainty and to protect future generations' interests, that may be disregarded by the discounting process characteristic of CBA (Randall, 1991).

The contribution that this approach may provide to a biodiversity conservation strategy is rather limited. First, it has already been noted that CBA presents more shortcomings than usual when employed to value biodiversity. Second, this approach, similar to that adopted by Randall and Farmer (1995) (discussed below), can only deal with 'the disappearance of a chip of biodiversity here and a chunk there' (Randall, 1988, p222). This is a rather limited contribution to a biodiversity strategy, which has to face the extinction of a large number of species and extensive degradation of ecosystems.

Randall and Farmer (1995) address two important questions. How should the SMS be set? What should be considered an intolerable cost?

The first question is addressed in terms of levels of resource use. That is, levels of resource use that may be adequate to the satisfaction of each generation's needs. This approach to the SMS differs from previous ones, which have considered the minimum threshold level for the conservation of the resource. Randall and Farmer (1995) suggest that the SMS of use should be set at that level that guarantees a sustainable and adequate level of consumption to different generations (D_{min}). D_{min} is such that a generation that uses less than that level would suffer extreme deprivation. If a sigmoid resource regeneration function is adopted, the chosen SMS (stock of resource conserved) results in a level greater than the one that would have been adopted by setting the SMS at a minimum threshold level.

The issue of intolerable cost is addressed by Randall and Farmer (1995) in terms of the level of SMS adopted. They note that the definition of intolerable cost depends on the specific ethical theory endorsed.[3] However, they find that the three ethical approaches converge on the same level of intolerable cost when resource degradation threatens the existence of human society. Each generation should limit its resource use to D_{min} and bear whatever costs are entailed. It would be considered intolerable for each generation to use less than D_{min}. None of the three ethical stances considered would demand sacrifice beyond that.

The approach presented above is theoretically interesting and enriches the debate about the application of the SMS. However, its application faces problems. First, detailed data about regeneration characteristics of each specific resource are required in order to set the appropriate SMS level. The information available for the limited number of species that have been studied scientifically exemplifies the fact that there is a great uncertainty about the levels of minimum viable populations and habitat requirements (Hohl and Tisdell, 1993). For the large majority of the species and ecosystems, there is a significant lack of information on their regenerative capacity. Second, the approach is applicable only to those resources that come under human use. Most of the species that become extinct or endangered are not directly used. It seems unlikely that the type and amount of information required to gauge their indirect contribution to life support functions and to economic activity, and then set the appropriate SMS level, will be available in the near future. Third, it can only address localized problems in biodiversity conservation. It is a piece-meal approach to biodiversity conservation in that it looks only at bits and chunks of biodiversity: it considers individual species and ecosystems – if their regenerative functions can be assessed. To face the challenge of reducing the rate at which biodiversity is lost, a strategic approach to biodiversity conservation is required (World Commission on Environment and Development, 1987; WRI et al, 1992). Thus, a different approach to the establishment of SMSs may be required.

PAs are an important component of a biodiversity conservation strategy (WRI et al, 1992). The adoption of a system of PAs by a country may be regarded as the adoption of an SMS for the conservation of biodiversity. Attempting to achieve intergenerational equity has implications for the economic assessment of PAs and for judging what may be considered an intolerable cost of conservation. These issues will be considered below.

The arguments developed above and in Chapter 1 suggest that biodiversity is an integral attribute of natural capital. To assess in a holistic fashion the implications of intergenerational equity for biodiversity conservation, this issue is approached in the wider context of the distribution and use of natural capital.

Natural Capital

The economic system can be described as being embedded in the ecological-social system.[4] The ecological-social system is constituted by natural capital (NC) and by human capital (HC). HC comprises the people living in the specific time and space with their culture, skills, knowledge and the institutions that regulate social and economic life.[5] NC is composed of renewable natural capital (RNC) and non-renewable natural capital (NNC) (Costanza and Daly, 1992).[6] RNC is self-sustained through the chlorophyll photosynthesis of solar energy and includes, for example, trees, fish and ecosystems. NNC is seen as inactive and includes resources such as minerals. The structure and diversity of ecological systems are crucial attributes of RNC, since they contribute to maintaining functional ecosystems.

The ecological system can exist independently of the presence of the social system, but the social system cannot exist without the ecological system. None the less, there exists a co-evolutionary interdependence between RNC and HC (eg Norgaard, 1984). HC adapts to the existing RNC and to changes in it. RNC too changes as a result of the influence of HC. HC is applied to RNC and NNC to produce manufactured capital (MC), and other goods and services. MC is operated by HC for the extraction and transformation of RNC and NNC in order to provide goods. Services are also provided by HC with the use of MC. The production of any piece of MC and of other goods is mainly a process of transformation of NNC and/or RNC through the application of HC. Finally, the economic and social systems degrade energy and produce waste. The latter is discharged into the ecological system.

Substitutability Between Natural Capital and Manufactured Capital

If NC and MC were perfect substitutes, an increase in the stock of MC that generates an equivalent decrease in the stock of NC, and a (temporary) increase in income would not pose a problem. The total capital stock (TC = NC + MC) would be left unchanged. Hence, from a Hicksian standpoint (Hicks, 1946) this would represent an improvement in economic welfare for the current generation and would not affect future generations. They would receive an equivalent capital stock.

It has been argued that NC and MC are complements in the early stages of economic growth, whereas in industrialized economies substitutability applies above a certain minimum threshold level of NC (Pearce, 1988). The latter is needed to sustain life support functions. It seems this claim of complementarity–substitutability is based on differences between industrialization stages. Industrialized countries are considered to be less dependent on the natural resource base than less-developed countries (LDCs) and to have a higher degree of resilience to environmental shocks. However, the use by industrialized countries of natural resources in absolute terms, and per capita, is far greater than that of developing countries (Sachs, 1992). Notwithstanding the actual dependence of different countries on natural resources, the relative dependence on natural resources does not imply a different relationship between NC and MC.

Some NC may be characterized as *critical* (Winpenny, 1991). This type of NC is described as irreplaceable and non-substitutable (eg the ozone layer). Winpenny asserts that the remaining NC, which includes renewable and non-renewable natural resources, can be replenished or substituted by MC. This approach is similar to that of Pearce's because it sets a threshold of NC (ie critical NC) that has no substitute. However, Winpenny grounds the notion of substitutability and complementarity on the physical properties of the resources. How MC might replace NC is not expounded by Winpenny.

The argument that MC can be a substitute for NC has been rejected on three counts (Costanza and Daly, 1992). First, if MC is a substitute for NC, then there would be no reason to produce MC given that NC is, by definition, naturally available. Second, MC is created by combining NC with HC, hence it is a contradiction in terms to say that MC can substitute for NC. Third, in the production process, MC and HC are combined to transform NC into products; MC is created to process an increased amount of NC, not to decrease the use of NC. The latter point is not in contradiction with the possibility of increasing the technical efficiency of MC, which results in a reduction of NC input per unit of output.

NC is at times replaced with MC in the production process. This should not be confused with the possibility of substitution between NC and MC in physical terms. The substitution of NC with MC in the production process is in fact a substitution between one type of NC and another type of NC, to which HC has been applied in order to transform it into MC. The application of MC cannot create physical matter but it may provide access or make useable elements of NC otherwise not amenable to human use. This means that an increased availability of economic resources may be derived from increases in the stock of MC and improvements in its technical efficiency. Thus, MC may enhance the stock of NC while not substituting for NC.

To summarize, NC may be subdivided into NNC and RNC, with the latter composed of critical RNC and other RNC. It has also been argued that MC is not a substitute for NC; however, MC and HC can be used to extend the life of NNC and to restore the stock of RNC.

Decisions about the distribution and allocation of natural capital are based on specific ethical viewpoints to which we now turn.

Ethics and Intergenerational Equity

Rawls' Theory of Justice

The agents considered by Rawls (1972) are rational self-interested individuals. However, this contractarian theory is developed as an alternative to utilitarianism as it seemed unlikely to Rawls that utilitarianism would be adopted as a rule for the basic structure of society. The reason proposed by Rawls is that it is implausible that rational self-interested people would embrace a principle which may require personal sacrifice in order to maximize the total utility of society and does not guarantee personal self-respect to everybody. The latter is seen as necessary if people are 'to pursue their conception of good with zest and to delight in its fulfilment.' (Rawls, 1972, p178).

Rawls assumes that individuals are brought together and are under a 'veil of ignorance'. They do not know the position they occupy in society or their endowments. However, they do know basic facts about society such as political, economic and psychological principles. This is called the Original Position and is a *fair* procedure which leads to the adoption of principles which can, therefore, be considered *just*. The two principles of justice, which Rawls specifies as the constitution of a society and will regulate all further agreements, are agreed upon in the Original Position.[7] They affirm, lexicographically, equality of rights in basic liberties among individuals, and that choices are to be made so that they benefit the least advantaged in society and provide for equal opportunities.

Given that the original agreement is drawn under uncertainty, Rawls suggests that rational agents would adopt a strategy that maximizes the minimum state, that is, the maximin strategy. In the Original Position, the maximin rule applies because: (a) there is no knowledge of the likelihood of the possible outcomes; (b) the principles of justice provide a satisfactory minimum, given that they result in a workable theory of justice compatible with the demands of efficiency; and (c) the principles of justice provide a satisfactory minimum when compared to the possible outcomes arising from the application of utilitarianism (Rawls, 1972). The principles adopted will benefit the least well-off and will not be regretted, once the veil is lifted and the agents' position in society is revealed.

In Rawls' theory, equity is expressed in terms of primary goods. These goods are regarded as things that every rational individual is assumed to desire. Primary goods include income and wealth but also rights, opportunities and the social basis for self-respect. As stressed above, basic rights are afforded priority over other primary goods. Hence, trade-offs between basic liberties and social and economic goals are not allowed. Rawls' theory differs from utilitarianism as advantage is not measured in terms of utility, but by considering an index of primary goods. Also, rights have intrinsic value, whereas utilitarianism simply affords them instrumental value. Rights also determine the opportunities open to people, and equality in outcomes is related to, but differs from, equality in opportunities.

Rawls noted that each generation should preserve natural assets, the gains of culture and civilization and just institutions. However, he addresses intergenerational justice as a question of determining a fair saving rate, where saving may take various forms, such as manufactured capital and education. Rawls stresses that saving is not required just to make future generations better off, but it is a condition needed to bring about a just society. However, focusing on saving formalizes the question of intergenerational justice in terms of making future generations better off. This misses the fact that, during this process of accumulation, disruptive ecological effects may occur and could negatively affect future generations. This approach to intergenerational equity does not recognize that the obligation to avoid harm may be more vital than attempts to improve well-being (Barry, 1977).

Rawls assumes that the persons gathered in the Original Position are contemporaries. To extend the analysis – which is mainly concerned with intragenerational justice – to intergenerational justice, a motivational assumption is introduced. Rawls assumes that agents in the Original Position do care for their offspring. This creates a problem of consistency in the theory. The aim of the theory is to derive all duties and obligations from a rational approach. However, assuming that rational self-interested individuals are concerned for the welfare of their direct descendants, inputs in the model the actual answer to the problem that Rawls seeks to solve (Barry, 1977).

The application of Rawls' theory to an intergenerational distribution of natural resources is due to Page (1977). He avoids the problem just discussed by assuming the agents in the Original Position are from all generations and are ignorant about which generation they will belong to. Page suggests that in the Original Position agreement would be reached on:

1   the provision of the conditions needed for permanent liveability – which may be taken as the assurance that life support functions would not be disrupted; and
2   the need for generational intertemporal self-sufficiency.

A criticism of the application of Rawls' theory to intergenerational justice is that there seems to be a problem of circularity. That is, the principles adopted in the Original Position may determine how many generations will exist and consequently how many generations will be represented in the Original Position. This argument is part of the Parfit Paradox (Pasek, 1992). These issues are considered below.

Some Critical Issues in Intergenerational Equity

How are the patterns of resource use that will allow the existence of future generations chosen in the Original Position? How much do the interests of the present generation diverge from those of the future ones?

If the rights to the use of a finite stock of NNC are extended to infinite generations, the share of each generation will tend to zero, assuming away recycling. All generations would forgo the benefits that could be derived from the use of NNC. This does not appear to be a satisfactory solution. Hence, what should be done with NNC?

Three alternative principles may be considered for adoption. Each generation could be asked to compensate the NNC used by investing in RNC, a prudent rule to guarantee sustainability (Costanza and Daly, 1992). The problem with this resource use pattern is that it is difficult to define the specific rule regulating compensation. A second approach may be to limit the rate of NNC consumption to the rate of improvement in technical efficiency achieved in its use. However, this resource use pattern presents implementation problems. It is not known in advance the rate of technical progress that a generation will achieve. Also, this policy would require a particularly interventionist approach.[8]

A possible alternative is the adoption of a more general principle that specifies that policies should be adopted in order to facilitate the transition to an economic system that relies almost entirely on renewable resources. This may be implemented by:

1   introducing depletion taxes on NC, eventually counterbalanced by a decrease in income tax (Costanza and Daly, 1992); and
2   shifting the focus of research and development from NNC-based activities to RNC-based activities.

Having examined the above approaches to NC management, it is obvious that, given the existing degree of uncertainty, it is not possible to guarantee that the chosen resource management conditions will allow the existence of an infinite number of generations. The fact of the matter is that due to ecological, economic and social uncertainties, it is impossible to define exactly the conditions that will lead to the indefinite existence of human beings, if this is indeed possible. It is only through a cautious, incremental and adaptive learning process[9] that the use of NC will be tuned to facilitate the existence of future generations.

A Rawlsian approach to intergenerational equity is useful in deriving general principles of justice, and to decide on the potential resource use patterns to be followed in order to achieve intergenerational equity. However, it cannot provide definitive answers to questions of intergenerational resource distribution. It is impossible to know the exact conditions that will allow the certain existence of future generations. In this respect, the critique of circularity levelled against the Rawlsian theory is of limited practical relevance.

A further weakness of the Rawlsian approach as developed by Page relates to the framing of the problem. The question of intergenerational equity is formulated as one of having to decide on the distribution of a limited quantity of resources across generations. This is obviously correct in relation to NNC. For RNC the distinction between the interests of different generations may not be so stark. It may be both in the interests of the present and future generations to maintain a non-decreasing RNC. For example, salinity in agricultural lands, and soil degradation and erosion negatively affect agricultural product and water quality, and are significant issues for present and future generations.

Implications for Biodiversity Conservation

The arguments of the previous sections may now be brought together to draw out the implications they hold for the distribution of NC across generations, for biodiversity conservation policies and for PAs.

Three Degrees of Intergenerational Equity

Choosing a pattern of resource distribution between generations is not only a question of finding the most equitable one. The agents in the Original Position 'will not enter into agreements they cannot keep, or can do so only with great difficulty' (Rawls, 1972, p145). In terms of the problem addressed here, this implies that it is necessary to identify which resource distribution pattern can actually be achieved. This is influenced by several factors such as the conditions of a specific country and the knowledge of the factors that make the sustainable use of ecosystems possible. This implies that one optimal resource use pattern – from an intergenerational equity point of view – cannot be identified. Three patterns of resource use are outlined below and are referred to as degrees of intergenerational equity. The specification of multiple resource use patterns is suitable to an incremental and adaptive learning process. It also facilitates the identification of objectives to be adopted in real-life political processes.

ve intergenerational equity, requiring equitable access to NC. This
e achieved by not reducing the stock of RNC and by progressively
ating the substitution of NNC with RNC in the economic process.
degree of intergenerational equity roughly corresponds to the
Lockeian principle that each generation should bequeath to the following
generations at least an equivalent resource base (Kavka, 1978).

- *Intermediate* intergenerational equity, requiring only non-negative changes
  in the stock of RNC. This could imply that the stock of NNC is progressively depleted without consideration of the impact on future generations.
- *Minimal* intergenerational equity, requiring the maintenance of critical
  RNC that provides life support functions. This concept of intergenerational equity is the one that is closer to the obligation not to harm future
  generations.

It is in the case of minimal intergenerational equity that the interests of the
current generation and of future ones coalesce the most, as it is indisputable
that all generations need life support functions. Also, different generations
may not have diverging interests in maintaining a non-decreasing level of RNC.

Implications for Biodiversity Conservation and Protected Areas

Biodiversity is a critical factor in securing the continuing functioning of life
support systems. The conservation of biodiversity at the bioregional level
would mean that considerable progress in achieving intermediate intergenerational equity would be made. In fact, protecting biodiversity at the bioregional
scale implies that RNC is managed on a sustainable basis. While PAs may be
regarded as providing an important contribution to the protection of biodiversity, they represent only a partial insurance against biodiversity loss. Efforts by
countries in protecting ecosystems and species in PA systems would thus
contribute to the conservation of part of their critical RNC. Therefore, this
would comply only partially with the requirement for the achievement of
minimal intergenerational equity.

The establishment of PA systems may be regarded as an SMS for the
conservation of biodiversity at the national level. Unlike other approaches to
the SMS, the one outlined here deals not only with endangered or threatened
species, and with species that are used by humans. By aiming at the protection
of ecosystems, it attempts to conserve the species that are used and those which
are not, the species that are unknown, and obviously the ecosystems
themselves. Information on the optimal design of a PA system may be lacking.
However, according to the precautionary principle, this should not be used as
a reason for postponing conservation initiatives that contribute to the achievement of a minimum degree of intergenerational equity.

Studies on the economics of biodiversity conservation have addressed the
question of how to allocate a given budget for the preservation of species.
They have noted that neo-classical economics cannot provide a basis for decid-

ing the amount of resources to be assigned to the conservation of species (Randall, 1986). The task of deriving an ethical basis for determining the resources to be allocated to biodiversity conservation has been attempted here. The adoption by a country of the principle that future generations have environmental rights (and most countries have done so by signing the Rio Declaration), seems to imply that they ought to *at least* plan and fund the attainment of minimal intergenerational equity. On this basis, it may be affirmed that the cost of establishing PA systems should not be regarded as unacceptably large.

The above argument implies that the approach to the economic assessment of PAs should be reconsidered. The establishment of PA systems fulfils, at least partially, the ethically and ecologically based requirement that society has for conserving critical RNC. Therefore, at this conceptual level, economic analysis should not be used to decide if PA systems should or should not be established. This question would necessarily be answered in the affirmative on the basis of the interests of future generations, which at this level tend to coalesce with those of the current generation. Economic analysis should investigate the most cost-effective way of establishing the PA. Depending on the specific type of PA, CBA could be eventually used to assess economic activities that may be carried out inside the PA within specified ecological constraints. Other issues regarding the economic assessment of PAs will be discussed in the next chapter.

Conclusion

The deductive approach to the development of ethical rules adopted in this chapter could appear to be in contradiction with the positions taken in Chapters 2 and 3. The arguments developed there suggest an approach to the generation of ethical rules for environmental management based on the participation of civil society. The deliberations of this process of participation would be expected to be rules that are grounded in the ethical base of a nation. That approach is certainly endorsed. The deductive approach is used here to generate alternative resource use patterns to those that could be derived by using other deductive approaches, such as those grounded in utilitarianism or environmental neo-classical economics.

An ethical base other than contractarianism could be used in considering the implications of intergenerational equity for resource use, and how this may be achieved. Rawls' theory of justice is adopted here because it is believed that it produces less demanding requirements than, for example, deep ecology (Naess, 1989) or the land ethic (Leopold, 1970). By taking this approach, the analysis cannot be criticized on the basis that it overstates the duties of the current generation towards future ones.

The analysis has been carried out by following a rationalist approach grounded on self-interested individual choice. The adoption of the ethical stances presented, for example, by Leopold (1970) and Naess (1989) would result in far reaching requirements for the conservation of natural capital and biodiversity. Therefore, the requirements derived here for the fulfilment of intergenerational equity should be regarded as lower bound requirements.

It is recognized that the ethical base derived for assessing natural resources distribution questions may not be transferable to different countries and/or cultures. What is important to stress is that because of the separation of economics from ethics, partly due to the positivist influence, the ethical implications of economic analysis are often not made clear or understood. The ethical underpinnings of economic analysis and the policies that may result should be exposed. These should be compared to the ethos of the specific society to which they are applied. This process could facilitate the identification of dissonances (which may hinder the successful application of the policies) and could provide viable alternatives.

Finally, concern has been expressed about the dominance of the preservationist approach in environmental policy-making, because it pays little attention to the needs of the local people. The emphasis of this chapter on intergenerational equity does not imply that the needs of local people are overridden by the needs and rights of future generations. The case for participation in research and decision-making has already been introduced in the previous chapters and will be considered in more detail in the following one.

Notes

1   See also Faucheux and Froger (1995).
2   See the papers published in the special issue of *Ecological Economics* containing the reprint of the article in question.
3   They consider consequentialism (eg Bentham, 1970), the moral duty approach (eg Ehrenfeld, 1988) and contractarianism (eg Rawls, 1972).
4   The material presented below is derived from Tacconi and Bennett (1995a).
5   Human capital could be subdivided into social capital, which includes institutions and social relations, and human capital proper, which includes people and their skills and knowledge (eg Carney, 1998). For the scope of the arguments presented here, an aggregated definition suffices.
6   For arguments in favour and against the use of the concept of natural capital see also Berkes and Folke (1994), England (1998) and Hinterberger et al (1997).
7   For a discussion of Rawls' work see Kukathas and Pettit (1990).
8   It has been argued that the question of equity in intergenerational distribution of NC is better addressed on a per capita basis (Young, 1992). This position appears to be valid if the population size of future generations is determined essentially by previous generations' activities. However, if future generations' size is partly (or to a large extent) independent of, say, the current generation's activities, this position has a more limited appeal.
9   The learning process approach 'presumes that neither the ends nor the means of social interventions can be fully known in advance, and that understanding and consensus on them must be built through practical experience.' (Uphoff, 1992, p12).

5

Economics, Land Use Planning and Participation

Introduction

Theoretical aspects of ECE and NEE and their implications for environmental decision-making were discussed in Chapter 3. Chapter 4 noted the difficulty of deriving monetary estimates of biodiversity values, and considered alternative instruments, before analysing in detail the question of intergenerational equity. It also derived some implications for biodiversity conservation policies and for the assessment and establishment of PAs.

This chapter concludes the first part of the volume by considering processes and tools applied to the distribution and allocation of natural resources, with particular attention to their practical applicability, intragenerational equity, sustainability and policy implications.

The problems encountered in the application of CBA are discussed first. Questions relating to land use planning are then considered before proceeding to a discussion of participatory processes and their use in conservation activities. Participation receives detailed attention as it has gained increasing importance in conservation activities, because conventional resource management approaches have failed, and are still failing, to stem environmental degradation. It seems that participatory approaches can contribute to improving this situation (eg Fisher, 1995, Walters et al, 1998). A brief summary of the major theoretical points emerging from Part I is presented at the end of the chapter. Each case study in Part II addresses a number of these issues.

CBA and the Valuation of Ecosystems

As noted in the previous chapters, efficiency is suggested as a primary rule in environmental decision-making, including whether to establish PAs (Dixon and Sherman, 1990). CBA measures efficiency by comparing the net present value of the resource use resulting in the modification (partial or total, reversible or irreversible) of the ecosystem (NPVMOD), with the net present value of the resource use conserving the ecosystem (that may or may not include human use of the area) (NPVCON). Modification of the ecosystem would be endorsed (and the establishment of a PA rejected) if:

$$NPVMOD - NPVCON > 0$$

The economic value of an ecosystem use, which provides the basis for the calculation of NPVCON, can be described by using the total economic value (TEV) (Pearce, 1990):

$$TEV = DUV + IUV + OV + EV$$

where DUV is direct use values, IUV is indirect use values, OV is option values, and EV is existence values.

Direct use values describe products and services derived from ecosystems, such as fish, timber and recreation values. They may be consumed or used as inputs in the production of other goods and services. Indirect use values relate to ecosystem functions that support life and enter indirectly into the economic system, such as nutrient cycling and watershed protection. Option values refer to the willingness to pay for leaving open the possibility of using the ecosystem in the future. Existence values represent the benefits derived by an individual from knowing that a certain species or ecosystem exists.

It is often assumed that the most problematic part in the application of CBA is the measurement of the TEV, and that the value of NPVMOD is not difficult to derive (but see below). Bateman and Turner (1993) point out two significant limitations of the TEV. First, use and non-use values cannot be easily aggregated because there may be trade-offs between them. Second, use values may be dependent on the level of services attributed to non-use values, therefore a clear-cut separation of use values from non-use values is rather dubious. The reliability of estimates of the TEV is still very much disputed (Common et al, 1993).

Some Problems Faced in the Application of CBA

The difficulties involved in calculating NPVMOD should not be underestimated. The evidence regarding the application of CBA to projects for the production of marketed goods and services shows a low success rate. There are large divergences between estimated *ex ante* and *ex post* rates of return (Pohl and Mihaljek, 1992; Porter et al, 1991).

A further issue relates to resource distribution. CBA is concerned with the efficient allocation of resources. Usually, resource distribution is of no interest or is seen as the outcome of the efficient allocation of resources. At the theoretical level, there have been attempts to deal with distribution within a CBA framework. However, the theory is fraught with problems (Stewart, 1975) and questions of distribution are not normally considered in applied CBA (Squire, 1988). Some problems that may be encountered in the application of CBA in relation to equity and the practical applicability of CBA are exemplified below.

National distribution

Non-timber forest products (NTFPs) provide at times sizeable benefits to communities that have traditionally consumed and traded these products. The clearing of a forest, for example by logging operations, may be an activity that competes with the gathering of NTFPs.[1] A decision to allocate the forest to NTFP collection or to logging activities would have totally different outcomes depending on the institutional, social and economic situation of the specific area. Assume that a logging company applies to the government for a logging licence in the community's forest. A CBA of whether to log the forest could obviously conclude in favour of logging or against it. If it finds against logging, the *status quo* would be preserved. A decision in favour of logging would mean the community, which had the *right* to control the resources, would lose this right and its resources. These resources may be the basis of the community's livelihood. In some cases, depriving a community of NTFPs could threaten its livelihood. de Beer and McDermott (1989) note that when NTFPs are an important component of livelihood, such as in the case of some subsistence economies, physical indices of dependence on these products may be more appropriate than the monetary values. The question whether the livelihood of a community should be traded-off against pecuniary benefits clearly has ethical and distributional implications. These issues cannot be simply reduced to a problem of efficient allocation of resources. In relation to the latter, whether the community would receive compensation depends on the specific institutional setting. If the potential Pareto improvement test were applied, actual compensation would not be required.

Finally, in relation to the viability of monetary valuations of NTFPs, which could be used to calculate NPVCON, several attempts have not produced satisfactory results (Batagoda and Turner, 1997), and this is further considered below.

Capacity to Provide Monetary Estimates

The economic rent from logging activities may appear to be relatively simple to assess in calculating NPVMOD, given that timber is a widely marketed good. However, many attempts have been rather imprecise (Tacconi, 1994). Timber prices are subject to wide variations. This could lead to a situation in which, during a period of buoyant timber prices, CBA could suggest that logging should be the favoured option. Alternatively, conservation could be favoured if the assessment were to be undertaken during a period of relatively lower timber prices. CBA provides an estimate at a point in time. As soon as the conditions change, a re-assessment of the options should be carried out. In practice, this is unlikely to be viable because of resource constraints. In theory, a re-assessment could take place if the conservation option had been favoured. However, if logging had been undertaken, an irreversible ecosystem change may have taken place and conservation would be foreclosed.

A final issue is the extent to which CBA could be used and the implications for market processes. In discussing biodiversity conservation policies, Randall (1986) recognizes the issue of species interdependence. Taking the argument that every species is interdependent to the extreme, he observes that if:

> *'the loss of any species initiates processes leading to* eventual *ecocastrophe, some choice can be made, by scheduling the disaster so as to maximize the net present value of aggregate human benefits between now and the end.'* (Randall, 1986, p101)

In other words, CBA could be applied in a global way to all the resource allocation decisions taken by society. Resources would be allocated through planning, which, according to this view, is a rational and objective allocation process (Kornai, 1979). The application of CBA to all the significant resource allocation decisions would imply that the economy is centrally planned. The attractiveness of such an approach is, to say the least, doubtful.

Summary

Advocates of CBA posit its use, implicitly or explicitly, on a site-by-site basis. Implicit in this approach is the assumption that each valuation may be considered as an independent endeavour. Also, there is no recognition of the specific social, institutional and ecological features that have shaped the use of the ecosystem. For example, CBA would be applied in the same way irrespective of the fact that a country may already have an extensive PA system or may have no PAs whatsoever. It would be applied in the same fashion to a densely populated area, with local people[2] having acquired rights to the area, or to a totally depopulated area. Finally, as noted in Chapter 3, applications of CBA do not discuss the place of efficiency in the decision-making process. Economics, and CBA, certainly have a role in ecosystem distribution and allocation processes, but it is a complementary role rather than an overriding one, as often argued in neo-classical economics. This role is discussed below and exemplified in Chapters 6 and 10.

These arguments suggest that the marginalist economic approach on its own does not serve natural resource management well. To summarize, this is due to the existence of:

- different values that actors may hold, and which are not necessarily reflected in monetary valuations;
- intergenerational and intragenerational distribution issues;
- significant uncertainties;
- possible irreversibility of changes in ecosystems; and
- limited practical applicability of the CBA framework to the valuation of tangible land use values.

Sustainable Land Use Planning

The focus on the sustainable use of resources that pervades national policies and international agreements has brought about renewed interest in land use planning, for simplicity used here to refer to marine resource use planning as well. The World Commission on Environment and Development (1987) stressed that altering land use patterns seems to be the best long-term approach to ensuring the sustainable use of ecosystems. In response to the demands for improved ecosystem management and stakeholders' participation, the 1990s have seen the emergence of bioregional planning. It is a form of land use planning that recognizes the need to manage whole ecosystems and their components sustainably. Whole ecosystem management originally was not considered by land use planners, who were mostly concerned with zoning and management of individual zones, without sufficient concern for the ecological linkages between zones. Bioregional planning is an organizational process seeking to draw stakeholders together in planning and managing their region, by taking agreed actions, evaluating progress, and refining the approach (Miller, 1996).

Sustainable land use planning encompasses the topics of sustainability and land use planning (van Lier, 1994). van Lier asserts that land use planning means active planning of land to be used to provide for people's needs, and that it has two major dimensions. The first relates to research and policy making aimed at deciding the allocation of land resources to specific uses. The second dimension relates to the understanding of current land uses and their changes. Sustainable land use planning involves (van Lier, 1994):

- the setting of policies for land use;
- the process of planning for various land uses and their locations; and
- the development of plans to improve spatial/physical conditions.

To lead to sustainable development, this process has to account for the needs of the present and future generations, and the maintenance of ecosystem functions over the long-term (ie environmental sustainability). In relation to the latter, three major ecological principles for environmental sustainability are particularly suited for consideration within a sustainable land use approach (Olembo, 1994):

1   maintenance of essential ecological processes and life support functions;
2   conservation of biodiversity; and
3   sustainable use of species and ecosystems.

In relation to the planning process, a technocratic approach could have the negative effect of causing the de-politicization of the debate (Rydin, 1995). In this context, the traditional technocratic approach to land use planning has come under severe criticism within the circle of land use planners themselves. This is clearly summarized in the proceedings of an international conference:

> *'Land use planning as a top down and static exercise has not only deserved its bad reputation, but it is also bound to fail.'* (Fresco, 1994, p6)

Indeed, reviews of experiences in land use planning reveal widespread problems and failure of traditional top-down planning exercises, in which technical experts have complete control over planning and decision-making, through steps such as the development of decision-making criteria, and the selection of alternatives with limited or no public consultation (Moote and McClaran, 1997; Dalal-Clayton and Dent, 1993; Dent and Goonewardene, 1993; RRA Notes, 1991; Chapters 6, 8, 9 and 10). Dalal-Clayton and Dent (1993) point out that, partly because of the failure of top-down planning, participatory (bottom-up) planning is now often promoted as an alternative. However, they stress that participatory and top-down planning are complementary rather than alternative. In fact, there are issues concerning national goals which cannot be completely delegated to the local level. On the other hand, local level issues have to be first addressed at the local community level, then they have to be made to carry weight at higher levels in order to ensure that policies are coordinated with local level activities. It has been suggested that to stress the importance of stakeholders' participation in planning activities, the term land use planning should perhaps be modified to land use *negotiation* (Brinkman, 1994).

Land use planning has been criticized with reference to the failure of central planning systems (Olembo, 1994). In fact, planning attempts based on regulatory approaches, for example applied to transport (Rydin, 1995) and to agricultural development (Dalal-Clayton and Dent, 1993), have often failed as a result of a lack of sufficient knowledge about the systems being planned, and especially because the plans were against the interests of the users. Therefore, we need to consider some of the economic issues concerning sustainable land use planning and the *form* this may take.

First, it has already been noted in previous chapters that market failure in relation to biodiversity occurs because of, among other factors, uncertainty and irreversibility of ecological processes. Second, it has also been noted that there are several potential economic development paths available to a country (or region). Once a society or country embarks on a specific path, the other ones may be foreclosed (North, 1990). Therefore, it is important for a society to develop a strategic vision of possible development paths, and to define policies aimed at steering the country in the direction of the preferred one (eg Cocks, 1999). This does not imply that the issue of efficiency is disregarded. The existence of different development situations (ie located on different potential development paths) implies that there are several efficient resource allocation positions. Therefore, the market may be relied upon to bring about an efficient allocation of resources along the specified development path. The generation of development visions cannot and should not disregard market realities as this would result in failure. However, they can certainly influence and develop markets. The following are examples of strategic decision-making. The decision to establish and plan the Great Barrier Reef Marine Park in Queensland, Australia, has influenced the development path of that region by favouring the establishment of the tourism industry against that of the oil industry (Raymond, 1996). The Australian Government is continuing on that strategic path through the development and implementation of the *Ocean Policy* (Chapter 7). With regard to forest ecosystems, the *National Forest Policy Statement* (Commonwealth of Australia, 1992a) has led to a large-scale land use planning programme, known as Regional Forest Agreements, which is aimed at allocating forest ecosystems to conservation and sustainable forest management (Chapter 6).

In relation to the *form* that land use planning may take, planners suggest the general rule that when resources are relatively abundant, compared with the needs of the people living on it, planning may be informal (Brinkman, 1994). An increase of pressure on resources should be met by a parallel increase in formal planning. This is exemplified by the fact that land use plans are more detailed in urban areas than in rural areas. It can be argued that land use planning activities should not only take place when the population is growing and resource use conflicts arise. It should also be carried out when there is uncertainty about the irreversibility or sustainability of human impacts on ecological processes and lack of, or failure of, markets in ensuring and maintaining ecological functions.

A Land Use Planning Framework

A land use planning framework is presented in Figure 5.1. In this conceptual model, actors' views, needs and wants, influence and are influenced by existing rules. Actors' views, needs, and wants and rules enter the decision-making system that influences the allocation and use of ecosystems. There is a co-evolutionary influence between actors and ecosystems, represented by the direct link between the two. Environmental changes influence actors and rules through the decision-making system. Ecosystems are allocated to different uses, which for simplicity are summarized as agriculture, conservation (including PAs) and forestry. These uses are shown to overlap to a certain degree because, for example, some agricultural practices conserve soils, agricultural lands are an important repository of biodiversity (eg Brookfield and Stocking, 1999; Thrupp, 1998) and agricultural and forestry activities take place in some (parts) of PAs. The overlap is not complete because the expansion of agriculture in all forest areas would result in the loss of forest biodiversity, and currently used forestry management practices often reduce environmental values.

The process of ecosystem allocation to agriculture, forestry and conservation is defined in the model as the *first decision-making level*. The *second decision-making level* concerns the practices adopted in agricultural, conservation and forestry activities. It is termed the second decision-making level because the allocation of resources to those activities is taken as given at the specific point in time. Over time, improvements in practices will affect the higher levels. This is an important element. For instance, an improvement in forest management practices may decrease the disruption of forest ecosystems, thereby reducing the impact on biodiversity. This would result in an increased overlap between conservation and forestry. In turn, this could change actors' views about the allocation of resources to the various uses.

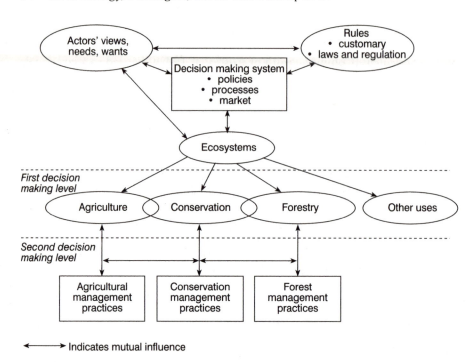

Figure 5.1 *A land use planning framework*

It may be noted that sustainable land use planning recognizes that multiple demands on ecosystems have to be considered. This engenders attempts towards formulating resource use plans in ways that allow the different needs to be addressed and possibly satisfied. Sustainable land use planning takes an encompassing view of available resources, rather than a narrow, piece-meal view characteristic of a neo-classical economic approach to resource allocation and use.

Decision support systems, often in the form of Geographic Information Systems, have become widely available (eg Cocks et al, 1995; Dalal-Clayton and Dent, 1993; Chapter 7). These decision support systems allow a certain degree of integration of environmental, social and economic variables. For example, cost-effectiveness analysis can be used to minimize the cost of achieving a specific conservation target. Also, trade-off analysis can be carried out in an iterative approach to the design of a PA system which takes into account ecological and economic costs and benefits. The availability of tools for sustainable land use planning is not a constraint, and probably is not the most significant issue. The reconciliation of the various actors' demands is the critical question. Therefore, an important issue is the process through which planning is carried out, because it can determine the values (broadly defined, eg ethical, environmental and economic) to be considered, the rules for choosing among alternatives, and the type and content of information admitted in the planning process.

Purposely, we close this section without providing steadfast rules for the solution of land use allocation and distribution conflicts, because they have to emerge necessarily from the specific situation.[3] The following section considers the issue of participation that is, among other things, relevant to defining processes for adoption in land use planning.

Participation

In development and environment management practice, and to a certain extent in research, the 1990s appear to have been the decade of participation, at least at a rhetorical level. Calls for greater citizens' participation are found in statements and resolutions of international and national organizations, agencies, and conventions (eg UN Global Consultation on the Right to Development, 1990; Rio Declaration on Environment and Development (Principle 10), 1992; World Bank, 1996). With the realization that by far the largest share of biodiversity is found in countries in the south, conservation organizations have in many cases joined forces with development aid agencies to protect biodiversity in those countries while fostering rural development, for example through the implementation of ICDPs (see Chapter 11).

Participation has several facets. Therefore, interpretations of the concept of participation, political issues and positive and negative aspects are considered in turn.

The Meaning of Participation

An early classification of participation was presented by Arnstein (1969). Her ladder of types of participation recognizes that there are cases where participation is used by those in power to appease rather than involve citizens in decision-making. The categories included on the ladder range from manipulation (classified as non-participation), through to consultation (a degree of tokenism) to citizen control (which is the highest degree of citizen power).

The rural development literature, which inspires recent conservation activities in developing countries, has focused particularly at the micro level where development projects, often aid-assisted ones, take place. Several types of participation, mirroring to a certain extent those of Arnstein's, have been identified (Cohen and Uphoff, 1980; Paul, 1987; Oakley, 1991; Cernea, 1991; Pretty, 1995), including:

- participation in terms of provision of financial incentives to project beneficiaries for their contribution or input to an activity; it is characteristic of community development projects calling on the supposed beneficiaries to provide material inputs into projects, whose objectives have been set by outsiders;
- involvement in setting objectives, implementation, sharing benefits and evaluation of an activity;

- participation seeking to empower people to address their problems and identify opportunities (self-mobilization).

Others see participation as a human right, and as such an end in itself (Taylor, 1995).

Cohen and Uphoff (1980) recognize the existence of a variety of participatory processes and provide a framework to describe and assess them. Their framework was prepared specifically for development projects but it can be adapted to other initiatives. It recognizes three fundamental elements:

1   the kind of activity involved: decision-making, implementation, benefits derived and evaluation;
2   the actors participating: local residents, leaders, government and foreign personnel;
3   the process involved: source of initiative and incentives, form of participation (direct, indirect), extent of participation (timing of actors' entry, duration and intensity; range of activities) and effect of participation (empowerment, interactions).

Classifications of participation are often used, implicitly or explicitly, with normative connotations, for example that self-mobilization should be preferred over consultation (eg Pretty, 1995). Manipulative approaches to participation may be disapproved on the basis of democratic and ethical principles. However, other types of participation, such as public consultation, have their place in democratic societies, and the specific context to which the process is applied should be considered in assessing their merit. The context involves a range of factors such as the type of activity (eg development project, policy-making), the scale of the issue (eg individual PA management, national conservation planning), and the stakes involved (eg benefits and costs, financial, time, as well as moral). The degree to which one type of participation is promoted over another one is influenced by social and political issues, as discussed below.

Politics, Planning and Participation

Until recently, participatory approaches to development, natural resource management and planning have omitted consideration of political and power issues (Thrupp et al, 1994). At times, this may be due to a lack of awareness of the pervasive nature of politics and power. However, some have clearly expressed the view that participation and community-based resource management should be preferably treated apolitically (eg Little, 1994), possibly because they hope this would avoid conflicts with politically powerful actors.

Participatory democratic philosophy underpins participatory processes seeking direct citizens' involvement in decision-making and management (Day, 1997; Moote and McClaran, 1997). When this takes place at a micro level, such as a development project, it may create power struggles for the control of project resources, but it might not conflict with established political and administrative arrangements, if the project is concerned with activities that are normally carried out within the realm of private initiative (eg farm management). Indeed, at this level citizens are normally the decision-makers. However, direct citizens' involvement in decision-making and management in public activities (such as public land planning and management, and development planning) can conflict with established rules of representative democracy, which is the dominant model in western countries and in an increasing number of developing countries. Some concerns about participatory democracy have been summarized by Day (1997) and include:

1   participation is skewed towards powerful interest groups;
2   broad participation makes the identification of the overall public interest difficult;
3   individuals and groups participating promote their own interests, rather than those of the disadvantaged;
4   as the number of participants increases so does the level of conflict and it becomes more difficult to reconcile interests;
5   democratization of administration is achieved at the expense of effectiveness.

The findings by Moote and McClaran (1997) concerning experiences in public land planning provide a good summary of the problems faced by top-down land use planning (or traditional public participation process), the solutions proposed by advocates of participatory democracy alternatives, and the problems and barriers the latter encounters (Table 5.1). These findings clearly show that although the traditional planning system presents considerable shortcomings, a participatory democracy model may stop short of its supposed benefits.

Concerns about participatory democracy models have also been raised by Porter and Onyach-Olaa (1999) in the context of development planning at the local government level, and are summarized below. They note that the cost-effectiveness of direct participation is to be proven, especially because it may divert resources away from the delivery of services. Very detailed participatory plans could be prepared but not implemented, partly because of a lack of resources, and the actual delivery of services is of greater concern to the constituency than participation in planning (although citizens appeared also to have concerns about how the needs to be serviced were chosen). However, they note, plans are often not implemented because of a lack of accountability on the part of political leaders and bureaucrats. Because of the difficulty in achieving objectives through the political process, rural development programmes often attempt to use administrative processes to achieve their objectives. This is reflected in the increasing popularity among technical staff of participatory rural appraisal methods. These methods promise direct access to needs, offer the authority of having spoken to people and hold a veiled

Table 5.1 *Traditional public participation, participatory democracy solutions and problems*

Criteria	Criticism of traditional public participation process	Participatory democracy solutions	Participatory democracy problems and barriers
Efficacy	Land use plans do not reflect the needs, concerns and values of the affected public. Appeals and lawsuits delay plan implementation	Resolving conflicts through the planning process will result in shared ownership and acceptance of the plan	Greater participation does not necessarily result in a plan that all will accept and support
Representation and access	Interest group domination of forums; few opportunities for direct public input; public access limited by financial and time barriers, and formal format	Involve non-represented, non-activist public. More access to agency staff and information. Modify agency attitude to encourage public input	Some affected interests may not participate; lack of time and financial resources restrict access, especially for non-affiliated citizens
Information exchange and learning	No opportunity for dialogue and no way for the public to correct misunderstandings. Agencies ignore public input	Encourage all interested parties to articulate needs, concerns, values; encourage informal dialogue and information exchange	Improved communication will not resolve differences rooted in fundamental conflicts of interest or values
Continuity of participation	Participation is confined to few points in the decision-making process; few opportunities for participation before publication of draft plan	Participation throughout planning and decision-making processes through network of formal and informal interactions	Transfer of agency staff reduces continuity, time requirements engender participant burnout. Agency mandates may require them to make a decision before public participants are ready to do so
Decision-making authority	Agency representatives maintain broad discretionary authority; public is not involved in decision-making	Share authority and responsibility for planning decisions among participants, agencies give up some discretion	Law does not provide for shared decision-making authority; no way to determine who is ultimately accountable for a collective decision

Source: Summarized from Moote and McClaran (1997, Tables 1 and 3).

threat of direct action by empowered communities. Porter and Onyach-Olaa (1999) stress that this approach could have the deleterious effect of further weakening the relationship between political leaders and their constituency. They stress that increasing accountability should be of greater concern than direct participation if service delivery is to be achieved. Accountability should be considered at three levels, between: political leaders and their constituency, administrative staff and political leaders, and various levels of government.

It may be noted that accountability is part of the broader subject area of governance. Decentralization has been considered extensively in development planning as a way to improve governance, and it may also have benefits for biodiversity conservation (Lutz and Caldecott, 1996, Chapter 8).

Further Positive and Negative Aspects of Participation

The NEE approach presented in Chapter 3 endorses the sovereignty of consumers and seeks to represent their views. However, participatory approaches seem to be better suited to reflecting citizens' actual views, because they are not derived through a model of simplified individual behaviour but by directly consulting them, and in some cases by involving them in the decision-making process.

Participation allows the stakeholders to express their actual objectives (ends) and to decide how these may be better achieved (means). NEE assumes that the ends are given (ie maximization of net present monetary value) and that the choice of means is not constrained by cultural and moral values. Cultural and moral values may, however, determine not only which are *acceptable* means but also which are *desirable* ends.

Participatory processes may allow people to evaluate the alternative ecosystem uses according to their specific needs and rationales. Byron (1991) notes that the net present value is only one of several decision criteria utilized to select a preferred option. Other criteria – such as the maximin rule or the minimum regret rule – are no less reasonable approaches than the net present value, an index that is appropriate when the objective is the maximization of monetary value. For example, income stability and food security are other criteria adopted by farmers in evaluating alternative options (Maxwell, 1990). Through participatory processes citizens may be enabled to express their views fully (for example, ranging from the selfish to the other-regarding ones). In this context, CBA may be applied to assess the efficient allocation of resources. It could be used to generate financial and economic information to be used in a participatory approach (Richards et al, 1999; Chapter 10).

Participatory processes may help in making decisions of a higher logical content than those made in a *snapshot* approach, characteristic of NEE. Participation facilitates interaction between individuals, between individuals and institutions, and between citizens and experts. This process may result in a re-conceptualization and better understanding of the problem faced, in exchange for information and in-depth analysis of the problem and data. This interactive process appears to offer support to the limited computational powers proper of each individual's brain.

With regard to the development benefits at the micro level, there are clear indications that participation is an important factor in delivering positive economic and financial outcomes, and in increasing the likelihood of the sustainability of activities (eg Cernea, 1987; Kottak, 1991; Krishna et al, 1997). In a study of 121 rural water supply projects in Africa, Latin America and Asia, Narayan (1996) finds that a high degree of participation:

1   contributed significantly to project effectiveness;
2   was an important determinant of good conditions in the water supply systems;
3   improved overall economic benefits;
4   increased the percentage of the target population reached;
5   had positive environmental effects;
6   contributed to the achievement of equality of access to facilities;
7   contributed to individual and community empowerment; and
8   strengthened community organizations, enabling them to carry out other development activities.

Participation was the most important factor contributing to the quality of project implementation, and it was more effective when taking place throughout the project cycle.

In relation to the costs of participation, these cannot be discounted, especially at levels beyond the localized activity. Porter and Onyach-Olaa (1999) note that the routine application of participatory appraisal tools to achieve intensive community-based development planning at a district level first, and then scaled up to the national level, is simply impossible. It would require an inordinate amount of time and resources. This point is similar to that raised earlier in the chapter in relation to CBA and central planning issues, the difference being that the issue raised here relates to an inordinate number of assessments to develop national plans from the bottom up.

Finally, in relation to rural development projects, Cohen and Uphoff (1980) conclude that participation is not a panacea. They note that its neglect may have devastating effects, but its introduction does not guarantee the success of a project because other factors are also important. This lesson needs to be taken into account by participatory conservation activities, to which we turn.

Participation and Conservation Activities

Participation in conservation activities is an issue in developed countries and developing ones alike; however, it has different connotations in the two sets of countries. This section considers the scope for participation in conservation activities and focuses on developing countries for the following reasons. In these countries, the debate considers the question of the different degrees of participation (as discussed in the previous section), which is also an issue in developed countries, but, in addition, it involves three other important aspects.

First, the issue of control (often ownership) of resources. In developed countries, institutional arrangements are often more developed and formalized than in developing countries, and there is less scope for stakeholders to influence these institutional arrangements. For instance, the state's control and/or ownership of natural resources is normally not questioned in developed countries,[4] whereas in developing ones it is often argued that the control of resources should be returned to local people (eg Colchester, 1994).

Second, in conservation activities in developing countries, there is often an expectation that local people and communities, who control or own ecologically important resources, will be willing to contribute considerably to conservation activities. This expectation is present to a greater extent in developing countries' conservation activities than in those taking place in developed ones.

Third, external stakeholders tend to have greater influence on local people's decisions in developing countries than in developed ones. In the former countries, local people (mostly rural) tend to lack knowledge of national and international conservation issues, and links to relevant conservation and also development institutions. The fact that they are often uneducated tends to limit their capacity to assess the information provided by the external stakeholders, for or against conservation initiatives.

Let us begin the analysis by presenting a description of community-based conservation (CBC):

> '*includes, at one extreme, buffer-zone protection of parks and reserves and, at the other, natural resource use and biodiversity conservation in rural areas. The term covers both new and traditional conservation methods, as well as conservation efforts that* originate within or outside the community, as long as the outcome benefits the community.
>
> *Community-based conservation reverses the top-down, centre-driven conservation by focusing on the people* who bear the costs of conservation. *In the broadest sense, then, community-based conservation includes natural resources or* biodiversity protection by, for, and with the local community.
>
> The deeper agenda, *for most conservationists, is* to make nature and natural products meaningful to rural communities. *As far as local communities are concerned,* the agenda is to regain control over natural resources and, through conservation practices, improve their well-being.' (Western and Wright, 1994, p7; emphasis added)

This definition is broad and while stressing the importance of local people, it does not specify what type of participation CBC may involve, apart from leaving the door open to outside intervention. It also clearly stresses the deeper agenda of most conservationists, which could be expressed as educating people (often changing their values) about the importance of conservation.

In relation to the performance of CBC, in a book dedicated to CBC, Little (1994) finds that only three out of twelve case studies resemble participatory

CBC, and they are not associated with national parks or PAs. To note, activities that include compensation or development activities in exchange for biodiversity conservation are not considered CBC by definition (Little, 1994).

A review of CBC in Africa (International Institute for Environment and Development (IIED), 1994) also summarizes some of the key issues affecting the performance of CBC and exemplifies the populist view of participation in conservation. The review could not identify examples of CBC initiatives involving *real active* participation, a concept meaning that the concerned community, without the intervention of outsiders, plans and carries out the management tasks aimed at the sustainable management of the resources. Conservation initiatives were initiated and funded externally, and categorized by the review as *towards active participation* – involving a substantial degree of participation, but not as extensive as favoured by the reviewers – and *passive participation* initiatives – said to focus on an efficient implementation of an externally-formulated project. Initiatives in the first category involved local people in resource management, without giving them *real* decision-making power. In several cases, local people had been given the responsibility to manage resources in order to ease the government's burden. In this way, communities have greater control over resources and distribution of the benefits. However, they also have an increased level of resource management costs. Some initiatives had tried to empower communities by devolving some power to the communities; these attempts relied on the development of consumptive and non-consumptive resource uses. The basic assumption behind this approach was that local people would benefit from the increased value of wildlife resources and, therefore, they would manage them sustainably. However, it was found that often the market did not favour conservation land uses compared to alternative land uses, and local people were not as interested in conservation as expected. To note, the achievement of greater community decision-making power has been difficult, because the authorities lack strong commitment to this objective.

According to IIED (1994), *passive participation* initiatives involved educating people and providing tangible economic benefits. These initiatives did not consider power-sharing in decision-making or self-determination. Their goal was to conserve biodiversity by reducing local opposition to PAs, and the introduction of conservation legislation and modern tenure arrangements. Specific activities included the following.

- Environmental education programmes: there were only few examples of good education programmes focusing on the benefits of conservation for people's livelihood; programmes had often concentrated on the aesthetic values of resources, simply creating confusion among the local people about the meaning of conservation.
- Compensation schemes: people were seen as passive beneficiaries; according to the review, these schemes reinforce powerlessness in relation to the authorities.

- Income generating projects: there were only a few cases where income generating projects had been successful.

Let us now consider some of the key issues underlying the arguments presented above.

There are significant expectations raised by CBC initiatives that local people will conserve, possibly through the establishment of PAs, the resources they control. This is due to the belief that local people live in harmony with nature (Agrawal and Gibson, 1999), that these communities focus on self-reliance, as exemplified by some ICDPs (eg Ellis, 1997), and that communities are homogeneous and often harmonious entities (Agrawal and Gibson, 1999; Guijt and Shah, 1998; Leach et al, 1997).[5] A review of an ICDP in Papua New Guinea,[6] considered also by Ellis (1997), notes that the project stresses self-reliance rather than dependency: without 'being the provider of services, development and conservation ... the project attempts to support and assist communities in coming to grips with the economic and environmental changes around them' (van Helden, 1997, p2). This implies that the local people are expected not to allow logging in their forests and provide their own resources to support alternative development activities; in this effort, the project would simply play the role of facilitator. A conservation agreement (such as a covenant, involving a payment to the owners of the forest) may not be acceptable from the ICDP point of view because it would be against the concept of self-reliance (van Helden, 1997). A rather different view of self-reliance is provided by Simpson (1997), in an aptly titled paper reflecting the views of (some of?) the local people. He remarks that local communities involved in logging projects regarded landowner companies[7] 'as a mechanism for establishing control over local social and economic issues and promoting a truly self-reliant community' (Simpson, 1997, p20). This means that a community may feel more self-reliant if it has control over its resources, and if it can derive greater benefits from them, as reflected in this extract from a letter sent by local people (landowners) to a Papua New Guinea Minister of Forestry:

> 'people are living like primitives who just came from the bush, while others are much well off than our people, where no proper health care, education, no proper social development, no good water during long drought, no proper economic and infrastructure development ... and we as natives of this country have every right to have any say over our property like land issues and the resources.' Cited by Wood (1997, p105)

It is obvious that the values of the proponents of CBC initiatives clearly colour the meaning of self-reliance and may overestimate the degree to which local people live, and want to live, in harmony with their environment (Agrawal and Gibson, 1999). Conservationists' views and beliefs may also obscure the degree to which local people's resource use strategies match those required to conserve biodiversity in each specific case. As discussed in Chapter 1, local people often do aim at using resources sustainably, but this does not mean that biodiversity will be automatically conserved (eg an agricultural system established through rainforest clearance may be sustainable but could reduce biodiversity). Also, the arguments presented here do not mean that local people are never interested in conservation in the form of PAs. In fact, there are cases in which they have timber resources, have decided to reject large-scale logging operations, and seem to be seeking alternative development options (eg Maisin and Conservation Melanesia, 1997; Chapter 10). In some cases local people may be interested in establishing PAs on lands they control and/or live on, but this should not be automatically presumed. It will depend on the local conditions, such as perceived development needs, alternative options available and local values. These values may be considerably different from those held by the promoters of a conservation initiative, and this should be recognized and factored in the participatory process aimed at developing, if possible, joint objectives.

Achieving meaningful participation in conservation activities is even more challenging than in rural development, because of the trade-offs between rural development and conservation objectives, often occurring in situations of prevalent poverty (Little, 1994; Reardon and Vosti, 1995). Little (1994) asks whether conservation programmes, through participation, can empower local people to achieve conservation, and whether participatory development can lead to conservation outcomes. These questions are fundamental to biodiversity conservation initiatives focusing on PAs. PA initiatives are more likely to generate situations with conflicts between conservation and development than conservation activities aimed, for example, at bringing about sustainable resource use such as soil conservation programmes in agricultural systems. Unfortunately, these questions are often avoided in conservation activities. For example, a review of ICDPs in Asia (Sanjayan et al, 1997) assumes that conservation-development is a single concept, and asserts that biodiversity conservation should be the primary objective of ICDPs. Then, it goes on to state that shared objectives should be developed, and participation is needed to develop these objectives and ownership of the project. Clearly, biodiversity conservation may not be a concern for targeted local stakeholders, and the development of shared objectives would simply mean trying to convince them of the goodness of the objectives imported by the project.

Together with social and ethical values, the institutional and economic incentives faced by local people are important factors in determining their choices about resource management. These are exemplified well by studies from Papua New Guinea about PAs and Wildlife Management Areas, which are PAs established, managed and controlled by the local people themselves on their traditional lands, and officially recognized in the legislation. These studies stress that resource owners have a variety of motives for establishing these PAs, and especially the desire to consolidate their ownership over a parcel of land and regulate the use of that land by outsiders (Babo, 1997), the prospect of gaining cash income from the area (WWF and DEC, 1992), and a hope that they would bring development (ie employment, and an improvement in services, which the government has failed to deliver to remote areas) (Johnson, 1997).

It is obvious that while some proponents of *pure* CBC (or *truly* participatory conservation) may see the provision of economic benefits, including income generation and compensation schemes, as creating dependence on outsiders, including the state, local people are concerned with the benefits they may receive from these initiatives. Rural development experience shows that the stakes involved are a significant factor conditioning citizens' willingness to participate (Matur, 1995; Uphoff et al, 1990).Therefore, a transparent participatory process would address these issues openly. This would involve provision of the necessary support to participate in the decision-making process, to analyse the relevant issues, and to deliberate in an informed fashion (Chapters 6 and 10).

Obviously, ever-present differences in the power and agendas of the relevant actors (such as the state, national and international NGOs and local people) determine the degree of transparency and openness of the participatory process. In relation to local people's economic benefits from PAs, it has long been recognized that they often benefit the least and pay the most (Wells, 1992). Due to the scarcity of resources available at the international and national levels, it is possible and unfortunate that the emphasis paid to changing local people's values (in the hope that they will endorse the agenda of the proponents of the specific conservation initiative) will continue to be much greater than that devoted to generating actual net benefits for the local people.[8] Clearly (conservation) education is important, but it should not be used to maintain the current trend of making local people pay for conservation that also brings considerable benefits to national and international communities. And if it can be shown that conservation initiatives offer an alternative and can generate real benefits over those of less sustainable activities, local people's participation will eventuate, even if the initiative was initially introduced by external actors, as has been demonstrated by experiences with rural development projects.

Concluding Comments

The shortcomings of the neo-classical economic approach have been outlined in the previous chapters and further considered in this chapter. Because of these shortcomings, the relevance of land use planning and participatory decision-making for the design of biodiversity conservation initiatives, and particularly for PAs, were considered. Economic analysis can find a useful application within land use planning and participatory decision-making. However, it would not dictate the values that should be adopted by society, and it can be used in a fashion that serves the values articulated through democratic participatory processes.

These values and biodiversity conservation objectives can be articulated through land use planning processes, which are more suited to addressing biodiversity conservation issues than the marginalist neo-classical economic approach. Reviews of land use planning have highlighted the need to adopt a more participatory approach to planning. However, they have also noted that simple bottom-up approaches are not the answer. There is a need to reconcile top-down and bottom-up planning processes, an issue that has also been recognized in the development literature (eg Uphoff, 1998). The planning literature, including development planning, shows that participatory democracy approaches are not problem-free; a very relevant problem is that no matter how detailed and participatory the initial planning process is, unless the findings are carried through to implementation, the planning process is irrelevant. This is particularly important for biodiversity conservation because there are many examples of paper parks (Chapter 2). In many cases these have been designed without the input of relevant actors. However, even if this input is sought through detailed participatory planning processes, if there is no commitment to maintaining the PAs and allocating the necessary resources, participation will not solve the problem.

Participation has been shown to be an important factor in the success of rural development projects. It may also help in empowering local people in making better use of their environment, and in controlling external forces, which may positively or negatively affect their livelihood. However, population changes, technological changes and institutional changes may influence the way the environment is used and some members of the community may not be aware of the possible impacts on the environment. Therefore, it should not be assumed that participation would necessarily lead to sustainable ecosystem use. In designing conservation initiatives, it is important to consider local people's livelihood systems and to understand how these are linked to ecosystem management. Local people's interests, needs and wants are not homogeneous, and may or may not coalesce with the interests of other actors of the current generation or with the interests of future generations. Mechanisms to enable these interests to coalesce and/or to resolve conflicts (Warner, 1997; Chapter 12) need to be designed on a case by case basis, including the appropriate degree of participation (eg Borrini-Feyerabend, 1996). Again, a mix of top-down and bottom-up approaches is required. Clearly, because of the stakes, values and power relationships involved, even an approach integrating conflict management activities may not lead to a consensus outcome.

Summary of Part I

The ecological economic framework for biodiversity conservation, specifically focused on the assessment and establishment of PAs, that arises from the analysis carried out in Part I, may be summarized as follows.

- The research and action methodology should be post-positivist, as exemplified by post-normal and constructivist methodologies.
- A range of forest actors, ranging from the individual to organizations, and relevant institutional features should be considered, rather than focusing on individuals as suggested by neo-classical economics.

- Ecosystem use patterns should be chosen on the basis of their sustainability and distributional aspects together with their efficiency aspects.
- Systems of PAs should be established in order to achieve, at least partially, minimal intergenerational equity.
- Intragenerational equity requires the correction of the asymmetrical distribution of the costs and benefits arising from the establishment of PAs. Local people often bear the costs of conservation, and it should not be assumed that they always benefit from the establishment of PAs.
- Land use planning is better suited to the integration and reconciliation of the multiple demands on the environment and to achieving biodiversity conservation than a marginalist neo-classical economic approach.
- The decision-making process should be participatory. The appropriate degree of participation will be influenced by a combination of factors, such as the scale of the problem and the resources available for the planning and implementation phases.
- Power and conflict (at different levels, from the local community to the national level) are important elements influencing ecosystem use and need to be addressed. It should not be assumed that the adoption of a participatory approach will automatically redress the distribution of power and solve conflicts.

The chapters in Part II consider in detail specific aspects of this framework and intend to show how such a framework may be put into practice. In this context, they also consider practical issues that may enhance the possibility of successful biodiversity conservation initiatives.

Notes

1   This is an example. NTFPs are often an important livelihood component (eg Dey, 1997). However, it should not be assumed that NTFPs from PAs are always an essential contribution to rural communities' livelihood, and that NTFP collection always conflicts with logging activities (Chapter 10).
2   We refer to local people as this is more inclusive than indigenous people, because it can also include people who have migrated to the area in question in a relatively recent or distant past.
3   General principles for land use planning are provided by Dalal-Clayton and Dent (1993, Box 30).
4   Notable exceptions are developed countries with indigenous people such as Australia and Canada.
5   Recent studies on development, such as those cited, highlight that communities most often have differentiated goals, power and access to resources.
6   Papua New Guinea is an interesting case among tropical forest-rich countries because the state controls very little land (1–2%), which is owned by the indigenous people whose rights are clearly recognized in the Constitution. The local people are referred to as landowners, given their control over resources.

7   Landowner companies are legal entities formed by local people who control/own forest resources. It needs to be stressed that sometimes these companies have been manipulated by large international logging companies.

8   A representative of an international conservation NGO stressed to the author that they cannot compete with logging companies in terms of financial benefits provided to landowners, therefore they are trying to convince them to conserve their forests through other means, such as conservation awareness programmes.

Part Two

Case Studies

6

Conflict and Agreement in Australian Forests

John Dargavel, Wendy Proctor and Peter Kanowski

Introduction

Australian forests are in a period of dynamic change. The old order of state and industrial forestry, dedicated to producing wood, had been engulfed in environmental conflicts which governments could not resolve. These were part of wider problems which led to changes in policies for several sectors. For the forests, they led the Federal and State Governments to declare the country's first national forest policy in 1992. Then they embarked on the Regional Forest Agreement programme; the most ambitious, comprehensive and expensive environmental and resource planning programme ever undertaken in Australia. It is to cover Australia's major forest regions and be finished by 2000. The programme spurred the development of new methods and incorporated various forms of public participation. It has led to regional agreements negotiated between the two levels of government which they hope will enable them to manage the conflicts. The initial results have been mixed. This chapter describes the programme and draws some preliminary lessons from it.

Australia's adoption of such an expensive and exhausting programme needs to be seen in terms of its historical and political circumstances, its scientific and forestry traditions, its industrial structures and public expectations. The following section sets this in context.

From Colonies to Country

Post-colonial Australia is deeply structured by its colonial origins. Three in particular concern the forests: the rights of the Indigenous people, the federal political structure and the imperial model of forestry which was adopted.

Australia is an extreme case of the demographic takeover of an Indigenous population by settlers. The British struck no treaties when they invaded in 1788 but simply arrogated all the land to themselves and parcelled the best of it out for sheep, cattle, wheat and all the appurtenances of modern society. By the end of the nineteenth century, 3.7 million white Australians had possibly the highest standard of living in the world, but the number of Indigenous people (Aborigines and Torres Strait Islanders) had fallen from perhaps 314,000 to 95,000 by murder, disease and despair. None remained as forest dwellers. Now there are 17.8 million people of whom only 353,000 are Indigenous. In an easing of colonialist and racist attitudes, the High Court ruled in 1993 and 1997 that Indigenous people could lay claim to *native title* rights in some land but negligible progress has been made (to 1999). The Indigenous cultural heritage has gained some recognition in forest policies, but not land rights, which are treated as a separate matter. The bitter legacy of colonization is yet to be dissipated.

The political dynamics of Australia's federal structure have a critical influence on resource and environmental policies. The six separate colonies founded between 1788 and 1859 became self-governing with their own parliaments. In 1901 they federated into the Commonwealth of Australia, becoming States in the process (for brevity, the Northern Territory and the Australian Capital Territory are included in the term States in the remainder of this chapter). They kept their own parliaments and responsibility for most affairs including land, forests, rivers and national parks. The new Federal Government took responsibility for defence, foreign affairs and trade but came to have most economic power. Local governments and regional bodies have little influence on forests.

Federal–State relations became more important as environmental concern increased from the 1970s because the large urban vote, particularly in Melbourne, Sydney and Hobart, was markedly pro-environment in contrast to the pro-development stance of the State governments. The political dynamics are complicated by the nature of Australian voting systems that enable some minor parties and interests, such as The Greens and environmentalists, to gain political leverage. They led the Federal Government to use its constitutional powers to influence the States' forest policies through national heritage and environmental impact legislation, by licensing the export of woodchips and by entering into international agreements such as the *Convention Concerning the Protection of World Cultural and Natural Heritage* (1972) and the *Convention on Biological Diversity* (1992). Not surprisingly, the States' governments were miffed at the loss of their autonomy in the forests.

It was a struggle to establish a policy of forest conservation in Australia against the dominant settlement and agricultural interests, but between 1870 and 1920 an imperial model was adopted in the various States (Dargavel, 1995). It rested on the reservation of state forests, their protection and management by professional foresters in government forest services, and long-term plans to sustain the yield of timber from each forest. The policy was only partly successful and its gains were slow. A national target of having 10 million hectares dedicated as state forests was only reached in 1966. The principles of sustained timber yield were not readily applicable to the condition of the forests, especially in the face of ravaging forest fires, and were difficult to impose on the sawmillers. Booming domestic timber demands in the 1950s and 1960s led to the forests being greatly overcut for sawlogs, only to be followed by an inevitable slump in production which will last well into the twenty-first century. The unmerchantable old trees left standing in the forests inhibited the regeneration of new trees and exacerbated the situation.

The state forest policy focused narrowly on producing timber from the 10 million hectares of state forests and largely disregarded other values, other forests and the woodlands. The cadre of professional foresters formed a close-knit, conformist group which advanced the cause of forestry in an energetic and practical manner but was ill-prepared for the environmental conflicts which burst upon them in the 1970s and 1980s (Table 6.1).

The conflicts were inflamed by the very energy with which the forest services promoted industrial development and tried to correct the forest problems. Some of the overcut native forests were replaced by fast-growing exotic pine plantations and large areas of the non-merchantable old trees were sold as woodchips to Japan. Both operations had drastic environmental impacts, particularly on the habitat of the endemic arboreal fauna (the koalas, possums, gliders, many birds and bats) which depended on the big old trees. The initial operations were rushed, crude, hideous and a ready target for the nascent environmental movement (Table 6.2).

The forest services were forced to stop clearing native forests for plantations and bought old farmland instead. However, the environmental critique widened and the conflicts spread around the country with particular focus on the limited areas of rainforests, old-growth and the continued clear-felling of forests primarily for woodchip exports. At the same time claims were made to expand the area of national parks, many of which were in forest regions. The overall effect was to reduce the wood resources which industries had come to expect and to challenge the legitimacy of the way the forest services managed the forests.

The offended forest services both improved their environmental practices and formed alliances with industry against the environmentalists. The forest industries were restructuring and drastically reducing the employment they provided, particularly in the smaller hardwood sawmills, but deployed the loss of employment as their major argument against the environmental claims. However, widespread public concern and well-publicized civil disobedience campaigns against logging raised the political temperature. Numerous State and Federal reports, environmental impact assessments and public inquiries failed to solve the conflicts between the interests. They also failed to solve conflicts between the Federal and State Governments, some of which ended in the High Court as constitutional challenges, and they failed to solve disputes within Federal Cabinet, some of which spilled over into the media. The political cost of the conflicts was too high; better ways had to be found.

Table 6.1 *Some forest conflicts and consequences*

Year and State	Conflicts	Consequences
1968–70 Victoria	Objections to agricultural clearing of mallee woodland in Victoria.	Political recognition of nature conservation and public participation. Review of all public land in Victoria.
1967–72 Tasmania	Objections to flooding of Lake Pedder in Tasmania.	Political rejection.
1973–75	Rising concern over environment.	Federal environmental and heritage protection legislation.
1973–	Objections to clearing native forests for pine plantations.	Numerous inquiries. Federal funding for State plantations ceases. States cease clearing and buy already-cleared land.
1973– 4 States	Objections to clear-felling native forests for woodchip exports. Blockades.	Numerous inquiries but industry expanded. Forest Practices Codes introduced.
1979–82 New South Wales	Objections to rainforest logging. Blockades.	Logging stopped. Area nominated as World Heritage.
1979–83 Tasmania	Objections to dam development on Franklin River in wilderness.	Area nominated as World Heritage. Constitutional challenge in High Court. Dam stopped.
1983–87 Queensland	Objections to logging and roads in wet tropical rainforests. Blockade of Daintree road.	Area nominated as World Heritage. Constitutional challenge in High Court. Logging and road stopped.
1987–89 Tasmania	Objections to pollution from proposed pulp mill. Federal–State and Federal Cabinet conflicts.	Pulp mill stopped. Push for better process.
1990–91 New South Wales	Objections to logging in high conservation value forests. Blockades at Chaelundi.	Public inquiries. Some state forest service operations controlled by wildlife service in order to preserve habitat for endangered animals.
1992 National		Federal and State Governments sign *National Forest Policy Statement.*
1994–95 National	Environmentalists object to woodchip exports. Loggers blockade Federal Parliament House. Federal Cabinet conflicts.	Prime Minister's Department takes charge of Federal position on forestry and oversees Regional Forest Agreement process.
1997–99		Regional Forest Agreements negotiated.

Source: Dargavel (1995); Robin (1998).

Table 6.2 *Public concerns about woodchip export industry*

Type	Concern
Environmental	
Soil	Declining fertility due to removal of nutrients and erosion
Water	Siltation of water courses, possible eutrophication due to increase in nutrients, depletion of value as water catchment and increased risk of flooding, increased turbidity and salinity
Flora	Depletion of species by replacement of non-commercial species, elimination of special habitats, introduction of exotic species
Fauna	Depletion of species including smaller less conspicuous ones
Disease	Increased risk of fungal pathogens
Pests	Increased risk of pests in uniform stands, consequent risks if insecticides or 1080 poison used
Fire	Increased risk of fire in young stands unable to regenerate naturally
	Escapes of fire and air pollution from burning cut over areas
Scenery	Loss of value of undeveloped environment
Wilderness	
Education	Loss of undisturbed environment for outdoor education in independence and survival skills
Science	Loss of study areas and gene pool
Resource	
Sawlogs	Over-exploitation threatens long-term future of sawmilling industry
Waste	Waste wood left in harvesting
Regeneration	Not all cut over areas regenerated
Social	
Recreation	Loss of value due to loss of scenery and tourism
Restructuring	Shift from small sawmills in rural towns to large mills in main towns
Economic	
Assessment	Lack of economic assessment before schemes commenced
Infrastructure	Road tolls insufficient to cover costs
Wood prices	Amounts paid for wood do not cover costs of regenerating stands which leads to deforestation on private land
Other industries	Reduction of honey and wildflower production, reduction of potential for pharmaceutical industry
Political	
Decision	Forests should be managed in the public interest and choice of how to do so should not be left to the forest services and industries

Source: Dargavel (1995).

Policy Revolution of the 1990s

Internationally, the Brundtland Report (World Commission on Environment and Development, 1987) launched the call for a policy of sustainable development. Australia ran a consultative process which led to a *National Strategy for Ecologically Sustainable Development* in 1992 (Commonwealth of Australia, 1992b; Dovers, 1995, 1997). In the fashionable *policy-speak* of the time, it proclaimed noble objectives such as improving welfare, providing inter- and intragenerational equity, and maintaining the nation's biodiversity and ecology. It went on to equally noble *guiding principles*: equity was to be considered in both the short- and long-term and was to cover economic, social and environmental dimensions; scientific uncertainty was not to be an excuse for failing to take care of the environment; global consequences were to be considered; there should be *broad community involvement* in making decisions; and pricing incentives should be improved. With a nod to realism, the policy was to be implemented in a *cost-effective and flexible manner*. The forests section took two lines. First, it recognized the need to conserve their biodiversity in what it called a *national framework* intended to cover both PAs and other forests on both public and private land. In practice, this was to mean establishing a system of PAs on public land. Second, it called for the forests to be managed in an ecologically sustainable manner. In practice, this was to mean strengthening Codes of Practice primarily for logging state forests.

The Brundtland Report set the stage for the 1992 UNCED conference in Rio de Janeiro. The *Global Statement of Principles on Forests* that emerged called for sustainable forest management. Australia supported this, the general *Agenda 21* document and ratified the *Convention on Biological Diversity* in 1993. Australia later joined the *Montreal Process* working group of twelve countries to develop criteria and indicators for assessing progress towards achieving sustainable forest management. Timber certification schemes were also being developed internationally which gave an economic impetus to consider the issues seriously.

To try and govern the environmental conflicts, Australia set up a specialized Resource Assessment Commission in 1989 whose first inquiry was into the forests and timber industry. It reported in 1992 that a fully representative system of reserves should be created and that the complex issues should be addressed region by region (Resource Assessment Commission, 1992). However, the relations between governments in the federal system were the critical political issue and this was addressed by an Inter-Governmental Agreement on the Environment that came into effect in 1992. The Federal Government agreed to limit its activities to representing the national interest, meeting Australia's international obligations, assisting to resolve transboundary issues, looking after its own environmental responsibilities and promoting a cooperative approach with the States. With the Inter-Governmental Agreement in hand, the Federal and State Governments were at last in a position to declare a national forest policy.

National Forest Policy

If a policy was to be successful in overcoming the conflicts, it had to address both the substantive issues of the environment–development conflicts and the thorny issues of governance; it had to address both content and process. The policy document proclaims broad principles for maintaining the forest estate, managing it in an ecologically sustainable manner and developing competitive forest industries (Commonwealth of Australia, 1992a). It sets out national goals as well as specific policies, objectives and strategies covering issues ranging from conservation and industrial development to tourism and research. It recognizes the extent of the changes which occurred since settlement: over one-third of the area covered by forest and woodland has been cleared, more in some types; 20 mammal, 9 bird, and 83 plant species have become extinct; and 57 species of vertebrate animals and 178 species of higher plants are threatened.

The content of the policy addresses the substantive issues on the one hand by endorsing conservation and on the other by promoting industry. Conservation is to be secured by establishing systems of dedicated, comprehensive, adequate and representative PAs, which means they cannot be logged, and by promoting ecologically sustainable management of the forests outside these PAs. Although encouraging statements are made about the virtue of further processing wood resources, industrial development is taken to occur much as given, provided the process of forest governance is right, which means that logging outside the PAs would not be disrupted by fresh environmental claims. The content addresses a range of other issues, mostly under the theme of conservation which embraces the full suite of values which forests can provide for current and future generations. Generally, people get short shrift. Displaced timber workers are to be trained or compensated from funds for industry restructuring. Indigenous cultural values, but not their land rights, are to be recognized.

The process has four elements. First, the policies are to be pursued on a regional rather than on a State-wide or national basis. Second, the Federal and State Governments and their bureaucracies are to work together in an *integrated and coordinated* manner, which is a tall order, given their fractious history. Third, binding agreements covering land use and forest management are to be negotiated, which means that the Federal Government would undertake not to impose fresh environmental requirements against the wishes of the States. Last, the public is to be educated in ecologically sustainable forest management and is to be provided with unspecified opportunities for effective participation in decision-making.

With the policy signed by every government (Tasmania eventually did) and various threats and cajolery, it was to be put into effect. First, some of the concepts had to be refined so that they could be applied in practice. The most difficult task was to define what would constitute a *comprehensive, adequate and representative* system of PAs. A council of eminent scientists decided that 15 per cent of the area of each forest community as it existed at the time of the European invasion should be reserved, although this definition was qualified by the bureaucracy seeking to implement it in a cost-effective and flexible manner (Kirkpatrick, 1998). Comprehensive assessments of each region were then undertaken, from which options for dividing up the public forests between PAs and state forest which could be logged were generated and agreements negotiated between the Federal and State Governments. Throughout the process, rational intent, bureaucratic manipulation and political negotiation were intertwined.

Rational Intent

The intent to provide a rational basis for the eventual decisions and agreements required the collection of a factual base (or assessment) for each component, a way of combining them and models to display the effects of various options.

Assessment

The assessment of each forest region had to cover ecological or biodiversity values, cultural heritage, indigenous heritage, social values, wood resources and other extractive uses. They were based on existing information as far as possible but had to be supplemented by new surveys where time and funds allowed. The willingness of the States to contribute their information varied considerably, Western Australia being notably retentive. The assessments were primarily spatial because the environmental conflicts were over the relative boundaries between PAs and state forests, and because place is inherent in the Australian definition of heritage. Geographic information systems were established as the core of each regional assessment.

Ecological or Biodiversity Assessment

Most effort was directed to biodiversity assessment because the whole process was primarily driven by the conflicts over logging and the new policy of creating the system of reserves. Few systematic assessments of ecological values on a regional scale existed. The foresters' timber stand-type maps had to be augmented with other surveys to gain a deeper understanding of the vegetation. Existing fauna surveys were reviewed, new ones carried out, and museum records searched. Particular attention was paid to the occurrence of rare and endangered species. Old-growth forests were delineated using the absence of past disturbance by logging, mining and similar activities. In the process, numerous historic sites were observed, described in reports and their position recorded. Wilderness was similarly assessed against criteria of remoteness from settlement or access, and apparent or biophysical naturalness.

The geographic information systems stored, assembled and displayed the voluminous layers of data, together with topography, climate, geology and soil data from which models estimated the area of each vegetation type at the time of the invasion and hence the area to be reserved under the 15 per cent criterion.

Cultural Heritage Assessment

Cultural heritage values were assessed using systematic surveys and community workshops in which people recorded places of importance to them. The old-growth and wilderness assessments provided further information. The types of historic places assessed included bridges, buildings, bullock wagons, cemeteries, charcoal pits, defence/war relics, ethnic settlement and workers' camps, explorers' routes, fences, fire towers, mines, railways and tramways, roads, sawmills and trigonometric stations, for example (Kowald and Williams, 1997). Novel methods were devised to assess aesthetic values in ways which could be related to particular sites (Lennon, 1999; Ramsay, 1999).

Indigenous Heritage Assessment

A systematic assessment of the history of Indigenous occupation of, and contemporary associations with and attachment to, forested lands was attempted for the first time in Australia, but it was difficult because Indigenous people rarely trusted governments, traditional knowledge of sacred places is held in confidence, and the accelerated timetables prevented adequate time for the consultations needed.

Social Assessment

Although less effort was directed to social assessment than to biodiversity assessment, a central social assessment unit was established and coordinators appointed to conduct the assessments and facilitate public participation in each region (Coakes, 1998). The literature on previous land-use decisions and their social consequences was reviewed. Demographic and socio-economic characteristics were tabulated from census and other statistical sources. Interviews and focus groups were arranged with key stakeholders and interest groups to identify issues of concern. Some surveys were conducted to ascertain community attitudes to forest management and aspirations for the region. Detailed surveys were conducted to document the location and type of industry, employment and some economic and educational factors. Selected case studies were conducted for communities which were particularly vulnerable to change as a result of the agreement process.

Wood Resources and Other Extractive Uses

The existing wood resource information and the models used by the States' forest services to project future volumes were largely taken at their face value. Indeed, given all the effort directed to the biodiversity values, there was little energy left to do much else.

From Intent to Decision

The assessments were demanding, but integrating them and developing options for allocating the forests between those which could be logged and those which were to be protected were formidable tasks. Technically, the various assessments had to be put on a compatible basis (the geographic information systems greatly helped in this) and models had to be developed to show the effects of possible changes to the boundaries. Socially and politically, processes had to be found for public participation, stakeholder involvement and eventual negotiation between governments.

Although cultural, Indigenous heritage, economic and social assessments provided essential information and were seen by Althaus (1999) to influence outcomes, the integration process was dominated by the targets set for having parts of each forest ecosystem allocated to PAs. The process applied solely to public forest, except in Tasmania. An illustration based on the case of the Eden region of New South Wales follows; the corresponding exercise in other regions followed different models, some of which addressed some of the limitations evident for Eden.

Integration in the Case of the Eden Forest Agreement Region

The integration of the various assessments for the Eden New South Wales Regional Forest Agreement followed a structured negotiation process with strict guidelines and was assisted by three existing computer-based scenario prediction models covering the design of the PAs, timber volumes and economic variables. The process was divided into two parts: reference points development and options development. Each part was conducted in meetings of representatives from the two governments and some of the stakeholders (Table 6.3).

Reference Points Development The first task was to find the range of what was possible for the region. For this purpose a set of what were called reference points, the outer bounds of the feasible region in modelling terms, were developed. Only when these were known would it be sensible to select the set of options to be discussed for the region. A series of meetings of the principals and stakeholders were held to define these reference points.

C Plan model
A PA selection model based on the geographic information system was used extensively for developing reference points. The model maps areas of differing irreplaceability and finds the smallest possible set of areas that will achieve a nominated conservation goal. The model also maps areas of old-growth forest, wilderness, potential mineral deposits, high cultural and heritage values, timber production areas, private and leasehold land as well as areas targeted for Aboriginal land rights claims.

Each area of high irreplaceability, wilderness, old-growth or with threatened species was investigated and documented for possible inclusion in the reserves. Reserve design was taken into account. Despite the technical and structured nature of the C Plan process, it included a degree of ad hoc selection and was influenced by the local knowledge of conservation groups and officers of the National Parks Service.

Table 6.3 *Principals and stakeholders in Eden region meetings*

Principals and stakeholders	Represented by	Role and power
Federal Government	Department of Primary Industries and Energy, Forests Task Force, Environment Australia, Department of Aboriginal Affairs, Department of Mineral Resources	Principal to agreement
New South Wales Government	National Parks and Wildlife Service, State Forests, Department of Land and Water Conservation	Principal to agreement
Conservation groups	NSW Conservation Council, Conservation Council of Canberra and South East Region	Major interest group
Forest industry associations	NSW Forests Products Association, National Association of Forest Industries	Major interest group
Unions	Construction, Forestry, Mining and Electricity Union	Major interest group which generally supported industry association positions
Indigenous people	New South Wales Aboriginal Land Council	Important interests marginalized in process
Farmers	New South Wales Farmers Association	Minor interest group
Excluded	Local Forest Forum	Regional issues developed by the Forum were displayed on a notice board at the side of the meeting room
Excluded	Some smaller interest groups, for example apiarists and the tourism industry	Not represented

FRAMES timber model

After several selections had been made, the extent to which conservation targets had been met were reviewed and the FRAMES timber volume model, developed by the forest service, State Forests of New South Wales, was run. It estimates the amount of commercial timber that could be harvested from the area of public forest remaining outside the reserves. It does not estimate the volumes on private or leasehold land.

FORUM (Forest Resource Use Model)

The results of the FRAMES runs for each reference point were fed into an economic model to determine the likely consequences on the value of timber production in the area as a result of the change in reserve selection. FORUM is a constrained linear optimization model. Given data on availability of timber supplies by type (provided by the FRAMES model) as well as cost and other data from individual sawmills, it provides an analysis of the commercial value of the forest harvest, net returns to the regional industry and employment implications. Once the results of the FORUM model were known, a wide range of feasible reference points was selected.

Options Development The next stage of the integration process was to prepare a set of options that could be documented and disseminated to the public for consultation. The process was similar to developing the reference points and relied heavily on manipulating the C Plan model. However, the negotiations attracted much closer scrutiny and more heated debates which often strayed from the objective, structured format of reference points development. The Indigenous representatives threatened to withdraw unless some formal mechanism was put into place to take account of their preferences. Until this stage, neither Government had attempted to explicitly address the convoluted issue of incorporating their preferences while their land rights claims were before the courts.

Unfortunately, the negotiation techniques adopted during the integration phase in October and November 1997 did not result in an agreed option or set of options as intended, but led the way to the development of four different scenarios, each representing the preferred position of a stakeholder or alliance of stakeholders. It was not until May 1998 that an options report outlining the four scenarios (but with no government-preferred scenario) was released for public comment, but even with these, the Governments could not agree. In October 1998, with an election looming, the New South Wales Government legislated its own Eden Forest Agreement, essentially one between the relevant State ministers. It was not until August 1999, almost two years after the integration meetings, that the Eden Regional Forest Agreement between the State and Federal Governments was signed.

State Differences

Whilst structured similarly, these integration processes varied substantially between States, and in some cases between regions within States. They reflected differences in the procedures agreed between the Federal and various State Governments and the degree of participation by non-government stakeholders. These differences led to markedly different outcomes.

Tasmania, Victoria and Western Australia excluded non-government stakeholders from direct involvement in negotiations, although they were consulted before and after the options development stage. The Tasmanian and Victorian processes were helped because they followed earlier consultative processes, and (in Tasmania and some Victorian regions) the viability of wood-based industries was not threatened by the additions to the reserve system needed to meet the conservation criteria. The Tasmanian Agreement is unique because it addresses conservation on private as well as public forests, complementing that State's regulation of logging on both tenures. Although an agreement was signed between the Federal and Western Australian Governments, it did not stand. The public thought it inadequate for protecting old-growth and biodiversity values in the taller forests and the State Government, with an eye to its electoral standing, subsequently extended the PA system and phased out some of the logging more rapidly, with immediate adverse consequences for timber industry employment.

The management and negotiation processes in New South Wales and Queensland included, at least initially, key stakeholders, representing the timber industry and environmentalists in Queensland and a broader group of interests in New South Wales. In both states, the State Governments ultimately proposed their own Forest Agreements for some regions ahead of endorsement by the Federal Government. The Queensland agreement was negotiated largely outside the formal Regional Forest Agreement process, and principally between environmental and timber industry stakeholders.

Influence and power

Although the integration phase involved stakeholders and the public to various degrees in a more or less open manner, the final agreements were negotiated directly between the governments concerned. The peak industry, conservation and union groups could exert their influence in private in ways that doubtless found some expression in the negotiations.

More obviously, the governments were subject to electoral and policy change. During the course of the process, the Federal Government changed from labour to conservative and took a more pro-development stance, and was less sympathetic to conservation and Indigenous concerns. Some of the State Governments were of the opposite political persuasion to the Federal Government, which created further difficulties.

Lessons and Questions

The Australian Regional Forest Agreement programme is not only the largest resource and environmental project ever undertaken in the country, it is also a serious attempt to address contemporary issues that apply in many other countries. The programme is not yet complete and it will be some years before it can be fully evaluated. In the meantime, we can draw six preliminary lessons with questions for the future.

Role of Economic Analysis

The first chapters of this book have discussed the place of environmental and ecological economics in managing natural resources. Although these fields are well-established in Australian research they found little direct place in the programme. This is surprising given that the programme was substantially funded and that the Resource Assessment Commission, mentioned earlier, had adopted several of the techniques in its inquiries, including that into forests. The economic analysis in the FORUM model only estimated the industrial consequences of resource changes. A broader conceptual framework that incorporates non-commodity values would seem to offer greater insights in future.

Biodiversity Conservation

Australia's biodiversity values were asserted strongly and taken seriously in the assessment and implementation of the programme. The comprehensive system of representative PAs was created, although the various trade-offs between the requirements of conservation and those of industry, which took place in the integration and agreement phases, weakened their adequacy in places.

Measures to develop sustainable forest management practices outside these reserves and on private land are evolving and cannot yet be evaluated.

Participation

Although the National Forest Policy called for public participation in forest management decisions, the degree to which it has been adopted by the various forest services ranges from merely providing information to consultation (Buchy et al, 1999). The nature and extent of participation in the Regional Agreement process also varied greatly at the different levels and between States. At the highest level, the final agreements were negotiated in private between Governments with an unknown amount of lobbying by peak groups. At the regional level, key conservation and industry stakeholders were involved in the integration phase in most regions. Public information sessions were also conducted. The assessment phase included community workshops to collect information on cultural heritage and, in places, on Indigenous values. In those states where Agreements for a number of regions were negotiated sequentially, processes for participation did improve successively on the basis of earlier experiences.

These participatory processes faced a number of difficulties due to the ability of some stakeholders to advance their interests more effectively through the political process, to the inherent loss of autonomy by government agencies and to the short times that were allowed, a matter that was particularly limiting to Indigenous participation. The reversal of the agreement in Western Australia was due in part to the way it was pushed through the consultative process, but also due to unresolved scientific doubts on the validity of the biodiversity assessments. Community support for politically agreed outcomes is clearly needed if they are to endure.

Political Cycle

The place on the political cycles of the negotiating governments was clearly a key issue in the way in which the processes were conducted in particular regions. The problems that arose are similar to those discussed under participation and could be overcome with a more open process conducted at arm's length from the political process. This is not impossible as the agreements, which last for 20 years, are to be revised at 5-yearly intervals. One might expect that once the initial agreements have been concluded, their revision would be less fraught.

Agreement or Conflict?

The process has led to agreements being signed between the two levels of government and can be said to have resulted in a resolution of conflicts between them. Its extensive assessments, modelling and the generation of options has also led to some apparent acceptance of at least the existence of a set of feasible options from which decisions are made. From a governmental perspective, the process has asserted a *language* of geographic information systems, modelling and options development which has made the forest conflicts governable, at least for the present. Whether they remain governable is subject to the continual dynamics of politics.

A Structured Process

Although various facets of the programme can be justifiably criticized, its most substantial achievement is to have established a structured process for dealing with a set of complex issues. Social and cultural values in the forests have been recognized to a greater degree than ever before and the preservation of the biodiversity in Australia's forests has been taken seriously. It is a platform on which Australia can build.

Acknowledgements
This paper draws on an earlier and longer unpublished paper, 'Australia: Settlement, Conflicts and Agreements', which was written with Irene Guijt and Digby Race for the International Institute for Environment and Development's project *Policy that Works for Forests and People*. We gratefully acknowledge the support of the Institute and the collaboration of our colleagues.

7

Marine Conservation through Collaboration and Partnership: Recent Australian Experiences

Nancy Dahl-Tacconi and Peter Taylor

Introduction

Australia has responsibilities for one of the world's largest marine jurisdictions. Under the United Nations Convention on the Law of the Sea (UNCLOS), Australia has either sovereignty or sovereign rights over 11 million square kilometres of ocean and a further 5.1 million square kilometres of claimable continental shelf. Australia's oceans contain resources of enormous potential benefit to Australian and global communities. The Australian Commonwealth Government (hereafter, the Commonwealth) recognizes the importance of managing these resources carefully and is committed to the protection of marine biological diversity and ecological processes, and the sustainable use of marine resources, through the goals and principles of Ecologically Sustainable Development (Commonwealth of Australia, 1992b). This commitment has been ratified through a number of national and international agreements and strategies, such as the Convention on Biological Diversity, United Nations Convention on the Law of the Sea and Convention on the Conservation of Antarctic Marine Living Resources.

These international agreements are implemented at a national level by the States, Territories and Commonwealth governments under the Inter-governmental Agreement on the Environment (Commonwealth of Australia, 1992c) and the Commonwealth Organisation for Australian Governments' Heads of Agreement on Commonwealth and State Roles and Responsibilities for the Environment. They are also implemented through the development of national strategies such as the National Strategy for the Conservation of Australia's Biological Diversity (Commonwealth of Australia, 1996) and through the

Taskforce on Marine Protected Areas, which was established in 1994 by the Standing Committee on Conservation of the Australian and New Zealand Environment Conservation Council.

This chapter outlines some of the Commonwealth Government's policies and programmes associated with integrated management and protection of the Australian marine environment. It considers some of the benefits of cooperative arrangements (informal collaborations and formal partnerships) and the challenges associated with the development of Australia's National Representative System of Marine Protected Areas. The case study of the Great Australian Bight Marine Park and other examples of issues involving stakeholders are presented to illustrate the progress being made and the challenges for the future.

Policy Background

Australia's Oceans Policy

In December 1998, the Commonwealth launched Australia's Oceans Policy in recognition of Australians' shared responsibility for ensuring the long-term maintenance of our oceans.[1] The Oceans Policy outlines a broad range of commitments that will translate into a programme of action to protect and sustainably manage Australia's marine resources. A central element of the Oceans Policy is the development of Regional Marine Plans. These Regional Marine Plans, based on large marine ecosystems, are expected to integrate commercial interests, community needs and conservation requirements.

To help implement the Oceans Policy, the Commonwealth has established a series of institutional arrangements with a view to encouraging the cooperation and participation of Australia's State and Territory Governments. These arrangements emphasize ministerial responsibility, stakeholder participation, and well-coordinated government support. The key institutional arrangements include a National Oceans Ministerial Board, a National Oceans Advisory Committee, a number of Regional Marine Plan Steering Committees, and a National Oceans Office (that will provide support to the Board, the Advisory Group and the Regional Marine Plan Steering Committees).

Putting the Oceans Policy into action will require both formal partnerships and more informal collaboration among all spheres of government, the private sector, and the scientific and wider communities. Some of the specific initiatives of the Oceans Policy to be actively pursued through the regional planning processes are (Commonwealth of Australia, 1998):

- improved understanding of the marine environment, including environmental baseline surveys, sustainability indicators, monitoring and improved assessment of the impacts of commercial and recreational activities;
- accelerated development and improved management of marine protected areas (MPAs);

- support for the development by the National Environment Protection Council of national standards for marine and estuarine water quality;
- support for the development of a single national ballast water management system;
- the phased withdrawal of the use of toxic organotin anti-fouling paints;
- trials to treat acid sulphate soil problem areas;
- support for a network of fisheries extension officers to promote environmentally sound fishing practices; and
- support for a National Moorings Programme for sensitive marine areas.

National Representative System of Marine Protected Areas

Australia's National Representative System of Marine Protected Areas (NRSMPA) is a core component of the Oceans Policy.[2] The establishment of a representative system of MPAs is widely regarded, both nationally and internationally, as one of the most effective mechanisms for protecting marine biological diversity (Kelleher et al, 1995). Development of the NRSMPA fulfils some of Australia's international responsibilities and obligations as a signatory to the Convention on Biological Diversity (UNEP, 1994), the Convention on Migratory Species (Bonn Convention) and bilateral agreements with Japan and China for migratory birds (ANZECC TFMPA, 1999). It also contributes directly to the Global Representative System of Marine Protected Areas, an initiative of the World Conservation Union through its World Commission on Protected Areas (Kelleher et al, 1995).

The *Strategic Plan of Action for the National Representative System of Marine Protected Areas: A Guide for Action by Australian Governments* has been developed to assist both government agencies and other stakeholders in the development of the NRSMPA. The plan was endorsed by the Australia and New Zealand Environmental Conservation Council in June 1999 (ANZECC TFMPA, 1999).

This strategic plan provides a basis for understanding the NRSMPA by describing its foundation in scientific studies, its status and its goals in the context of international and national conservation initiatives. It sets out a framework for the establishment of the NRSMPA by identifying and prioritizing key phases and specific activities necessary to achieve the goals of the NRSMPA. The specific actions identified in the plan fall into the major areas of:

- establishing a comprehensive, adequate and representative system;
- information requirements and management;
- involvement of stakeholders;
- classification of MPAs;
- managing the NRSMPA; and
- performance assessment.

A broad range of stakeholders will be involved with progressing specific actions in each of the above areas. Teams have been established to ensure that the interests of all stakeholders are represented for each of the plan's actions. Some of the critical actions identified in relation to fundamental stakeholder communications and initial involvement are:

- *harness community knowledge* through documentation of knowledge from traditional and local communities;
- *analysis of information programmes* by assessing present educational programmes focused on marine conservation and promotional activities aimed at best practice models for activities in marine environments;
- enhance *stakeholder understanding* of government policies and priorities by increasing dialogue regarding social, economic and cultural values of marine environments throughout the processes of developing and managing MPAs; and
- increase *information availability* by promoting awareness and use of national electronic directories such as the Australian Coastal Atlas and Blue Pages.

The capacity of the Commonwealth to accelerate the declaration of Commonwealth MPAs has been advanced significantly through the establishment of the NRSMPA as a strategic policy framework and through a firm commitment to management of appropriate multiple uses in MPAs.

Commonwealth Marine Protected Area Development Programme

The Commonwealth MPA Development Programme is a significant component of the NRSMPA that focuses on Australian waters from three nautical miles to the outer limits of the Exclusive Economic Zone. These MPAs are being developed with the primary goal of establishing and managing a comprehensive, adequate and representative system of MPAs in Commonwealth waters in order to contribute to the long-term ecological viability of marine ecosystems, to maintain ecological processes and systems, and to protect Australia's biological diversity at all levels (ANZECC TFMPA, 1999).

The Commonwealth's processes for the establishment and management of MPAs commence with a proposal for an MPA that has been developed with the advice and consideration of relevant stakeholders. The proposal outlines the objectives, boundaries and the conservation values being protected. It also canvasses potential socio-economic issues. Once this has been prepared it is released publicly as a Notice of Intent to declare an MPA and public comment is invited on the proposal. Following a public submission period the Commonwealth can recommend the declaration of the MPA to the Governor General. Once proclaimed by the Governor General, a plan of management is prepared which provides details of zoning arrangements, specific management prescriptions and monitoring regimes for the MPA. The plan must be tabled in both Houses of Commonwealth Parliament before it can be enacted. Management of the MPA is then legally directed by the agreed plan of management and implemented through cooperative arrangements between Environment Australia and other stakeholders.

The Commonwealth is pursuing its MPA Development Programme through the adoption of multiple use principles where these are deemed appropriate. This programme is underpinned by four fundamental principles embracing:

1   maintenance of ecosystem integrity;
2   wealth generation and resource use;
3   equity, and
4   a participatory framework for decision-making (Sainsbury et al, 1997).

This latter principle refers to a consultative and participatory process that involves all stakeholders so that decision-making processes are not dominated by particular interest groups. Such a process is meant to ensure that all stakeholders have equal access to information and opportunities so they can participate meaningfully in the design, management and assessment of MPAs. This approach aims to ensure protection of biological diversity while allowing for the management of a range of appropriate uses on a precautionary basis, so that activities are consistent with conservation objectives.

In the development and management of MPAs around Australia, the Commonwealth uses the precautionary principle, as outlined in the Intergovernmental Agreement on the Environment (Commonwealth of Australia, 1992c):

> '*Where there are threats of serious or irreversible environmental damage, lack of full scientific certainty should not be used as a reason for postponing measures to prevent environmental degradation.*
>
> *In the application of the precautionary principle, public and private decisions should be guided by:*
>
> 1   *careful evaluation to avoid, wherever practicable, serious or irreversible damage to the environment; and*
> 2   *an assessment of the risk-weighted consequences of various options.*'

The precautionary principle is particularly relevant in remote Commonwealth waters where there is a degree of risk to species from external influences, insufficient scientific data to fully assess the risk, and a chance of irreversible damage being caused before more detailed information is available. The principle is also particularly relevant in Commonwealth waters where many stakeholders are active or interested in the same area, which tends to increase the number of available options and intensify the consequences of management decisions.

There are currently eleven Commonwealth MPAs and a further six protected areas with marine components (Figure 7.1). These areas are located

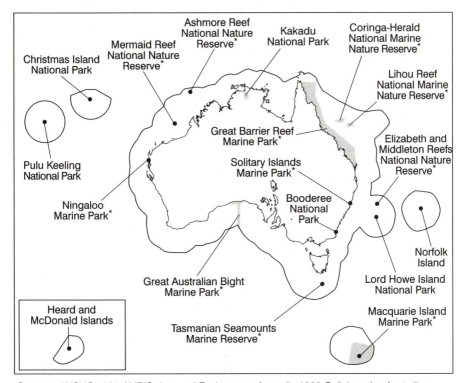

Sources: AUSLIG 1998 AMBIS data and Environment Australia 1999 Collaborative Australian Protected Areas Database. Copyright Environment Resources Information Network, Environment Australia, 1999.

Figure 7.1 *Existing Commonwealth marine protected areas (indicated by *) and Commonwealth protected areas with marine components*

around the continent from the eastern limits of the Coral Sea to the western reaches of the Indian Ocean, from Ashmore Reef in the north to Heard and McDonald Islands in the Southern Ocean. Historically, Commonwealth MPAs have been generally of two main types. *Marine Parks* are large, nationally significant areas declared primarily to balance protection of the marine environment with sustainable development (ie IUCN Management Category VI, based on IUCN, 1994). *Marine National Nature Reserves* are nationally significant areas declared primarily for nature conservation and scientific purposes (ie IUCN Management Category Ia based on IUCN, 1994). Future MPAs in Australia will continue to be developed and managed in accordance within the IUCN guidelines, but they will not be restricted to the two categories mentioned above.

In April 1998, the Great Australian Bight Marine Park was declared. At that time it was the second largest MPA in the world. Shortly after, the Environment Minister announced the Commonwealth's intention to accelerate the development of new Commonwealth MPAs by declaring five more. These areas were chosen because conservation assessments identified significant natural values and because the ecosystems were either non-represented or under-represented in the existing national system. The first of these declarations have been the Tasmanian Seamounts Marine Reserve declared in May 1999 and the Macquarie Island Marine Park declared in October 1999, which contains the world's largest marine no-take area. The three other areas being explored as prospective Commonwealth MPAs include the waters around Australia's sub-Antarctic territory of Heard and McDonald Islands, the waters around Lord Howe Island off the coast of New South Wales, and the region of Cartier Islet and Hibernia Reef in the Indian Ocean.

The case of the Great Australian Bight Marine Park (Commonwealth Waters) (GABMP) is discussed below. It is useful to start from this specific case because the experience gained through it has had a significant influence on the activities that have followed. A discussion of broader issues concerning the establishment and management of Commonwealth MPAs is presented later in the chapter.

Great Australian Bight Marine Park

The Commonwealth Waters of the Great Australian Bight extend from Cape Pasley in Western Australia to Cape Catastrophe, at the entrance of Spencer Gulf in South Australia and from 3 nautical miles offshore to the extent of the Australian Exclusive Economic Zone around 200 nautical miles offshore. This region is of great conservation significance. It provides important calving habitat for the endangered southern right whale and supports colonies (including pupping areas) of Australia's only endemic pinniped – the Australian sea lion. It supports some of the highest levels of marine biological diversity and endemism found anywhere in Australia.

In 1998, the Commonwealth declared the GABMP under the *National Parks and Wildlife Conservation Act 1975*. It is adjacent to the State Marine National Park, which was declared in 1996 and encompasses waters out to 3 nautical miles. The objectives of establishing the GABMP were to complement the State Park's protection of the southern right whale and Australian sea lion and also to protect a representative sample of the unique benthic flora and fauna and the unique sediments found in the region.

Initial Views of Stakeholders

The first engagements the Commonwealth had with stakeholders (late 1995) coincided with a move within Environment Australia (EA) to enhance its strategies for fulfilling marine conservation responsibilities while accommodating multiple uses and ecologically sustainable development. Like the State Government at this time, the Commonwealth had no structured mechanisms or policy framework for pursuing MPA development or multiple use management. A Commonwealth Government Steering Committee was established to oversee the development of the GABMP and it was critical in ensuring that all Commonwealth interests and responsibilities were considered, and that conflicts were resolved, in the development of the proposed park.

It was agreed at the Commonwealth level that the design and development of an MPA proposal should be achieved through negotiation and consultation with the affected stakeholders. With the support and guidance from other Commonwealth agencies, EA then made contact with all relevant stakeholders in the regions that would potentially be affected by the proposed park. EA consulted peak stakeholder groups (fisheries peak bodies, oil and gas peak body, tourism agencies, indigenous organizations, regional economic development bodies, scientists and conservationists). In addition to consultations with peak bodies, considerable time was spent consulting fishers in their towns, Aboriginal communities and various regional organizations.

Initially (1995–97), there was fierce resistance to the concept of an MPA in State and Commonwealth waters, particularly from the fishing industry. The wide perception among the fishing community and in parts of the South Australian State Government was that MPAs were necessarily no-take reserves that would exclude commercial activities and would not allow for any uses. The oil, gas and fishing industries willingly engaged in dialogue, primarily to defend their interests, but were deeply suspicious of the Commonwealth's new strategy regarding multiple use MPAs.

Reasonable oil and gas prospecting opportunities exist offshore in the Great Australian Bight region and the oil and gas industries actively engaged in consultations on the premise that the proposed park would accommodate multiple uses where appropriate. Despite their willingness to engage, consultations with all fisheries operating in the region were fraught with significant conflict. There was negative media coverage by the fishing industry and extremely defensive attitudes based on fears of a loss of livelihood and a lack of understanding of all the issues involved with establishing a new MPA. Because of these perceptions, they remained cynical throughout initial consultations and disagreed with the need for a park. They did express their appreciation, however, for the commitment by Commonwealth officials to come to their towns and regions to consult with them.

Throughout consultations, conservation groups in South Australia remained adamant that the GABMP should be a strict no-take reserve and that no resource extraction of any kind should be allowed. In the lead up to the declaration of the State MPA these conservation groups had been criticized strongly by industry for their strict anti-multiple use stand. While opposing multiple use generally they opted not to challenge, formally or strongly, the multiple use components of the Commonwealth's MPA strategy.

During these initial consultations, some funding was directed to two minor economic impact assessment studies. Neither of these covered all the issues and did not satisfy the concerns of any stakeholders, because they failed to utilize all the available data. The most effective process for determining potential economic impacts appeared to be EA working with a combination of other Commonwealth agencies, peak bodies and local stakeholders to access detailed information and identify where socio-economic impacts were most likely to occur.

Despite the initially opposing views, all stakeholders remained engaged in the consultation process because EA continually provided opportunities for their input into the design and management of the park. The process eventually resulted in the determination of boundaries, objectives, zoning and management intentions.

Changing Views of Stakeholders

By late 1997, after the public Notice of Intent to declare the GABMP had been released, a shift in stakeholder attitudes began to emerge. The Notice contained clearly defined objectives for the park, which stakeholders could recognize as complementary to their own interests. It was acknowledged that most commercial activities would not be contradictory to the proposed park's conservation objectives.

The oil and gas industry had already been engaged positively and issued a press statement supporting the need for the MPA. The fishing industry also made statements in the media about benefits to be gained from cooperating with EA in the management of multiple use MPAs. Despite being principally opposed to the multiple use components of the proposed GABMP, conservation groups did not actively campaign against the declaration; some saw the park as an adequate first step for an ongoing conservation effort in the Great Australian Bight. At this stage most stakeholders had increased trust and confidence in the overall consultation processes that led up to the public notice and felt that they each had some influence on the final proposal.

The GABMP was declared in April 1998. Little negative press followed. Many of the general management prescriptions, including the zoning of the park, had already been negotiated during initial consultations. The process of developing a plan of management, including details of the day-to-day operation of the park, then began. The planning process involved two planners from EA travelling around the relevant regions of South Australia consulting with all key stakeholders. During these consultations, the general framework of the plan of management was discussed and input was sought on issues that were worrying stakeholders, including ideas as to how they might contribute to monitoring and management of the park. The consultative mechanisms established and the relationships built between EA and other stakeholders helped to facilitate the fine tuning of the draft plan, particularly with regard to multiple use management.

The fishing industry in South Australia recognized the need to take a more pro-active approach to working with EA in monitoring and managing the GABMP. A consortium of peak fisheries bodies sought funds from within industry, EA and the South Australian Government to employ a fisheries liaison officer for the purposes of building capacity within the fishing industry to make positive contributions to the management of the GABMP. The proposal was developed with input from EA and the South Australian

Government. Both Commonwealth and State governments funded the proposal.

Throughout the planning process, conservation groups continued to oppose the multiple use approach adopted by EA for the GABMP. They have particularly opposed the prospects that oil and gas exploration and production might be permitted in the Benthic Protection Zone of the GABMP. The plan of management for the GABMP indicates that activities in this zone will be considered on a case by case basis and stringent conditions will be imposed, by which companies must demonstrate that their activities will not compromise or threaten the conservation values being protected in the GABMP.

Some of the lessons learnt from the GABMP inform the discussion below and are further considered in the final section.

Establishment and Management of Marine Protected Areas

The Commonwealth MPA development programme is new and a great deal has been learned since the programme commenced in 1997. The following is a summary of some of the experiences and challenges (categorized broadly under the processes of declaration, planning and management) which have contributed to this evolving programme.

Declaration of MPAs

The Commonwealth established new legislation in July 1999 entitled the *Environment Protection and Biodiversity Conservation Act*. This will replace several pieces of Commonwealth environmental legislation and will embrace a very wide range of Commonwealth environmental responsibilities, including MPAs, replacing the *National Parks and Wildlife Conservation Act 1975*. The latter Act was limited in its capacity to balance the sometime conflicting priorities of environmental conservation and commercial interests. The new Act gives greater power to the Commonwealth environment portfolio to intervene in any commercial activity that is deemed to be detrimental to marine biological diversity or is considered unsustainable.

As outlined above, the Environment Minister agreed in 1997 to an initial programme of five areas that were to be actively considered for establishment as MPAs. EA began by establishing a multidisciplinary negotiation team made up of individuals from different work and educational backgrounds such as environmental science, economic development, social and cultural policy.

This team has been responsible for implementing the Commonwealth's agenda in addition to seeking from the Minister a commitment to resources and a process for working with stakeholders to ensure that the MPA agenda is successfully achieved. It was also important to establish a whole-of-government (Commonwealth) approach to the MPA programme and its processes to ensure that all Commonwealth interests are considered and responsibilities satisfied. This was achieved through the establishment of an inter-departmental steering committee as mentioned above. The representatives on this committee are all expected to contribute directly to the design and development of MPA proposals, in addition to seeking support for the proposal from their respective Ministers. The committee also plays a critical role in identifying relevant stakeholders and advising on potential conflicts as they may arise from different sectoral interests so that balanced decisions are made in situations of conflict or competing interests.

The involvement of a variety of stakeholders, each with different objectives and interests, in the early stages of developing MPAs has often been conflict ridden. This has largely been due to traditional views that industrial activities and conservation efforts must be naturally at odds with each other. An important part of the consultation process in the early stages of declarations has been to sift out the complementary interests from amongst these initial conflicts. The existence of common goals, such as ecologically sustainable development and recognition of multiple varied interests has helped to facilitate the process of effectively engaging stakeholders from the beginning of the MPA development process.

One of the significant lessons learned in relation to working with stakeholders has been the importance of establishing working relationships with peak bodies that represent stakeholder groups. Experience has demonstrated that the support for MPA proposals from these bodies is important as they are often the best equipped to identify specific stakeholders that may be affected by the proposal. When working with peak bodies effort is made to identify where common goals can be agreed and where the areas of possible conflict may arise in the development of the proposed MPA. In some instances the peak bodies became strong allies with the Commonwealth in assisting to promote initially unpopular decisions, such as a closure of a fishery or a controversial zoning arrangement, to their members. Peak bodies are often much more powerful than the Commonwealth in convincing their members of the strategic benefits of cooperating with conservation efforts. They are also better equipped to actively build the capacity of their members to contribute effectively to decision-making processes. These organizations contribute to the development of innovative solutions to conflicts and complex problems.

The steps, timing and the mechanisms for stakeholder engagement in the design and development of proposed MPAs are different for each candidate MPA because the ecological, economic and social issues are different for each. The ability of EA to be adaptive to the unique regional circumstances and the nature of stakeholder needs has been an important development in the building of trust and confidence of stakeholders. In the development of recent MPAs, stakeholders have consistently demanded to have a clear understanding of the steps and objectives of the consultation and negotiation processes. They particularly have wanted to know what their role is and to have assurances that EA will genuinely incorporate their input to the MPA proposals. To build stakeholder confidence, EA has provided regular feedback and demonstrations of where stakeholders have directly influenced the design of MPA proposals. An example that frequently arises is the benefit of utilizing stakeholder expertise to assist in designing practical zoning arrangements and even boundaries for proposed MPAs.

The advice and input of stakeholders in the early stages of the design and development of Commonwealth MPAs, such as the GABMP, the Tasmanian Seamounts and the Macquarie Island Marine Park, has contributed significantly to the satisfaction of those stakeholders and their support of new MPAs. Some of these early experiences helped lead to a major agreement between EA and the Australian Petroleum, Production and Exploration Association, Australia's peak oil and gas industry body. In 1996, this peak body and the Australian Nature Conservation Agency (which was responsible for MPAs at that time) formalized a commitment to greater cooperation with the aim of facilitating sustainable development and increasing understanding of each other's objectives. Before this, neither organization had contemplated such an innovative alliance.

The outcomes of this commitment, and the re-signing of the agreement with the whole of EA in 1998, have opened new opportunities to explore innovative strategies extending beyond the more traditional and adversarial approaches to environmental management and protection. The most important outcomes arising from the 1998 agreement relate to the building of mutual trust, cooperation and willingness to share and exchange information, and include:

- an agreement to collaborate with the oil and gas industry in establishing an off-reserve marine conservation strategy in a region of Western Australia where intense oil and activities occur amidst significant conservation values;
- the secondment of an EA officer to work with the peak body for short periods (three to six months) on mutually beneficial policy related projects;
- an article prepared by EA on the benefits of collaboration with industry presented at the 1998 Australian Petroleum, Production and Exploration Association conference and published in the peak body's journal; and
- the productive engagement by the oil and gas industry in negotiating multiple use prescriptions in management plans for new MPAs.

The Australian fishing industry is fragmented and has no single peak body that fully represents the interests of all fishers. Despite this, discussions have been progressing between EA and the Australian Seafood Industry Council, a national body with strong affiliations to a range of influential peak fishing bodies around Australia. These discussions have been focused on progress toward agreements on policies and processes for fishers to engage in the declaration, planning and management of MPAs.

Planning for MPAs

The planning process informally begins early in the design phase of each MPA. The Notice of Intent to declare an MPA, on which stakeholders have had input, outlines the boundaries, the intended zoning arrangements and where proposed restrictions might occur, for example types of fishing and or mining in particular zones.

The formal planning process then commences following the declaration. The broad management framework outlined in the proposal for the MPA is used as the basis for this process. The time taken to complete a plan should be as short as possible and should honour the intentions described in the proposal, in order to avoid uncertainties for stakeholders or any loss of their confidence in the processes. Where significant conflicts arise, they should be addressed as soon as possible in order to avoid delays in the process. EA's experience has also demonstrated the importance of continuity across the development and planning processes. If staff members or approaches are different across these phases (ie processes handled by different groups or organizations), there is a likelihood that stakeholders will lose trust and confidence. EA's experience indicates that building and maintaining stakeholder trust and confidence is an issue that needs constant nurturing.

EA has used the planning process to pursue the development of detailed prescriptions for the management of each MPA. To this end, the stakeholders involved in the development of the MPA are engaged in determining how particular commercial activities may operate in the MPA without compromising or threatening the conservation objectives of the MPA.

Because most of the Commonwealth MPAs are in remote locations, alternative approaches to management must be pursued. In many of these instances the fishing industry and the oil and gas industry will be the only human presence in or near these MPAs. In addition, the amount of data and information available to further understand or monitor these MPAs is often limited and expensive. Gathering and consolidating information from various sources can be onerous and complicated. There are often opportunities to coordinate with industry, scientists or other interested stakeholders to acquire current information and involve them in the planning and management of MPAs. Accessing information and data from stakeholders who already collect marine related information has added to EA's capacity to make informed planning and management decisions.

Similarly, the task of planning for the monitoring of large MPAs in remote locations requires a great deal of coordination. The initial cooperation and agreement of all stakeholders in the design and purposes of a PA is a first step to reducing the resistance, costs and difficulties of monitoring for compliance. Cooperative arrangements with users can also significantly reduce the cost of monitoring for scientific information and increase the amount of data made available for the purpose of assessing the performance of the park according to predetermined objectives. In return for this cooperation, users may receive financial support, opportunities for further influence in the management of

MPAs, direct indications of whether an MPA is having an impact, and they may also enjoy a cooperative image that could lead to other similar opportunities for their business in the future.

Some of EA's planning experiences have reinforced the importance and benefits of incorporating expertise and ideas from stakeholders into the planning process. A good example of this was the consultation process for the GABMP, in which the oil and gas industry and the fishing industry each made significant technical contributions and provided innovative solutions to problems of conflict.

Management of MPAs

The Plan of Management, once allowed by both Houses of Commonwealth Parliament, sets the prescriptions of what can and cannot happen within the MPA for a period of 5–7 years. The prescriptions are enforceable via the relevant legislation.

EA, at the time of writing (1999) has just commenced the process of managing its new multiple use MPAs. The work that has been carried out to date has provided a basis to negotiate assistance from the industry in the monitoring and management of remote MPAs. The benefits of such arrangements for industry include improved public image, direct input into the management of MPAs and greater influence in decision-making processes that may affect both fisheries management and oil and gas activities. Other commitments have been made to EA by other organizations concerning management, research and surveillance. These include assistance from the Royal Australian Navy to transport EA research teams to and from remote MPAs for ongoing research activities, and utilizing Coastwatch patrols for surveillance and monitoring of a number of remote MPAs.

There has been increasing pressure from stakeholders, particularly the fishing industry, during recent declarations and planning processes to develop a programme of performance assessment for each MPA that will allow managers to demonstrate, over time, whether MPAs are achieving their objectives. The first step in implementing a performance assessment programme has been to establish or reinforce clear and specific objectives for each individual MPA or system of MPAs. With clear strategic objectives in place, a selection of meaningful performance indicators (or measures for sampling programmes) can be chosen. These indicators should be selected based on predetermined criteria, such as relevance to objectives, cost-effectiveness, ease of interpretation etc. It is the Commonwealth's intention that the results from ongoing monitoring of these indicators will allow the MPA or system of MPAs to be assessed in a meaningful way, so that the success of the MPA can be demonstrated and future management decisions can be guided and justified. A major challenge in this process is the translation of objectives into indicators that it will be possible to monitor and analyse in a clear and understandable way. During the process of selecting appropriate indicators, stakeholders with expertise and local knowledge will play a crucial role in helping to identify potential indicators and possibilities for cooperative arrangements to collect data.

To ensure the ongoing integrity of its MPAs, the Commonwealth will need to continually evaluate the progress of performance and be prepared to modify management strategies to ensure that the primary goals of the MPAs can be achieved while accommodating the objectives of other stakeholders where possible. In this respect, three key challenges face the further development and management of MPAs in Australia.

First, community and industry knowledge should be harnessed. The Strategic Plan of Action for the NRSMPA recognizes the importance of this, as indicated above. Mechanisms are needed to encourage stakeholder contributions and document relevant knowledge and expertise of industry and local communities, including indigenous communities. These resources can provide a significant contribution to informed decision-making and conservation efforts.

Second, there is an urgent need to develop models for the industry's cooperative involvement in and contribution to the monitoring and management of MPAs in remote areas of Commonwealth waters. In many instances industry groups are likely to be the only stakeholders in the vicinity of some of the Commonwealth MPAs.

Third, an enhanced understanding and ability to apply and monitor performance indicators is critical not only for determining whether MPAs are achieving management goals and objectives, but also to inform further management decisions regarding the ongoing operation of MPAs. EA is currently developing mechanisms by which the results of monitoring programmes can be fed back into ongoing management and decision-making processes for MPAs.

Conclusion

The last three years have seen an acceleration in Australia's commitment to managing its oceans. The establishment of Australia's Oceans Policy and a commitment to implementing large-scale regional plans have provided the Commonwealth Government with a powerful mandate to work with the users of our oceans. There are a range of initiatives and resources linked to the Oceans Policy that provide the government with mechanisms designed to achieve integrated and sustainable management of our oceans.

An important initiative arising from the Oceans Policy is the establishment of the National Representative System of Marine Protected Areas, a key focus of this chapter. Progress to date has been substantial, with all Australian Governments agreeing to a Strategic Plan of Action for establishing the NRSMPA. This plan provides the policy framework and mandate for each government jurisdiction to declare MPAs. The Commonwealth Government has made a strong commitment to pursuing its obligations under this plan and has declared three large MPAs since 1998. Substantial stakeholder participation has been involved in their development, planning and management.

In illustrating EA's experiences with stakeholders, the chapter discusses the development of the GABMP. A range of important lessons and challenges from this experience provided the government with the confidence to formally commit to a substantial programme of new MPAs within a multiple use framework.

Some of the key lessons learned during the GABMP development process include:

- the importance and benefits of openly acknowledging conflicting interests, recognizing common goals toward conservation and sustainable development and reaching acceptable compromises through exploring innovative options;
- recognition of the need to resource adequately processes for stakeholder participation in order to ensure that stakeholders remain engaged;
- recognition of stakeholders' specialized expertise and acknowledgement of their desire to contribute to conservation efforts; and
- the importance of a multidisciplinary team of EA negotiators with knowledge of environmental, social and economic issues, which allow for systematic, thorough and balanced stakeholder engagement during consultations.

While substantial progress has been made in establishing Commonwealth MPAs, much more work needs to be undertaken particularly in the areas of management and performance assessment of declared MPAs. The challenges that lie ahead for EA regarding management and performance assessment are also dependent on relationships with stakeholders and their capacity to contribute to the maintenance of the long-term integrity of the conservation values in MPAs.

Historically, the Commonwealth Government agency responsible for Commonwealth MPAs had pursued strict no-take reserves with minimal consultation or cooperation with other stakeholders. Australian experience in establishing MPAs and many of the more controversial terrestrial national parks has tended to be very costly, both financially and in terms of human resources, because of stakeholder conflict. Embracing conflict as an instrument to learn from while being supported by a government mandate for multiple use management has probably been the most important development in the current MPA agenda. The conflict which emerged early in the MPA programme through establishing the GABMP provided a basis by which EA could restructure its stakeholder consultation processes based on direct experience rather than through a policy process which at times may not accommodate the wisdom derived from experience. With subsequent experiences gained through developing the Tasmanian Seamounts Marine Reserve and the Macquarie Island Marine Park, EA was in a stronger position to review the processes of stakeholder participation. The strategies toward stakeholder participation that are now seen by EA as central to the success of MPAs include:

- clear understanding of all socio-economic issues relating to individual positions;
- mechanisms to identify and acknowledge common goals throughout consultation processes so that conflicts can be addressed without jeopardizing established agreements;
- commitment to addressing conflicts as they arise in order to minimize speculation, rumour and uncertainty;
- promotion of the principle that all stakeholders have a responsibility to protect and manage marine biological diversity and that MPAs are critical tools to achieving this shared responsibility; and
- provision of opportunities to allow stakeholders to make tangible contributions to the design, planning and ultimately the ongoing management and monitoring of MPAs.

The importance of stakeholder contributions to the design and management of MPAs is now more clearly recognized. The practical application of stakeholder expertise in the management of MPAs remains a significant challenge for the future. More effort is needed to encourage some stakeholders to contribute their expertise and input. The Australian conservation movement, for example, remains generally opposed to large-scale commitments to multiple use MPAs on the basis that any use may be contrary to serious conservation objectives. EA recognizes that more work needs to be done to promote a better awareness of its emerging multiple use approach and the benefits this can bring to marine conservation.

The future success of the Commonwealth's MPA development programme will depend on a range of challenges discussed in this chapter (from technical to political). The dominant factors that will drive the success of this MPA agenda will be a continued whole-of-Government approach to conservation and multiple use management, and the capacity of EA to honour its commitments to stakeholders and to continue to run processes that ensure trust and confidence are built and maintained. The breaching of these commitments at any stage in the MPA processes and at any level of action (Ministerial through to actions of individual officers) could jeopardize the integrity of the whole agenda. The involvement of stakeholders in developing and managing MPAs is a delicate balance, one that needs a constant and high level of nurturing.

Notes

1   Information on Australia's Oceans Policy can be found at
      http://www.environment.gov.au/net/oceanspo.html
2   Information on the NRSMPA can be found at
      http://www.environment.gov.au/marine

8

Biodiversity Conservation in Indonesia: Policy and Politics

Petrus Gunarso and Jim Davie

Introduction

While a number of the older PAs were located opportunistically, Indonesia has been endeavouring, since the 1970s, to establish a scientifically selected representative network of PAs (MacKinnon and Artha, 1982). Indonesia has 304 terrestrial PAs, 30 marine PAs, 30 terrestrial National Parks and six marine National Parks (Ministry of Forestry, 1997). These PAs cover 16.6 million ha of land and 8.2 million ha of sea. A further 30 million ha has been set aside for the protection of watersheds and other environmental processes. The gazettal of these areas is authorized by the *Basic Forestry Act No. 5 of 1967* (hereafter, the Forestry Act[1] created by government policy) and the *Conservation of Living Organisms and their Environment Act No. 5 of 1990* (hereafter, the Conservation Act). They are administered by the central government through the Directorate-General of Forest Protection and Nature Conservation in the Ministry of Forestry and Estate Crops (MOFEC), formerly Ministry of Forestry.

Unfortunately, such an impressive achievement in the gazettal of a vast area for conservation purposes does not on its own deliver conservation. The widespread degradation of forest resources, including those in national parks and other smaller PAs has been widely reported (Barber et al, 1994; Giesen, 1991; Whitmore and Sayer, 1992; Wibowo et al, 1997). The continuing social, economic and political crisis in Indonesia is further eroding the values of PAs as local people, and locally powerful forest companies, seek to meet their needs where they can (Kompas, 23/2/99; 29/4/99; 25/8/99a). In our view, the accelerated degradation, which is now occurring, is a consequence of the power vacuum that has occurred as a result of the decline of the Central Government's authority in the forest sector since the end of the *new order* government of President Suharto.

There are powerful reasons to believe that decentralization may be the best management option. Miller et al (1997) have suggested that decentralization to the local level will increase the probability of achieving development targets. This result is possible mainly because local governments have more direct contact with people surrounding the PAs upon which their welfare depends. Despite the initiative by the reformist government of President Habibie to decentralize power to the district level, each sectoral ministry has been slow to determine which powers will be devolved. The MOFEC has so far devolved only a few of its most trivial responsibilities (Gunarso and Davie, 1999).

In this chapter we focus on the policy and politics of biodiversity conservation, and we consider how they affect the process of decentralization, community resource use and participation, and the continued existence of PAs. First, we review Indonesia's achievements in biodiversity conservation and some of the most pressing issues challenging its capacity to deliver on international expectations, arising from the 1992 Earth Summit in Rio de Janeiro (Ministry of Forestry, 1997). This analysis includes an assessment of national and local level issues, using the case of the Hutan Bakau Pantai Timur Nature Reserve as an example. We then examine the obstacles created by the government's policy to reconciliation between local communities and the government itself. Finally, the potential for devolved power in conservation management is considered, as it could assist local level governments and communities to exercise control over the presently alarming rate of degradation of forests and PAs.

National Biodiversity Issues

Policy

At the policy level, the Indonesian government has shown leadership over many years in the way it has embraced international initiatives. Significantly, Indonesia is signatory to the Convention on International Trades of Endangered Species (CITES), the Convention concerning the Protection of the World Cultural and Natural Heritage, the Ramsar Convention on Wetlands and the Convention on Biodiversity. To support these commitments, the Indonesian Government enacted the Conservation Act. By 1993, it had produced the Biodiversity Action Plan and the National Strategy on Management of Biological Diversity (Ministry of National Development Planning, 1993; State Ministry of Environment, 1993). Consistently with the commitment to Agenda 21, in recent years the priority of the conservation programme has shifted increasingly to focus not only on statutory PAs, but also on agro-ecosystems and the broader landscape, *ex situ* strategies, the encouragement of traditional knowledge and the sustainable utilization of biodiversity (Ministry of Forestry, 1997).

The extensive area of forest lands and marine environment within the PA estate further emphasizes the willingness of the government to implement its

Table 8.1 *Gazetted and proposed protected areas in Indonesia,*
December 1996

Types	Gazetted area (000 ha)	Proposed no. of locations	Area (000 ha)	No. of locations
Nature Reserves (terrestrial & marine)	4900	180	9400	154
Wildlife Sanctuaries (terrestrial & marine)	3480	50	8070	90
National Parks (terrestrial & marine)	14,080	36	3220	15
Recreation Parks (terrestrial & marine)	720	90	3490	45
Grand Forest Parks	220	9	500	2
Hunting Parks	230	13	430	11
Total	23,630	378	25,110	317

Source: (Ministry of Forestry, 1997).

policies with respect to biodiversity conservation as presented in Table 8.1. It is proposed that by 2000 the gazetted and proposed PAs in Indonesia should cover a total of 48.3 million ha of terrestrial and marine environments.

Unfortunately, the gazettal of the PAs alone will not be sufficient to ensure that conservation objectives are met and sustained. There are at least four issues that must be addressed before any further real progress is made.

Is it Realistic to Set Aside a Very Large Area of the Country for Nature Conservation?

More than 74 per cent of the terrestrial area of Indonesia is designated as state forest, 25 per cent of which is either PAs or protection forest. Only 9.9 per cent is legally designated as arable land (SESRTCIC, 1999) or 0.12 ha per capita (Pingali et al, 1997). In a country with a population in excess of 200 million, of which more than 50 per cent are in rural areas, it is not difficult to understand why the pressure on forest land is high and increasing. The attempt to ensure conservation through this level of reservation is very ambitious. This can be appreciated by noting that among the nine most populated countries, the percentage of land allocated to conservation (at least on paper) in Indonesia (9.67 per cent) is second only to the USA (11.12 per cent), but the latter has a land resource per capita of 3.41 ha, compared to the 0.88 ha for each Indonesian.

A Large Number of People Live in Enclaves within PAs or along the Statutory Borders.

Notwithstanding some experience with ICDPs, strategies for the management of PAs do not acknowledge that large numbers of people live in and beside most PAs. The PA management model is based on the exclusion of people and dates back to Dutch colonial times. This approach is supported by the Forestry Act. The Conservation Act (which introduced the concept of the national park into Indonesia) is more flexible, but in practice the resettlement of local communities outside the borders has continued to be commonly adopted (Wardhana, 1998; Wind, 1990).

There is a Need for New Ideas, Supported by Local People, about what can be Realistically Achieved in Nature Conservation

The agenda for nature conservation is still largely driven by the western international community, despite foreign funding contributing only 20 per cent of the biodiversity budget in the Sixth Five-Year Plan (Repelita VI). Foreign funds have been directed mostly towards national strategic planning and national park planning (Wells et al, 1998), with a strong focus on zoological and botanical aspects. Sociological issues receive little attention despite their over-riding importance for sustainable resource use and conservation.

The Central Government no longer has the Economic Power, Human Resources, or Infrastructure to Regulate the Activities of Provincial and Local Governments, and Local People

The continuing political and economic crisis, which has been unfolding since the middle of 1997, has translated into a management vacuum in PAs throughout the country. Forest destruction through over-exploitation and conversion is occurring in all categories of PAs, including national parks, and also in permanent production forests. It has been reported that 15 out of 36 national parks are now in very poor condition as a result of illegal logging (eg Kompas, 25/8/1999b), and more than 16 million ha of production forest are also degraded (Media Indonesia, 1999a). There is undoubtedly a significant need for sustenance being demonstrated in local people's actions. However, the extent of the destruction may also reflect a backlash from local people, who have felt that their rights to natural resource use were unjustly denied when the PAs were established. There are very strong messages in these events for the future practice of nature conservation.

Integrating Protected Areas into the Wider Landscape

Indonesia, like many other countries, is struggling in the transition from the practice of conserving biodiversity within the boundaries of PAs to reducing the impact of human activities in the broader landscape through better environmental planning. The concept of *protected landscapes* (Lucas, 1992) has considerable potential in densely populated tropical countries. In Indonesia, the legislative basis for this approach is still fragmented despite valuable progress in this direction with the *Spatial Planning Act No 24 of 1992*. There remains a poor understanding of how this approach might be translated into day-to-day management practice. During the 1990s, the Indonesian government has sought to address this issue in two ways.

First, the creation of the national park category has allowed the aggregation of smaller PAs into larger units, for example:

- Gunung Leuser National Park; the 1,790,000 ha Leuser Ecosystem includes the 905,000 ha of park plus adjacent production and protection forest; and
- Ujung Kulon National Park; this 120,000 ha park combines 44,000 ha of marine area and 76,000 ha of terrestrial area.

Second, the concept of modifying the impact of local people on biodiversity values has been embraced in a series of projects linked to the major national parks. The implementation of this approach has taken several forms:

- Biosphere Reserves (UNESCO) have been created around the national parks of Ujung Kulon; Gunung Gede/Pangrango/Halimun, Komodo, and Siberut Island;
- ICDPs (World Bank) linked to the national parks of Kerinci Seblat, and Wasur;
- Integrated Protected Area Systems (Asian Development Bank) implemented at Siberut and Ruteng national parks;
- Integrated National Park and Community Development Planning (USAID), Natural Resource Management Project Phases 1 and 2 at Bunaken National Park; and
- World Heritage Site (USAID, UNESCO, GTZ, and WWF Netherlands) implemented at Lorentz national park.

The details of these activities differ from one project to another. However, the general concept conforms with that of ICDPs (Wells et al, 1998). The essential concept is to conserve biodiversity, in and around PAs, by focusing on the social and economic development of the local people, who have an interest in, or a potential to impact on, the resources contained in the PA. In its many forms this approach has focused either on zoning of uses to ensure that high value, core areas are preserved (Wind, 1990), and the development of resource substitution approaches (Davie and Djamaluddin, 1999; see also Chapter 11).

An evaluation of the ICDPs has indicated that the approach has had little impact on reducing the rate of resource depletion (Wells et al, 1998). This is because local communities' impacts on national parks are still small relative to the threats from transmigration projects (eg Lore Lindu and Siberut national parks), mining (eg Kutai, Gunung Halimun and Dumoga Bone national parks), and from large forest concessions (Gunung Leuser and Kerinci Seblat national parks).

Little attention has so far been directed towards modifying commercial level resource extraction techniques to minimize impacts. However, such an approach is now seriously being considered at the international level in relation to sustainable forest management and forest conservation (ITTO, 1992; Commonwealth of Australia, 1999)

Some progress could be made in consolidating the force of the law through stricter implementation of PA management regulations. However, the present emphasis on increased policing needs to shift towards industry and community extension focused on collaborative solutions. A new emphasis on extension will itself require a substantial philosophical shift away from the current Forestry Act, which states that it is the public's responsibility to listen to forestry officials. Explicitly, Article 37 (para 1) states that through extension, the government has to direct and mobilize people, and make them participate in the conservation of living natural resources.

Lack of Consultation and Information

The identification of the boundaries of PAs is based on the interests of educated nature conservation professionals. The uniqueness of proposed conservation sites is a major consideration. The delimitation of the boundaries is based primarily on reconnaissance surveys employing aerial photographs or satellite imagery. Little consideration is paid to social, cultural or customary rights, or to demographic surveys. The small-scale maps, on which the boundaries are drawn, rarely register important local features that might form the basis for a negotiated solution acceptable to local people. Following the identification of potential new PAs, based on scientific criteria, the normal process for informing the public is a declaration by the central government through the media. The needs of local communities are ignored, and frequently they are subjected to involuntary resettlement. The human implications of this approach concerned the former State Minister for Environment and Population, Professor Emil Salim, as long ago as the early 1980s (IUCN-COE, 1984).

There is a gap between the educated public sector élite and the general community. The concept of PAs for nature conservation is understood by the élite, who accept the global responsibility which Indonesia has for biodiversity conservation and appreciates its long-term economic and ecological importance. However, this understanding has not been projected to the community, particularly local communities, many of whom depend on land and forest resources for their livelihood. To people living in remote areas of Sumatra, Kalimantan or Irian Jaya, the potential of conservation activities to provide future opportunities for social and economic development, as well as the basis for sustaining the ecological processes necessary for productive landscapes, appears a land use luxury being imposed by a distant government responding to the wishes of the developed world.

The top-down, autocratic approach to PA management, and indeed all other classes of forest land, has contributed to the present explosive situation. Local communities, local officials, and private sector organizations do not respect boundaries designed to protect biodiversity. The case study presented below exemplifies how the central government's intentions are being ignored, and represents a situation from which there is no chance of reconciliation without a new, locally-based form of management. Despite the circumstances described below, the MOFEC has shown no inclination to move towards an alternative form of land designation that might preserve at least some of the important biodiversity values for which the area is still listed. Unfortunately, this case study represents an example of the *paper park* situation that occurs widely in the country.

Hutan Bakau Pantai Timur Nature Reserve

Hutan Bakau Pantai Timur (HBPT) is a Strict Nature Reserve (IUCN Category 1a), located on the highly dynamic east coast of Jambi Province. The PA has been attracting the attention of international organizations for many years. The main purpose of the PA is to conserve mangrove forests and the mudflats that provide feeding and resting areas for migratory waders on the Asian–Australian flyway. This PA is among the few Indonesian Nature Reserves that have received international funding for management planning.

The PA is unique in shape, a long narrow strip along the coast in excess of 80 km and dissected by 13 estuaries. Extending over almost 90 per cent of the province's coast, it was declared in 1981 by Decree of the Minister of Agriculture. Boundary marking was conducted intermittently over four fiscal years from 1985 to 1998, despite the central administration's policy of assigning top-priority to boundary marking of Strict Nature Reserves.

Initially, the PA covered 6500 ha, but in our most recent survey in August 1998 the remaining area of native forest was only 1800 ha. Most of the PA had been converted into coconut plantations, fishponds, reforestation pilot projects, settlements and even channels and roads. Depending upon the source of authorization, local or central government, these conversions can be interpreted as either legal or illegal. The projects most easily viewed as being illegal were those carried out by the local people. Non-local development projects were generally treated as being legal. Settlement and conversion to coconut plantations and fishponds by local people are based on the authority of the *Kepala Parit*, the informal village leader responsible for opening the land for agriculture, subject to authorization by the *Kepala Desa*, the village head. Road and channel construction are official government projects and are not considered illegal. When the Provincial Office of Forest Protection and Nature Conservation has objected strongly, the construction of channels has been halted. However, when this has not occurred, and a current road project is an example, encroachment has proceeded.

Government officers' interpretation of what is legal or illegal is remarkably different from the views held by local people. When the local people were asked about their conversion activities, they felt that their actions were legal. About 68 per cent of respondents indicated that they did not feel guilty about being in the PA. This perception was based on their belief that they were not encroaching on state land because they got it from the *government*. In their terms, *government* is the *Kepala Desa* or even the *Kepala Parit*. Their purchase of land was confirmed by receipts, signed by either the *Kepala Parit* or the *Kepala Desa*. There were also some villagers who had left their proof of purchase in the hands of the *Kepala Parit*. In the survey, 72 per cent of the local respondents said that they convert forest land in the PA because they need land to cultivate crops; 52 per cent admitted that they had seen boundary marks, but purchased the land anyway. While the purchase is considered illegal by the central government, 68 per cent believed that the purchase was legal according to the local government.

The purchase of land through the *Kepala Parit* or the *Kepala Desa* may create problems if the land is needed by other people who can access a higher level of government support. Local people's land receipts would be ignored, or they would only receive a small amount of compensation. They have no rights to object to official project proposals.

The establishment of the PA was based primarily on scientific aspects of conservation. Social considerations were, and continue to be, ignored by the MOFEC. The Ministerial Decree establishing the PA noted that its purpose was the protection of unique flora and fauna. No mention of social considerations was made. The problems with the design of the PA are also illustrated by the fact that it covers almost all of the coastal area of Jambi province, thus severely restricting people's access to the sea.

The unplanned loss of much of the PA has clearly impacted on its values, but the central government has paid little attention to this issue. When the problem was pointed out to government officers (in a workshop discussing the findings of a World Bank funded management plan), the authorities expressed surprise, but so far neither the provincial government nor the central government has taken action.

During the fieldwork, workshops were conducted with all levels of government to gather the views of the different public sector stakeholders. The most significant result was the pervading view that the local community was not considered to be a stakeholder; therefore, consultation about management issues has not reached village level.

How representative this case study is of the many hundreds of PAs in Indonesia is not certain, as evaluations of their status have generally not occurred. Evaluations have focused on national parks. The results from 20 national parks that have adopted ICDP approaches are consistent with the general picture which the case of HBPT paints. Without further information to the contrary, we believe that the situation of HBPT is likely to represent that of many other PAs.

Can there be Effective Protected Area Management? Problems in Reconciling the Stakeholders

The current approach to nature conservation through gazettal of extensive PAs in Indonesia, and in many other developing countries, marks the acceptance of international practice, largely developed and endorsed in western countries. There are some advantages in adopting this approach (Cribb, 1988).

International acknowledgement has accompanied the effort that Indonesia has made towards meeting its global responsibilities under Agenda 21. Large sums of foreign assistance from multilateral and bilateral sources have increased the government's capacity to implement its programme, and presented it with opportunities to increase its institutional capacity, through staff training and education.

However, this approach has exposed considerable differences between central government decision-makers and the local communities. The reality is that many PAs are being openly destroyed by neighbouring communities. Reconciliation between local communities and the government will continue to be very difficult while the social and economic environment remains uncertain. For example, in the Kerinci Seblat National Park, capital accumulation is the main reason for local people to encroach on the PA, and convert the land to cinnamon (Wibowo et al, 1997). Resettlement has occurred in Bogani Nani Wartabone National Park and at Lore Lindu National Park. In these cases, important cultural relationships with the land have been severed, leading to social distress. The failure of the Forestry Act to recognize customary rights has resulted in the alienation of local communities from forest resources.

Unless broader community input into conservation planning and management is legitimized, the present process by which community expectations are accommodated by local authorities through non-institutional, non-legal authority will continue (Gunarso and Davie, 1999). PAs will continue to be treated as open access resources and illegal conversion of natural ecosystems will continue.

In considering the obstacles facing reconciliation between the main stakeholders, the central government and the communities, the following aspects of the central government's policy are particularly significant.

The first aspect relates to land tenure, which the government does not consider appropriately. Land tenure problems are common throughout the country, although they are more serious in the outer islands, where the largest percentage of land is classified as forest land, rather than agrarian land as in Java and Bali. Land ownership is a significant factor in conferring privilege within a society. In Indonesia, most PAs are established on state forest land, with no acknowledgement of long-established land right claims by local people. In most cases, following gazettal, local people are required to abandon the land and move to another location. Where enclaves of people remain on traditional land, within the boundaries of the PAs, they are technically without legal rights. They are always in a poor bargaining position in relation to the nature conservation agency of MOFTEC.

The discrepancies over local community rights between the Forestry Act and the Agrarian Act are an important factor contributing to land tenure problems. The rights of local communities are dealt with differently depending upon the extent to which local people claim customary rights which predate the enactment of national legislation. The existence of customary rights is recognized by the Agrarian Act, but it achieves less importance in the Forestry Act, that states:

> '*Customary law where it still exists and governs the rights of the community to benefit from the forest, either directly or indirectly, shall not alter the efforts of the forestry sector to achieve the development objectives as referred to in this Law.*' (Article 17)

The Forestry Act allows the MOFEC to grant tenure to forest companies, without acknowledging customary law. Encroachment, even by customary owners, has resulted in involuntary resettlement. Despite intense protest in support of customary rights, a new Forestry Act is being considered in which customary land is still classified as state forest. The extent of the disempowerment of local people which stems from the law can be appreciated by noting that about 74 per cent of the land is *state forest land* and subject to the laws administered by the MOFEC.

In practice, the capacity of the government to implement the legislation has declined to such an extent that it is basically ineffective in all but the most intensively managed locations (eg some of the national parks on Java and Bali). In other cases, the government has had to redraw the boundaries to accommodate settlement (eg Berbak National Park), and in other locations attempts to remove people have not been successful, and re-population of the PAs has taken place.

The second aspect concerns centralized conservation management. Despite an extensive shift towards a devolution of power in the past two years, the *Act No.22 of 1999 Concerning Local Government* stipulates that conservation will remain centralized. With limited budgets available for nature conservation, most of the available funds will be invested in national parks and small PAs will suffer. The issue of decentralization is considered in the next section.

Third, local communities have not been acknowledged as primary stakeholders by the government. Natural resource management is carried out through up to sixteen sectors of government. Despite administrative attempts to increase coordination between the Ministry of State for Environment and the National Planning Board, there is no legislative hierarchy among the sectors. Rather, each sector, represented by its ministry, operates through vertical management from the centre to the provinces and administrative districts. Within the forestry sector, forest land use is determined under the Forestry Act, through a system of Forest Land Use by Consensus, recognized by seven of the land resource sectors. Within an administrative district, the Land Use by Consensus maps represent the ratified view of the central government. There is no avenue for the involvement of local people.

Fourth, most new laws and regulations emphasize the need for greater community participation. In practice, however, participation continues to be a somewhat alien notion, especially among local communities. In the Conservation Act, community participation is defined such that the agency is required to direct and mobilize people by involving groups, to make them actively participate in the conservation of natural resources. In Government Regulation *No. 69 of 1996 Concerning the Rights and Responsibilities of Communities and People to Participate in Spatial Planning*, community is defined as a private, legal institution or government organization. Included in community participation is technical assistance and management assistance from the community to the government to carry out spatial planning. Such involvement is expected at each level of government (central, provincial and district). The capacity of the community to provide technical input to government is likely to be limited, even in developed nations. It seems that it is the élite who are expected to participate, given that they have the capacity to do so. The Act Concerning Local Government also requires community participation, but its definition is subject to further legislation. It is not surprising that confusion about the role and contribution of the public continues. Participation has simply been used in development jargon to please donor countries.

Finally, and unfortunately, the incorporation of foreign ideas about conservation practice into Indonesian forestry has failed to include those aspects of traditional practice which also support conservation goals. Conservation is practised by many indigenous groups. For example, *Sasi* is a form of marine conservation practised in Maluku (Pannel, 1997). Traditional resource management practices are also used for river belt protection in the Hutan Bakau Pantai Timur PA described above.

Institutional Change: Decentralization

Indonesia is involved in a process of institutional devolution of authority. This change began under the Suharto presidency in the Sixth Five-Year Plan (Repelita VI 1994–1999) as a means of holding together the state. In the present political climate, decentralization is a very topical issue (eg Suara Pembaruan, 1999).

Much of the literature dealing with decentralization issues has focused on governance in a political-economic framework (eg Rondinelli et al, 1989; Samof, 1990). However, some recent literature addresses decentralization in relation to management of PAs and biodiversity conservation (Press et al, 1996; Miller et al, 1997; Lutz and Caldecott, 1996). Miller et al (1997) suggest that the devolution of natural resource management is a valuable strategy for achieving environmental and developmental goals. They argue that decentralization is important and necessary for implementing provisions of the Convention on Biological Diversity, although they recognize that this can only be achieved if there is an improvement in administrative capacity.

Most of the analyses deal appropriately with strengthening institutions and capacity building, but the application of these models to Indonesia remains problematical. The centralized government structure is inhibiting the decentralization of decision-making and regional capacity building. There are several reasons why centralization is proving difficult to break-down. Apart from obvious issues associated with the rearrangement of entrenched personal power, a significant impediment to decentralization lies in the cultural history of the archipelago. Historically, political power has been wielded from Java.

An established pattern of conquest through the outer islands was reinforced by the Dutch and continued in modern, post-colonial Indonesia. As a consequence, it is rare that a local community can exercise its own decisions with no ratification by higher authorities. That communities may not necessarily distinguish between national institutional authority (backed by legislation) and non-institutionalized decision-making at the provincial or district level (by powerful people), further complicates the process (Gunarso and Davie, 1999). Suspicions about the sincerity of the central government's willingness to transfer decision-making power through decentralization have also been increased by the fact that the 1999 Act Concerning Local Government and *Act No 25 of 1999 Concerning the Distribution of Finance* devolve authority to the district level. However, they present important inconsistencies, there are many exceptions listed in both acts, and many government regulations will be required for their implementation.

In relation to biodiversity conservation, Caldecott (1996) has identified some rational and practical considerations for planning decentralization. However, a process of non-institutionalized decentralization has already been occurring, with land use decisions being taken beyond the control, or intent, of the central government by government officials at provincial, district and even village levels (Gunarso and Davie, 1999). These government officers have always, even if unofficially, exercised a high degree of autonomy in decision-making, because the central government lacks the capacity to implement appropriate controls. The consequence of this process in the forestry sector has been unplanned land use changes, and often the result is the loss of permanent production forest (Gunarso and Davie, 1997) and degradation of PAs as in the case study presented above. The NGOs and other community sectors have very limited control (Barber et al, 1994).

The actual implementation of decentralization has been very limited despite sweeping decrees in its favour. In the forestry sector, where centralized control has long been an important feature, its expression relates only to the devolution of control over activities that are trivial with respect to their capacity to yield economic returns (bee-keeping, silk production, forestry extension, community forestry and forest restoration). This partial devolution has increased confusion in the sector (Gunarso and Davie, 1999).

Formal, institutionalized decentralization has not yet resolved the problem that local administrators outside the forestry department continue to make illegal, informal decisions of major significance to resource conservation. The only way that legal controls can be effectively implemented at the local level is through a comprehensive formal delegation of powers to the local forestry service, together with the provision of the necessary resources (Gunarso and Davie, 1999). Unfortunately, the 1999 Act Concerning Local Government has exempted conservation activities from decentralization. But it seems clear that with limited budget and personnel, if all PAs have to be managed from the central office in Jakarta, they will become (or remain) paper parks. Decentralization is needed to encourage local community participation, and to attempt sustainable resource management.

Conclusion

Despite the achievements registered at least on paper in biodiversity conservation, it is obvious that centralized management of PAs is not a satisfactory strategy. There are several factors explaining the adoption in Indonesia of the centralized approach to natural resources management, and PA management in particular. The first, and obvious one, is that the country has been governed in an authoritarian style since it became independent. A second contributing factor is that many of the PAs were established during the colonial administration, while many others were created during the 1970s and 1980s and are a result of foreign inspired plans. A third and important issue is that most of the experts working for the development of national conservation activities have backgrounds in zoology and botany. Therefore, these activities reflect a natural science approach, with little or no input from the social sciences.

It seems that in the post-Suharto political environment there is some willingness to decentralize decision-making. However, the extent to which the central government is actually willing to transfer power to local level governments remains to be seen. As far as conservation activities are concerned, it seems that the new legislation has almost closed the decentralization option. In the short term, given the fact that local governments are not yet ready to take on responsibilities for conservation, the decentralization of nature conservation to local communities should, in any case, be exercised with caution. Otherwise, many PAs will be further degraded.

In the medium to long term, to avoid *paper conservation*, the management of PAs has to be based on appropriate planning and community participation.

PA planning and management needs to take into account biophysical aspects, as well as social, economic and cultural concerns specific to the area. Investments such as boundary marking in vast areas of Irian Jaya and Aceh should not be accorded high priority, which should instead be given to extension and public education.

It will take time to change the traditional conservation approach of attempting to lock people out of the environment. The current system of government and imported systems of PA management do little to enhance community participation. While participation is mentioned in new laws and regulations, attempts aimed at increasing it have so far only reached the early stages of token participation, information sharing, and participation for material incentives.

Notes

1   A new Forestry Act was being debated at the time when this chapter was drafted.

9

From Top-down to Participatory Planning: Conservation Lessons from the Adirondack Park, United States

Jon D Erickson and Sabine U O'Hara

Introduction

The Adirondack Park located in Northern New York State of the United States of America (approximately 4 hours north of New York City) is a unique combination of protected State and privately owned land regulated by zoning laws (Figures 9.1 and 9.2). This combination of ownership models has made the Adirondack Park a unique application of land use planning compatible with large-scale biodiversity protection. By implementing a network of public and private lands, New York has been able to protect the ecological integrity of the largest park in the contiguous United States during the past 100 years. However, these gains in environmental protection were achieved at the expense of individual liberties of private landowners and local communities. This has led to repeated tensions between public agencies and representatives and between local stakeholders and citizens. One reason for these tensions is that today's Park has evolved from a rather top-down planning process that considered little input from local communities, who were left to bear the burden of real or perceived conflicts between a State agenda of environmental protection and a local agenda of economic development. More recently, both sides have become aware that the long-term viability of local economies within the healthy and functioning ecosystems of the Park will depend on a new era of community involvement and collaborative, participatory decision-making.

This chapter summarizes the significance of the Adirondack experience as an example of biodiversity protection. It offers an historical overview of the decision-making process responsible for today's patchwork quilt of the public and private lands within the Adirondack Park. It discusses recent developments in research and decision innovation that seek to bridge the knowledge gaps between various stakeholder groups, decision-makers, and those most affected by land use decisions. Four current examples of this bridge building process are discussed to illustrate the potential that community-based research and policy making offers for improving sustainable development efforts within the Adirondacks.

The Global Significance of the Adirondack Park

New York State was the breeding ground for the American industrial revolution. The timber resources of the northeast United States, the extensive waterway system providing transport to mid-western states and the birth of the 20th century's financial centre of New York City, all contributed to the accumulation of wealth and power characteristic of the Empire State. New York has been home to the Rockefellers, Vanderbilts and other oil, rail and industrial empires that became synonymous with a turn-of-the-century free-market ideology perhaps never before and never since experienced. This chapter of New York history is well known and continues to shape the discourse within boardrooms of Fortune 500 companies, the New York Federal Reserve and the trading floors of Wall Street and the New York Stock Exchange.

A lesser-known chapter of New York history stands in contrast to the well-known culture of human expansion, exploitation and domination. New York State is also home to the largest park in the contiguous United States. The century-old, 6 million-acre Adirondack Park of Upstate New York is larger than its better known cousins Yellowstone, Yosemite, Grand Canyon and Smoky Mountain National Parks combined. In fact, the American concept of wilderness and land conservation can be traced to the constitutionally protected New York Forest Preserve, upon which the Adirondack Park was built (the Adirondack lands within the Forest Preserve are highlighted in Figure 9.2). Created in 1892 through an amendment to the State Constitution, the New York Forest Preserve in the Adirondack and Catskill Mountains today stands as one of the strongest protections of land in the world (Brown, 1985; Terrie, 1994). Article XIV of the New York State Constitution reads in part:

> *'The lands of the State ... shall be forever kept as wild forest lands. They shall not be leased, sold, or exchanged, nor shall the timber thereon be sold, removed or destroyed.'*

Throughout the 20th century, the development and lumbering restrictions set forth by Article XIV withstood many challenges from timber interests and hydropower projects, and more recently, large-scale tourism development interests (Schaeffer, 1989). Any change to the Constitution of New York requires the passage of amendments in consecutive State legislatures followed by a statewide public referendum. This rather rigorous process has made it possible for Article XIV to stand against such challenges. In fact, the signifi-

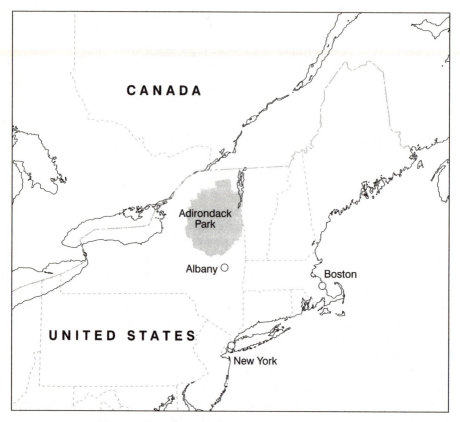

Figure 9.1 *Adirondack Park of New York State*

cance of Article XIV has extended well beyond the Park's boundaries. It is widely recognized that its language, and decades of legal experience in its defence, laid the foundation for the US National Wilderness Act of 1964.

Yet despite its strength, the New York Forest Preserve faces similar challenges to those faced by many national and international nature protection efforts. Like most conservation strategies, the Forest Preserve depends in large part on State government purchases (or seizures) of land and on the cessation of economic activity within protected land boundaries. Such strategies have proven effective at best for small parcels of land. However, government finances and the availability of land for sale typically limit them.

The Adirondack Park is no exception. Its boundaries were originally drawn with the ultimate goal of complete State acquisition. However, through the years, as the Park boundary expanded, land values increased, Adirondack towns and villages developed, and large tracts of land were retained in the private sector, it became clear that this ultimate goal was infeasible. The Adirondack Forest Preserve did continue to expand, but today accounts for just under half of the 6-million-acre Adirondack Park.

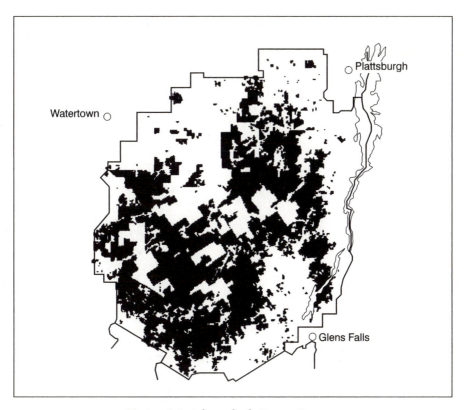

Figure 9.2 *Adirondack Forest Preserve*

While the level of protection afforded to the public Adirondacks is unique, the incorporation of private lands within a protected Park system sets the Adirondacks apart from the typical public park model. By including both public and private lands within the Park boundaries, comprehensive planning had to evolve in order to protect a large relatively intact ecosystem from incompatible uses on privately owned land.

Prior to the 1970s, public land in the Adirondacks was simply protected with no intent of incorporating recreational land use on protected lands into the Park's land use regulations. Yet given the Park's unique structure of private lands intermingled with publicly owned tracts of land, new forms of land use and protection were needed. Private lands consist of small tracts around hamlets, large open spaces owned by timber industries, a few remaining wealthy estates and recreation clubs.

Following the completion of interstate highway 87 in 1967, which runs through the eastern border of the Park connecting large population centres in New York City and Montreal, new threats to the Park's ecological integrity emerged. Public lands were suddenly accessible to a larger and demographically and economically more diverse segment of the northeast US population. New subdivisions and sales of private lands for second-home and seasonal

Table 9.1 *State and private land classifications, 1992*

APA classification			
State land (47%)	Private land (53%)	% of park	Compatible uses
Wilderness		17	Camping, hiking, canoeing, fishing, trapping, hunting, snowshoeing, ski touring
Primitive & canoe		1	Similar to wilderness uses
Wild forest		21	Similar to wilderness uses with the addition of some motorized vehicle access
Other		7	Water (6%), Pending (0.68%), State administration (0.01%), historic (0.01%), and intensive use (0.33%: ski centres, public campgrounds, developed beaches, boat launching)
	Resource management	28	Forestry, agriculture, game preserves, recreation, very low density development (42.7 acre average lot size)
	Rural use	18	Similar to resource management, low density development (8.5 acre average lot size)
	Low intensity	5	Low density residential development (3.2 acre average lot size)
	Moderate intensity	2	Concentrated residential development (1.3 acre average lot size)
	Hamlet	1	All uses compatible, no APA development intensity limit
	Industrial	<0.5	Existing industrial uses (ex/mining), future industrial development

Note: Based on personal communication with John Barge, APA and Collins (1994).

housing development, town expansions, and recreational land use development rapidly altered the character of the private land pockets within the Park. In reaction, New York State commissioned a study of the Adirondacks resulting in the creation of the Adirondack Park Agency (APA) in 1971. The APA was charged with the task of zoning the public Adirondacks for recreational use and the private Adirondacks for various intensities of development. The results of the newly formed APA's work were two comprehensive plans: the Adirondack Park State Land Master Plan (1972) and the Adirondack Park

Private Use and Development Plan (1973). Table 9.1 lists the public and private zoning classifications, current percentage of Adirondack land within each, and a brief description of use intensity by zone.

At the dawn of the twenty-first century, the story of the Adirondack Park is one of seeking to live the generally abstract concept of sustainability rather than conservation. People are trying to make a living within a protected area rather than keeping human use and nature protection neatly separated. Today's Adirondack Park is home to over 135,000 permanent residents in 105 towns and villages, and host to over 200,000 seasonal homes. Seventy million people live within a day's drive from the Park. Almost by accident, the region has evolved into an application of modern multiple land use models extolled by conservation biologists to protect large ecosystems through networks of cores, corridors and buffers (Erickson, 1998). McKibben (1995), Schneider (1997), Terrie (1997) and others have looked at the Adirondack experience in search of compromise between economic development and environmental protection. In the search for operationalizing vague principles of sustainable development, the Adirondack story is shedding some much-needed light on its application at a regional level.

The Adirondack Park Agency and Top-down Land Use Planning

The modern era of the Adirondack Park began with the enactment of the Adirondack Park Agency Act in 1971. The main purpose of the act was to establish an agency within the executive branch of the State Government that would be responsible for zoning and enforcing land uses compatible with public and private interests within the Adirondacks. Although the act resulted in master plans for both public and private land use, it was the private use plan and an accompanying park-wide map that stirred the most serious controversy since its inception. The APA plan recognized

> 'the complementary needs of all people of the state for the preser-
> vation of the park's resources and open space character and of
> the park's permanent, seasonal and transient populations for
> growth and service areas, employment, and a strong economic
> base, as well.' (APA Act, sec. 801)

However, despite this language, the local perception was one of the State Government protecting the land conservation interests of tourist and downstate residents at the expense of local Adirondack residents' economic interests and private rights. For instance, a 43-acre parcel of land that could once have been subdivided into numerous plots for sale or construction was suddenly limited to one principal building. Private local landowners' rights were severely limited for the sake of the larger social good.

The drafters of the APA act recognized and partly addressed this conflict between private and public interests by incorporating concerns for a local government voice. The APA commissioners consist of the state commissioner of environmental conservation, the state commissioner of commerce, the secretary of state and eight members appointed by the governor (APA Act, sec. 803). Among the eight appointees, five must be full-time Park residents and three must be non-Park residents. The act also called for the establishment of an Adirondack Park Local Government Review Board consisting of twelve members, each representing one of the twelve counties fully or partially located within the Park. The purpose of the review board was to advise and assist the APA in carrying out 'its functions, powers and duties' (APA Act, sec. 803-a). Most significantly, sec. 807 of the APA Act provided for agency review and approval of 'any local land use programme proposed by a local government and formally submitted by the legislative body of the local government'. Approval was subject to meeting a number of criteria essentially assuring that local programmes were at least as strong as APA regulations.

Despite such attempts to flavour the make-up of the APA with some local voices, the magnitude of its centralized decision-making authority and power sentenced the APA to tremendous local animosity from its inception. The perception has always been one of credentialled, outside experts talking down to local people. Appointments to the APA are highly political. The Local Government Review Board has always acted only in a review capacity, with no voting power. Only a handful of Adirondack towns have taken the necessary steps to write and seek APA approval for local zoning laws. Those towns interested in superseding APA regulations with their own have found the legal and administrative expense to be prohibitive. Thus, as much as the APA Act has been an unprecedented story of zoning over 3 million acres of private land, the result has also led to a lesson in polarizing stakeholders.

This polarization was magnified by the active participation of national environmental groups, such as the Audubon Society and Sierra Club, in designing Park policy. Table 9.2 is a snapshot of the types of non-governmental groups that have been involved in Park-wide issues. Many very organized, well-funded groups such as the Association for the Protection of the Adirondacks have been involved in Park politics throughout this century, while other organizations were formed only recently, in the modern APA era. Groups such as the Adirondack Solidarity Council, the League for Adirondack Citizens' Rights and the Adirondack Minutemen were formed with the sole mission of abolishing the APA. Their tactics were not limited to political discourse. Stories of personal threats, rock throwing and spray painting were common amongst first generation APA commissioners.

Amidst the hostility and defending numerous legal challenges to their zoning authority, the APA was able to slow the pressure for the subdivision of properties, but the practice of top-down planning has left a legacy of distrust in the Park that has subsequently hampered new top-down plans from the State. Despite zoning laws, sales of subdivided property in the Park tripled between 1982 and 1985, and then doubled again by 1988. These alarming

Table 9.2 *List of private Park-wide interest groups*

Interest group	Central mission
Adirondack 46ers	Promote and maintain recreation access and trails
Adirondack Council	Environmental and open space protection
Adirondack Development Corporation	Community economic development
Adirondack Land Trust (Nature Conservancy)	Environmental protection, land acquisition
Adirondack Liberators	Property rights advocacy
Adirondack Minutemen	Property rights advocacy
Adirondack Mountain Club (ADK)	Promote and maintain recreation access and trails
Adirondack North Country Association	Community economic development
Adirondack Research Consortium	Promote interdisciplinary research on the region
Adirondack Solidarity Alliance	Property rights advocacy
Association for the Protection of the Adirondacks	Protect the New York State Forest Preserve
Association of Adirondack Towns and Villages	Local government advocacy
Blue Line Council	Economic development
Citizens Group of the Adirondacks	Property rights advocacy
Earth First!	Environmental rights advocacy
Empire State Forest Products Association	Promote forest products industry
League for Adirondack Citizens' Rights	Property rights advocacy
National Audubon Society	Environmental protection, biodiversity preservation
Wildlife Conservation Society	Environmental protection, biodiversity preservation
Northern Forest Alliance	Alliance of environmental groups
Residents Committee for the Protection of the Adirondacks	Environmental protection
Sierra Club	Environmental protection, biodiversity preservation
Wilderness Society	Environmental protection, biodiversity preservation

trends spurred the creation of a second study commission, the Commission on the Adirondacks in the Twenty-First Century. The Commission reported that at full build-out under then current APA zoning laws, there would be 156,598 houses in resource management and rural use zones (see Table 9.1 for definitions), and an additional 250,000 homes along shorefronts and roadsides in and around hamlets (Commission on the Adirondacks in the Twenty-First Century, 1990). This scenario was projected to increase the 1990 Park population by five-fold.

Following some time for public review and comment, at times witness to violent public outbreaks against the Commission's work, *The Adirondack Park in the Twenty-First Century* was released, including two volumes of technical appendices. The report contained 245 recommendations, including the addition of 654,850 acres to the Forest Preserve at an estimated cost of $196 million, the purchase of transferable development rights in the range of $27–42 million, and acquisition of conservation easements at about $100 million. Peter Berle, President of the National Audubon Society and an active proponent of the original APA Act in 1971, served as the Commission's chairman. This appointment by the Governor had tainted the Commission's work with suspicion of a hidden, downstate environmental agenda. The backlash from Adirondack property rights interests was considerable. For instance, an anonymous group formed calling themselves the Adirondack Liberators, whose mission was to write threatening letters to Commission members (Dobbs and Ober, 1995). The coalitions that attempted to abolish the APA in the 1970s were born again.

Adirondack citizens and downstate New Yorkers alike began to feel that the State had overstepped its bounds. In 1990, for the first time in State history, New York voters failed to pass an environmental bond issue that would have provided the funds for significant additions to the Forest Preserve. Next, legislation based on the 21st Century Commission's recommendations was defeated in the New York Senate in four consecutive years. In 1994, New York's three-term Democratic governor who had created the 21st Century Commission was defeated by a Republican, pro-business platform with the help of a high voter turnout in the northern New York counties. The demise of a dominant top-down planning process in the Park was imminent.

Community Participatory Processes: A New Policy Era?

Given the tensions, controversies and political shake-up that resulted from the Adirondack Park's top-down protection efforts, decision-makers agreed that a more open and participatory process was needed for guiding the Park's future development and conservation strategies. For example, in the wake of the defeat of the 1990 Environmental Bond Act, New York citizens demanded a more clearly defined rationale for land and water conservation needs, and the means and strategies for their attainment. In response, in 1992 New York produced the first statewide Open Space Conservation plan with the input of Regional Advisory Committees jointly appointed by the State and local governments.

The first steps of moving toward a more participatory decision process were undoubtedly motivated by political expediency. Clearly, local participation can result in lower implementation and acceptance costs of potentially conflicting protection and development agendas. However, beside such political expediencies, the participation of those most affected by land use decisions has other advantages. First, local experts may add invaluable information about specific context attributes such as historical events, social characteristics of specific communities, or spatial and ecological specifics, which non-local experts may not be aware of. Second, an open communication process between mutually respectful individuals allows a discursive reason to become operative that goes beyond individual conceptions of reason and a discursive ethic that goes beyond preconceived ethical norms (Habermas, 1984, 1996; Apel, 1973, 1980).

The reason for this expanded discursive rationality is that discourse allows the larger social and environmental context of people's lives to become visible. Individuals make judgements and assess options not in isolation but within a network of communicative relationships and interactions (Dryzek, 1997; O'Hara, 1996; Ulrich, 1989). Individual perceptions and valuations are altered when these contextual relationships are expressed in a mutually accepted communicative process. Behavioural research, for example, has demonstrated that such communicative interaction changes decision outcomes. For example, the opportunity to discuss decisions has altered people's willingness to contribute to public goods (Caporael et al, 1989; Dawes et al, 1990).

Three types of context criteria may become evident in a discourse involving nature conservation and development decisions:

1   economic factors such as job creation and income generation;
2   socio-demographic factors such as the region's population density, age distribution and education; and
3   environmental factors such as pollution impacts, plant and animal species survival, and aesthetic changes.

Community-based indicators of development and sustainable development have generally reflected these three categories, varying with respect to specific indicator categories reflecting physical/chemical environmental, monetary and non-monetary economic, and social impacts (Cities International, 1996; Selman, 1996).

Communication between researchers and local stakeholders can aid the selection process of relevant indicator categories. Indicators can then be used to evaluate land use planning decisions from a local perspective while taking non-local conservation and protection interests into account. By using a flexible design and an open feedback process, the models can offer refined and integrated development scenarios as input for an informed decision-making process. Sustainable development options can then be identified, evaluated and adjusted rather than offered as the pretence of decision results. In this way, the interaction between credentialled experts and local experts allows for a process of valuation and re-evaluation of development options in which unsustainable practices can be detected and corrected early.

Generally, it has been the outside expert community that has selected relevant indicator categories, as well as evaluated the impacts associated with alternative land uses. Often this expert-based valuation process, however, is not made explicit to those most affected by land use decisions. Instead, it remains hidden behind disciplinary assumptions and implicit valuation methods. Economists, for example, have generally sought to evaluate a selection of economic, social and environmental impacts of alternative land use options by assigning them a common monetary value. Similarly, planning and development interests may use property values, tax revenues or infrastructure as a reference point for evaluating development alternatives. Conservationists may use the impact on wildlife, species diversity, or open space as their primary reference point. By using one commensurate measure of value, or narrowly defined set of valuation criteria, to express the wide variety of quantitative and qualitative effects associated with different land use and development options, complexities are veiled and often simplified to the point of distorting reality. Valuable information is lost in the process and it becomes difficult to correct misperceptions. Assumptions about how different development and conservation options are evaluated become hidden from public scrutiny and are not openly communicated to local decision-makers and those most affected by development decisions.

In contrast, an open and non-coerced discourse of affected individuals and stakeholders invites participants to express their concerns and priorities in an integrated way. People can voice their opinions as citizens rather than as landowners, or as neighbours rather than environmentalists. Broader social interests can be brought to the foreground by admitting the complexities of local and non-local participants' life-worlds to the decision process. Sagoff (1998) coined the term *citizen preferences* to point to the social preferences operative in discourse processes. In this way, the communicative interaction between expert-based models and local-expert valuation may form a much needed basis for improving information about the decision norms and decision criteria that may be operative in land use decisions and land use conflicts.

Participatory Sustainable Development in the Adirondacks

Despite the advantages of participatory decision-making processes, not all processes are created equal. Renn et al (1995) offer an extensive discussion of a variety of discourse models, including citizen advisory councils, planning cells, citizen juries, citizen initiatives and regulatory negotiation. In the worst case scenario, discourse models have been criticized as being manipulative and dishonest and providing a thinly veiled cover-up for pre-decided decisions. To help avoid such a scenario, Renn et al (1995) stress the importance of evaluating different techniques of participatory decision-making based on clearly defined standards of competence and fairness.

Citizen advisory councils, for example, are relatively restricted to a selected group of participants who are generally expected to contribute a particular credentialled expertise to the valuation process. In contrast, citizen juries and planning cells tend to be less exclusive and generally represent a broad cross-section of the affected public. However, citizen juries tend to limit the valuation process to deciding between a limited number of pre-selected options. Acceptance and implementation barriers are typically associated with the selected options. Focus groups tend to select group participants from a broad spectrum of citizens, but generally organize participants into small groups of six to ten according to characteristics associated with typical demographic, socio-economic or other subgroup attributes. Focus groups can thus lack the broad representation of viewpoints that facilitate the communicative reason of discursive interaction. They also tend to be very research-oriented.

Citizen initiatives tend to be more action-oriented and are generally open to and inclusive of a wide variety of perspectives. Initiatives, such as round-table meetings, generally try to inform as well as organize citizens on pertinent environmental and development issues. From this commitment to educating the public, citizen initiatives generally work hard at representing a spectrum of local, experiential and technical knowledge. This can create a powerful force to overcome competence barriers. Projects undertaken by citizen initiatives are often carried by the sheer energy of determined citizens with little institutional support. Citizen initiatives can take the form of activist groups who seek to identify and implement an agenda, or study groups focused on identifying solutions and educating the wider public on the available options. Both types of initiatives are often associated with a roundtable type process in which citizens meet in a format similar to a focus group but with a longer-term commitment to meetings over the duration of a particular agenda item (for examples see IREE, 1996 and Douthwaite, 1996).

Even after designing an appropriate participatory process, many challenges remain. For instance, decision-makers and agencies representing environmental policies or official development agendas may dismiss citizen initiatives as biased or representing limited local views. Efforts at establishing a more participatory process for the evaluation of public and private land use options in the Adirondack Park must therefore go beyond implementing mere local participation and be conscious of the biases to local participation innate in various types of participatory processes. Some examples of ongoing participatory processes in the Adirondacks are presented below. These examples particularly highlight the role of community input into informing and making use of regional research.

Adirondack Research Consortium

In 1994, a small group of academics and representatives of Adirondack non-governmental organizations and state policy organizations met to discuss forming an interdisciplinary society committed to promoting and disseminating research on the region. At the time, extensive research in diverse disciplines was being conducted in the region with little communication to local stakeholders or researchers across disciplines. A local perception had evolved that viewed the academic research community as acquiring research from the region and only reporting the results to national and international meetings and journal publications. There was little incentive and few formal mechanisms to report research back to the Adirondack community.

As a result of this meeting, and with the support of regional colleges and universities with an active Adirondack research agenda, the Adirondack Research Consortium (ARC) was founded to address barriers to information transfer between diverse organizational, political and disciplinary boundaries. The ARC has since sponsored six annual conferences, helped develop the bi-annual *Adirondack Journal of Environmental Studies*, organized an electronic listserv discussion forum, and hosted a web page[1] to aid in regional research. The annual conference has accounted for the bulk of the ARC's activities, where diversity of disciplines and attendance has been the overarching goal. For instance, the third annual conference held in May of 1996 featured a forum with the chairman of commissioners and the executive director of the APA, executive directors of the Adirondack Council and Residents' Committee to Protect the Adirondacks and an Adirondack town supervisor. Paper session and forum participants totalled 62, including: 24 faculty and nine students from fourteen regional universities and colleges; nine representatives from state and federal agencies; fifteen people from not-for-profit organizations; and five representatives of local governments.

By promoting various communication mediums, the ARC has been effective at linking academicians, NGOs and policy-makers, mainly due to the fact that each of these levels is well-organized and can take advantage of electronic communication media. The link from the research community to the local towns and villages is less developed, and possibly inherently flawed due to its top-down nature, although a highlight of the fifth annual conference was a series of forums addressing community development issues which were well attended by citizen activists.

The ARC might be characterized as a citizen initiative; however, the initiative has come largely from a credentialled expert community. There is no pre-selected research agenda, only an obligation to lower the walls between disciplines, the research community and regional stakeholders. Aside from discussion forums, conferences have largely been organized into research reporting sessions where the expectation is to communicate in a non-expert language.

Oswegatchie Roundtable

In the northwest corner of the Park lies a largely undeveloped region in the Oswegatchie and Black River watersheds. This region has a similar land ownership pattern to the Park as a whole, with approximately one-third state and two-thirds private land. In 1996, the Wildlife Conservation Society (founded in 1895 as the New York Zoological Society) helped initiate a series of roundtable meetings involving participants representing private land-holdings, commercial timber companies, state and regional agencies, local governments, conservation organizations and research institutions. The goal was to design and implement a cooperative land stewardship research initiative to identify and implement ecologically and economically sound forest, water and land management policies and practices.

This is a fairly well-defined, sparsely populated region of the Park, creating a higher likelihood for reaching consensus on a land use agenda. Research stemming from roundtable discussions has contributed to better understanding of:

1 poor forest regeneration and productivity;
2 ecological and economic impacts of logging scale, intensity, frequency and regulations;
3 influence of long-term environmental change; and
4 consensus on sustainability criteria and their impact on local communities, business and the Adirondack citizen.

For instance, long-term research plots have been established on private lands to investigate contributing factors to sugar maple regeneration failure (Jenkins, 1995). Roundtable discussions have also provided input into an ongoing, highly politicized discussion of wolf reintroduction in the Adirondacks (Hodgson, 1997).

Lake George Watershed Research

Lake George represents the largest water body wholly within the Park at 32 miles in length and over a mile wide in some areas. The lake and surrounding communities represent the most accessible area of the Park to New York City and New England States, and have long been struggling with population and resource demands from recreation use. At one time considered as one of the world's premier vacation destinations, the region has been left with a legacy of ill-planned development and water quality issues.

The Darrin Fresh Water Institute in Bolton Landing, a research station of Rensselaer Polytechnic Institute, is located on the western shore of Lake George. Founded in 1967, the Fresh Water Institute has been largely concerned with monitoring changes in the lake's water chemistry. During its first 25 years of operation, this research station has produced over 100 graduate theses, 600 scientific reports and exposed more than 250 undergraduate students to a direct, hands-on environmental experience.

Much of this initial research focus was precipitated by local property owners' concern about the deteriorating water quality of Lake George and the resulting threats to the tourism-based local economy. While researchers at the Fresh Water Institute may select a specific water quality research focus and methodology, the Institute's fresh water focus is itself defined by local residents' perty owners' interest in protecting the oligo- to mesotrophic lake's pristine water quality. More recently, the Institute's research agenda has moved from a pure science focus to one that considers both the natural and anthropogenic causation of water quality change. Research now considers both the measurement and the mechanisms for how negative impacts can be avoided without jeopardizing the region's economic viability (O'Hara and Vazquez, 1998; O'Hara et al, forthcoming).

The Institute's long-term presence in the community has allowed for fewer barriers between credentialled experts and local experts. However, despite creating the conditions for participatory decision-making, implementing a truly participatory decision process is not an easy task. The challenge is to balance access to decision-makers with a strategy of including a broader constituent of groups whose views are less represented or even excluded from the decision process (O'Hara, forthcoming). One way of navigating these challenges is by first identifying research agendas and then presenting research findings for scrutiny and possible redefinition to a select group of stakeholders. The process can further be open to broad-based participation by involving local media and citizen groups.

Economic Renewal Programmes

The Rocky Mountain Institute of Colorado has developed a particularly innovative participatory process called Economic Renewal (Kinsley, 1997). The process entails a series of town meetings where participants envision their preferred future. In the process, participants inventory the community's problems, needs and assets. Participants study successes from other towns and discuss ideas for projects to strengthen the community and its economy based on their own inventory of community assets. Initiatives are then designed that make the most sense for their particular circumstances. The intended result is the development of action plans for identified projects.

In 1996, Cornell University's Local Government Programme helped to coordinate the services of the Rocky Mountain Institute to run economic renewal workshops in the Adirondack villages of Indian Lake and Minerva. One of the explicit criteria of the process is to create an atmosphere that invites voluntary community participation. With sufficient citizen interest, a successful economic renewal programme can help identify a set of shared values amongst community stakeholders who may have been at odds with each other in the past. The ultimate goal is to build enough community capacity so that the services of an outside expert are no longer needed.

Indian Lake residents have had a fair amount of success with the economic renewal process. Project leaders were able to define the community's direction and legitimize actions to implement projects. A sample of resulting projects include a new youth centre, the remodelling of an old movie theatre into a centre for community events, a town beautification project, a craft cooperative and a community directory for townspeople and tourists. In addition, veteran business people are now assisting with start-up business plans.

Lessons to be Learned and Challenges to Come

These participatory research initiatives provide some encouraging examples of how to include local voices in research and policy-making. The Adirondack Research Consortium represents an attempt to improve communication both within the research community and between local stakeholders, policy-makers and academic institutions. The Oswegatchie Roundtables are helping to design a well-informed research and policy agenda for the northwest portion of the Park based on a long-term, participatory process. The Darrin Fresh Water Institute represents an encouraging partnership of an applied research station with watershed communities. Assistance from the Rocky Mountain Institute has helped to start a process of economic renewal in the original study communities that is spreading throughout the Park. Each of these examples recognizes the respective roles of credentialled experts and local experts, the power of local citizen participation, and the benefit of carefully designed participatory processes to future Park policy.

These initiatives are coming during another critical era in Park history. During the past two years, over 10 per cent of private Adirondack land has been for sale, most in large, undeveloped lots. For instance, 144,000 acres of land owned by the multinational pulp and paper company, Champion International, was on the market, the sale of which had been structured as part State acquisition and part conservation easement. Unlike the early 1990s, the State has acquisition money available through an Environmental Protection Fund established in 1996 and annually financed primarily by a tax on real estate transfers. A 1996 public referendum also passed a $1.75 billion environmental bond act, of which $150 million was earmarked for open space acquisition (Cox, 1998). The State also has in place a process to prioritize purchases (Kane et al, 1998).

These rapid changes in land ownership and use patterns are resulting in a new economic and stakeholder structure to Park communities, changes that are only beginning to be studied (Erickson et al, 1998). Given the complexity of sustainable development and the historical tension between conservation and development interests, the process of bringing together credentialled and local experts is critical in this new era. Neither community by itself has the technical expertise or the political know-how to ensure a lasting economy–ecology relationship. Participatory planning processes can promote an awareness of local dynamics and the importance of balance. Most importantly, this new policy era is supporting a critical realization of the necessity of context when considering economic, social and environmental dimensions of sustainable development.

Notes

1   http://www.rpi.edu/~erickj/arc/archome.html

10

Policy, Institutions, Values and Biodiversity Conservation in Vanuatu*

Luca Tacconi

Introduction

Participation in conservation activities has been widely applauded but, generally, poorly implemented. A significant challenge to the implementation of participatory approaches is matching the various *external* agendas, such as national conservation and resource use policies and views held by national and international NGOs, with local people's needs and aspirations. For example, in many countries where biodiversity conservation is not progressing well and the state claims control over ecosystems such as forests, conservationists argue for greater participation of local people in resource management, and in many cases call for the devolution of control over forests to local stakeholders.

The objective of this chapter is to discuss the approach adopted in reconciling the national agenda for biodiversity conservation with local needs for development and conservation in Vanuatu, a small island state in the South Western Pacific, and to draw policy implications.

The application of constructivist methodology is discussed before considering the details of the case studies. Relevant institutional and policy aspects are considered, then local people's views and their implications are presented. The case studies of Erromango island and Malekula island highlight a series of issues to be considered by conservation initiatives, and the implications for the theoretical framework presented here are then drawn. A discussion of issues relevant to ICDPs and national conservation policy concludes the chapter.

Methodology

The research process was guided by a need for policy relevance (it had to produce information for decision-making by the Government of Vanuatu), and rigour (Box 10.1), which is a necessary condition for good quality academic research (also expected by the funding agency). Constructivist methodology guided the research process, and it had important implications for the research process.

The relativist ontology made the author aware of the need to understand and document the different perceptions of the natural environment held by the local people and government officers. This informed the application of a dialectic methodology whose aim was to achieve consensus between the views and expectations of the local people and those of government officers. Throughout the research, it was accepted that the findings are influenced by the interaction between the parties to the process. For example, when the landowners[1] asked our advice 'whether it was good or bad to establish a PA or to go ahead with logging', we sought to provide all the information available to us in a balanced way. Had we tried to apply a positivist methodology, we would have simply sought landowners' views and values – possibly just through a questionnaire survey – and would have avoided answering their questions so that we did not affect the research output (by biasing the sample data). The continued interaction between the landowners and ourselves had two beneficial effects. First, it improved their knowledge about conservation and logging issues. Thus, in the case of Erromango, their decision to accept the land lease agreement was based on an information-set richer than the one they had at the beginning of the research process. Second, it helped us in improving our understanding of landowners' needs and wants by discussing with them our views and thoughts. Had we simply carried out questionnaire surveys – as befits the positivist approach as utilized by environmental economics – these useful, and pleasant, interactions would have not eventuated. These interactions are essential in building reciprocal trust, which is a fundamental element in achieving (relative) consensus, an important factor contributing to the solution of environmental issues.

Finally, the research process did not attempt to test specific hypotheses, for instance whether community-based conservation as specified in theory (see Chapter 5) could be applied to Vanuatu. Rather, it sought to find practical ways to assess and establish PAs by taking into account the rights of local people to their land and other resources, the rights of future generations (as recognized in the Constitution), and the need to ensure equity.

Institutions and Policies Affecting Conservation

According to Article 7(d) of the Constitution, one of the fundamental duties of every citizen of Vanuatu is: 'to protect the Republic of Vanuatu and to safeguard the national wealth, resources and environment in the interests of the present generation and of future generations'.

Chapter 12 of the Constitution deals with the issue of land. The first three sections of that chapter state the fundamental principles guiding the post-independence land tenure system. They respectively affirm that:

Box 10.1 Description of research rigour according to constructivist criteria

Prolonged engagement. The author was based in Vanuatu for two and a half years, and interacted on a continuous basis with the relevant stakeholders.

Persistent observation. Six months were spent in total in the research areas considered in this chapter, and several meetings, workshops and discussions about the issues described below were held.

Triangulation. Several tools were used, including rapid rural appraisal, a questionnaire survey, quantitative data for timber volumes assessment and cost–benefit analysis. Key informants were contacted, workshops involving local village people were held, Mr Livo Mele (Research Assistant), with his knowledge of the local culture and environment and continued engagement in field research, helped in cross-checking whether some inferences drawn by the author were sound.

Peer debriefing. This took the form of debriefing by colleagues in the Vanuatu Department of Forestry and the PhD supervisor.

Member checks. The data, interpretations and possible solutions to the questions being analysed were discussed with the stakeholders.

Reports with working hypotheses and thick information. Material summarized in this chapter has been published in academic journals, working papers and conference proceedings.

Impact on stakeholders' capacity to know and act.
1   The local people in Erromango
   •   formed a management committee, which is still active;
   •   increased sandalwood planting for cash income as a result of research;
   •   have good links with relevant government officers in the capital.
2   A land owning group in Malekula
   •   has built two small bungalows to attract visitors to their area, and
   •   is actively engaged in learning about tourist activities and is seeking to attract more visitors.
3   The Department of Forests is in a better position to act on conservation issues because the research presented here appears to have increased
   •   the awareness about conservation issues among forestry staff, and
   •   Mr Livo Mele's (Research Assistant) knowledge of conservation issues and planning (through formal and informal training). At the completion of the research project, Mr Mele set up a Conservation Unit within the Department of Forests with the support of other staff. (After further studies, he has become Director of the Department of Forests.)

Inquiry audit. The research outputs were discussed at a workshop that concluded the activities of the project and involved representatives of national and local level government, donor organizations, NGOs, staff of the Department of Forests and one representative of local people. A review of the research activities was also conducted later by the funding agency and provided a very thorough assessment.

1   all land belongs to the indigenous custom owners and their descendants;
2   custom rules are the basis for the ownership and use of land; and
3   only indigenous citizens, who have acquired land in accordance to custom
    rules, can have perpetual ownership of the land.

A first-hand explanation of the constitutional development process is provided by Narokobi (1981), who worked with the Constitutional Planning Committee. He points out that the particularly strict principles regarding land tenure established in the Constitution are the outcome of the strong bond that ni-Vanuatu[2] have with their land, and the episode of land alienation experienced under European rule.

The relationship between ni-Vanuatu and their land is a fundamental and permanent aspect of Melanesian culture, which colonization and recent history have not been able to change (Bonnemaison, 1984). In the words of the first Minister of Lands of the independent Republic of Vanuatu, 'it is with the land that he [a ni-Vanuatu] defines his identity and it is with land that he maintains his spiritual strength' (cited by Van Trease, 1987, pxi). These sentiments are reflected in the fact that land is not normally sold in Vanuatu.

The rights of landowners to their land are attenuated by the constitutional Articles 76 and 77, which enable the Parliament to legislate in relation to land ownership. They assert that compensation should be paid to those persons whose interests are adversely affected by such legislation. The *Land Acquisition Act* (1992) gives power to the government to declare any area in the country public land, if it is recognized to be of public importance. In theory, this legislation could be used to acquire land for conservation purposes, provided that appropriate compensation was paid to the rightful landowner(s). However, it seems rather unlikely the government would be willing to face the negative political consequences arising from the enforcement of this legislation with the objective of establishing PAs. Because of the strong attachment that people appear to have to their land, attempts at enforcing this legislation even for development purposes (eg building rural airstrips) could result in social and political unrest.

The need to establish PAs is outlined in the *National Conservation Strategy* (Environment Unit, 1993), developed through an extensive community consultation process. However, before the introduction of the *National Parks Act* (1993) Vanuatu did not have any law enabling the government or private organizations to establish PAs. Nevertheless, landowners and chiefs traditionally have had the capacity to declare a particular site (or resource) a taboo area (resource). This prerogative has been used extensively throughout the country, normally to regulate the use of, or to protect, small areas of forest, reefs and specific species. An emerging problem affecting the use of these traditional methods is that the respect for the traditional rights of landowners and chiefs is being eroded in several areas of Vanuatu. This is due to cultural changes, partly brought about by an increased reliance on the cash economy and the resulting increase of demands on natural resources.

People's Views and Use of Forests

People's views about, and knowledge of, logging operations, the contribution of non-timber forest products (NTFPs) to local people's livelihood, and their views about conservation are all factors that influence decisions concerning the allocation of forest ecosystems to different uses. Conservation initiatives cannot assume that local people will conserve the forest because they own it. Therefore, their views were actively sought at the outset of the research process.

The views of the local people are detailed below by relying mainly on answers to a questionnaire. Seventy-five household heads were interviewed. This sample represents about 34 per cent of the households enumerated in Erromango during the 1989 national population census. The total population of the island has been estimated at 1254 inhabitants. The population density is low at 1.4 inhabitants per km².

Views and Knowledge about Logging Activities

Of a total 75 respondents, 28 did not own land with merchantable logs. Therefore, only the views of the people owning forests with merchantable timber are considered in relation to views about logging activities. These are summarized in Table 10.1 and are rather self-explanatory.

Landowners appear to have a reasonable degree of understanding of the potential positive and negative aspects of logging activities. However, this seems to be more so in relation to positive aspects than negative ones, as indicated by the higher 'do not know' percentage. The income generating potential of logging activities appears to be the main concern. This was often cited together with the expectation that the logging company would build a road. Currently, the majority of the villages in Erromango do not have road access and pack animals are not available.[3]

Use and Collection of Non-Timber Forest Products

Potential and actual uses of NTFPs have been found to be sizeable in several studies (eg de Beer and McDermott, 1989; Grimes et al, 1994). Other authors have questioned the economic viability of NTFPs collection as an option to be undertaken on a large scale or even at the micro-level (Browder, 1992; Pinedo-Vasquez et al, 1992).

The frequency of collection of NTFPs and the location where this occurs, and recreational visits to the forest were considered in the questionnaire (Table 10.2), and were validated through rapid rural appraisal, as described later in the chapter. The question relating to NTFPs aimed at ascertaining whether local people made extensive use of closed canopy (relatively undisturbed) forests (ie *dark bush*). These are the forests which may be of greater conservation value, and are richer in timber relative to disturbed forests, which are normally closer to villages and have been used for gardening purposes (ie shifting cultivation).

Table 10.1 *Views and knowledge about logging activities*
(Number of respondents: 47)

Have you recently signed a logging contract?

Yes 37 (78.7%)   Not yet 6 (12.8%)   Not interested 4 (8.5%)

How do you plan to use the area once it has been logged?

Activity	Number of citations	Percentage
No current plan	19	33.9
Cattle project	16	28.6
Replant logged areas	10	17.9
Coconut plantation	4	7.1
Plant sandalwood	4	7.1
Plant kava[a]	1	1.8
Plant coffee	1	1.8
Make garden	1	1.8

What are the positive aspects of logging?

Positive aspects	Number of citations	Percentage
Do not know	3	4.2
I do not like logging, no positive aspects	3	4.2
It generates income	27	38.0
The logging company will build a road	25	35.2
Sawn timber will become available	7	9.9
Logging brings employment	3	4.2
The company will replant trees	2	2.8
The company will build a school	1	1.4

What are the negative aspects of logging?

Negative aspects	Number of citations	Percentage
Do not know	10	13.7
No negative aspects	1	1.4
Some damage; ok if distant from village	1	1.4
It pollutes rivers	24	32.9
Trees left standing are damaged	11	15.1
It damages the environment	7	9.6
Fish die	6	8.2
The soil is negatively affected	3	4.1
It damages custom sites	3	4.1
It pollutes the sea	2	2.7
It creates problems for the birds	2	2.7
It damages fruit trees and other useful plants	2	2.7
Timber cut is left in the forest	1	1.4

Note: a *Piper methysticum*

Table 10.2 *Frequency of visit to the dark bush for collection of NTFPs and recreation (percentages in parenthesis)*

Purpose	Daily	Weekly	Monthly	Biannually	Yearly	Never	Number of respondents
Custom leaves[a]				2	14	58	74
				(4.1)	(18.9)	(78.4)	(100)
Building materials[b]					14	59	73
					(19.2)	(80.8)	(100)
Firewood						73	73
						(100)	(100)
Hunting[c]	24	21	5	1		23	74
	(32.4)	(28.4)	(6.8)	(1.4)		(31.1)	(100)
Fruit and nuts			5	26		41	72
			(6.9)	(36.1)		(56.9)	(100)
Prawns and fish[d]			23	13	3	34	73
			(31.5)	(17.8)	(4.1)	(46.6)	(100)
Rest[e]			4	9	7	53	73
			(5.5)	(12.3)	(9.6)	(72.6)	(100)

Notes:
a   Medicinal plants and other plants that are used for customary uses, eg spiritual.
b   Used for the construction of traditional housing, eg thatched huts.
c   Wild pigs and feral cattle.
d   Fresh water ones.
e   The Bislama (pidgin English) word used in the interview was spell, which refers to rest and relaxation.

The general picture derived from the table is that the majority of the respondents visit the *dark bush* rather sporadically with the aim of collecting NTFPs. The explanation of this behaviour, provided by several respondents during the questionnaire survey and informal discussions, is that NTFPs are normally available – wild or planted – in garden areas or in secondary vegetation near the villages. Thus, local people do not derive many NTFPs from the *dark bush*, and if logging operations were to be carried out, the availability of NTFPs would not be reduced. This argument is strengthened by the fact that clear felling operations do not take place in Vanuatu.

Views about Conservation and Future Generations

The question whether 'it is important not to log *part* of the forest' (Table 10.3) was drafted with the objective of ascertaining people's views in relation to conservation within a *real world* framework. Logging operations are being carried out in Vanuatu. It was assumed that this would continue and that the landowners being interviewed may be eventually interested in having at least part of their forest logged. The answers are reported, as closely as possible, according to the original wording used by the respondents. Answers that may be interpreted as based on similar reasons have been grouped together. Some respondents provided multiple reasons.

Table 10.3 *Attitudes towards avoiding logging in part of the forest*

Do you think that it is important not to log part of the forest?	No 1	Yes 67	Don't know 7
Number of respondents: 75			
Reasons for not logging part of the forest (yes answers only)			
No reason given	8		

		Total	Percentage
Group A			
A1: Wait and see if the logging company operates well	1		
A2: Do not log in areas which are difficult to access	1		
A3: I would conserve the forest that is not good for logging	1	3	4.2
Group B			
B1: Keep some forest as resource for the future (eg garden, timber)	8		
B2: Conserve some areas to protect timber and fruit trees	7		
B3: Conserve forest close to village, rivers and sea	5	20	28.2
Group C			
C1 Tourists may want to visit	5	5	7
Group D			
D1: It is good for the environment	10		
D2: I like the forest the way it is	2		
D3: Protect birds and animals	8	20	28.2
Group E			
E1: To conserve our heritage	3		
E2: Our children will see the forest	16		
E3: Our children will have good areas to make gardens, to collect seed	4	23	32.4
Total		71	100

Answers A2 and A3 appear to express no interest in the long-term conservation of forests that hold timber resources and are accessible. Answer A1 appears to express interest in logging activities provided the logging company can be expected to adopt good logging practices. Group B includes answers that appear to indicate interest in conserving part of the forest for its direct and indirect values. Clearly, future utilization of the forest for gardening activities would result in a modification in the forest structure. The respondents seem to associate avoidance of logging activities with potential tourist activities, Group C, in relatively few cases. The answers that appear to express an

Table 10.4 *Importance of establishing a protected area for the children*

Could you tell us whether you think that it is not important, not really important, do not know, important, or very important, that the government establishes a protected area for the children to see the kauri trees.
(Number of respondents: 75)

Not important	Of little importance	Don't know	Important	Very important
0	0	15	6	54
		(20%)	(8%)	(72%)

interest in the conservation of the environment are in Group D. These could express a variety of values.[4] Group E seems to express a clear interest in not logging part of the forest in order to ensure conservation that would benefit part of the current generation – the children already born – and future generations. Answer E3 does not necessarily imply that there is an expectation the forest will be conserved in the future. The data presented may be interpreted as indicating that the majority of the respondents (Group D and Group E) support the conservation of part of the forest because of their concern for the environment and the benefit of future generations.[5]

The analysis presented above suggests that the people of Erromango are interested in conserving the forest, among other things, for the benefit of their present and future children. This view is supported by the fact that the respondents reported their interest in this issue without actually being asked directly. A further question, aimed at openly eliciting people's views about future generations[6] corroborates this conclusion (Table 10.4). The large majority of the respondents thought that it was either very important or important to establish a PA so that the children could see Kauri trees (*Agathis macrophylla*).

Reflections

In concluding this section, we note three major issues. First, local people are both interested in using and conserving the forest. Therefore, there is a need to work with the local people to develop plans that allow for timber production, subsistence use, conversion of forested areas to agriculture and forest conservation.

Second, people seem to display both self-interested and other-regarding behaviour. Conservation initiatives may benefit from supporting those people who express conservation interests. The strengthening of their capacity to protect their environment may result in the establishment of PAs. However, it should not be forgotten that people's self-interest has to be taken into account. There are cases where people may want to sell their forest resources to derive cash income. If the forest in question is important for biodiversity conservation, alternative sources of income need to be provided to the owners of the forest.

Third, lack of information may be at times a constraint on informed decision-making. However, it should not be assumed that simply supplying more information will be sufficient to allow local people to make informed decisions. Making informed decisions is a combination of availability of information and capacity to process it. There may be cases when the landowners do not have the capacity to assess the information, because of a lack of familiarity with the issues in question, or a cultural barrier between them and the external people wanting to exchange information with them. In these cases, improved decision-making will be the result of a long-term learning process that will have to bring down cultural barriers and improve people's ability to process the information. Participatory approaches are important to address this issue, but it should not be assumed that they necessarily lead to well-informed decision-making over the short-term. A long-term commitment is required. Within this long-term commitment, it should be recognized that landowners, when well-informed, or at any time during the process, may choose to have logging undertaken on their land. If the aim of the specific project is to achieve a conservation outcome, then, as noted above, financial incentives may have to be provided to the landowners to achieve this objective.

The case studies discuss in detail the above issues as well as other aspects concerning conservation activities.

The Erromango Kauri Protected Area

The first case study relates to an area of kauri forest on the island of Erromango, the Erromango Kauri Protected Area (EKPA).

The issues researched and the research approach and tools adopted depended partly on the historical conditions existing at the beginning of the research process. Specifically, as a result of negotiations that had been occurring between the landowners and the government (since the mid-1980s) before the onset of the research process, the landowners expected the government to lease their land to establish the EKPA. This influenced the approach to the assessment of local development and conservation needs and the design of the incentive framework.

Given that the landowners had already been offered an agreement to lease their land for conservation purposes, it may not have been in their interest to reveal whether they would protect the forest without government intervention. In fact, this would have reduced the likelihood of them receiving compensation payments. Therefore, the assessment of their development and conservation needs through a participatory research approach appeared not to be appropriate. It may be noted that one of the landowners suggested that he was thinking of protecting the area even if the government did not intervene. This intent could have been due to an interest in conserving the environment in its current state and/or in protecting the land in order to pass it on to his children. However, other landowners either did not openly express their intent in relation to the area or had previously signed a logging contract.

Therefore, it was decided to consider the contribution of subsistence uses of forest products to the local people's livelihood, using rapid rural appraisal tools, and the potential value of logging royalties. This assessment was thought to provide an indication of whether the landowners would conserve the forest without external intervention.

The assessment showed that the local people depend on the secondary forest close to the village for their subsistence requirements. Shifting cultivation, fuelwood collection and provision of building materials do not take place in the EKPA. The collection of medicinal plants and food in the EKPA is also very limited. This implies that landowners would not face shortages of subsistence produce were they to allow logging in the EKPA. By not allowing logging, they would forgo financial benefits in the form of logging royalties. These had to be estimated to assess the amount of compensation to be provided to landowners.

Two issues relating to the question of compensation had to be clarified before proceeding to the definition of the compensation package. First, it was not evident that a land lease agreement was the option favoured by the landowners. Also, it was unclear both to the landowners and the Department of Forests how much, in terms of lease payments, would represent a sufficient compensation for the benefits forgone by the landowners. The assessment of these issues was carried out with the landowners through a participatory approach.

Discussions were held with the landowners on the possibility of developing an income-generating project in exchange for the landowners' undertaking to protect the forest. They did not favour this option. They argued that the development of economic activities in the area is constrained by the lack of roads and access to markets. Also, it is obvious that, for the landowners, an income-generating project is riskier than a lease agreement. The option of building a road to link their villages to the closest airstrip and boat landing was then considered. A road could be built in exchange for the landowners' commitment to conserve the forest area. One of the landowners noted that this option would have been accepted if it had been presented to a village meeting. However, he did not agree with it. He is the owner of the land and the road project would not provide him with the benefits he expected.

The option of a lease agreement was therefore considered in detail. The land use options open to the landowners were:

1   signing a lease agreement with the government (with the details to be defined), or
2   allowing logging operations to go ahead, without the possibility of leasing the land afterwards.

The discounted values of a 75 year lease[7] on the land and of logging royalties were calculated and presented to the landowners (Table 10.5). They decided that a land lease agreement satisfied their financial expectations and agreed to offer their land for lease to the government at the rate of 100 vatu/ha/year. The signing of the agreement took place in 1995. This rate is to be revised in accordance with any increases in lease payments for unimproved agricultural

Table 10.5 *Present value of protected area lease and timber royalty*

Proposed protected area	Discount rate		
3257 ha	0	4%	8%
Present value of:			
Fixed rate lease	24,427,500	8,021,217	4,383,261
(100 vt/ha/year; 75 years)			
Increasing rate lease	44,376,625	11,364,178	5,303,464
(100 vt/ha/year and 25 vt/ha/year increase every 10 years; 75 years)			
Timber royalties			
Low range	9,429,022	8,382,366	7,485,062
High range	16,689,517	14,836,920	13,248,677

Note: Vatu (vt) 115 = US$ 1
Source: Tacconi and Bennett (1995).

land on Erromango set by the Department of Lands. The lease agreement – drafted together with the landowners, one of the two village chiefs, a representative of the youth and the women's representative– allows, within limits, the use for subsistence purposes of the EKPA. These activities are regulated by the management committee of the EKPA. The structure of the management committee is such that the landowners maintain their customary control over the EKPA.

Protected Areas in Malekula Island

The approach to the identification, assessment and establishment of PAs developed for Malekula island is designed to establish PAs that are consistent with local people's needs and wants in relation to development and conservation. The individual PAs were identified and assessed through a participatory planning process. Whether a PA should or should not be established, its boundaries, the resource use rules to be applied and the term of the PA were defined through research carried out with the landowners and chiefs.

First meetings were held with landowners who had approached the provincial government, or the author, asking for assistance in establishing a PA, or had rights to areas that had been indicated as potential PAs by the provincial government. We carried out a first round of visits to the areas proposed for conservation status in order to introduce ourselves to the villagers, to identify some of the owners of the areas identified by the provincial government, and to find out whether the landowners were interested in pursuing some form of conservation.

At the beginning of the first meeting for each PA, we stressed that the objective of our work was to help landowners assess their conservation needs and wants, if they were interested in doing so. At the beginning of these meetings, we noted that:

- the provincial government intended to establish PAs, and it had identified certain areas; and
- one objective of the visit was to assess with the landowners whether they were interested in protecting these areas, or other areas, and to find out what other conservation issues they needed to pursue.

In presenting the second point, we made clear that we had no intention to impose any decision on them and that the provincial government did not have the power to do so. We emphasized that landowners would be helped in protecting their resources, if they needed and wanted to do so. In every area visited the response of the landowners to our visit appeared to be positive. Therefore, arrangements were made to carry out detailed work in their areas.

During further visits to each of the areas, the assessment of conservation needs and ways of achieving these were carried out jointly by the landowners and ourselves through group and individual meetings, analysis of topographic maps, analysis of livelihood sources and development aspirations and options, and surveys of forest, agricultural and marine resources.

The following issues were discussed before actually proceeding with the detailed assessment of local conservation needs:

1   positive and negative aspects of logging operations, in relation to both ecological and socio-economic impacts;
2   meaning of the concept of resource conservation; and
3   meaning of the concept of PA.

The following major issues were addressed in group and individual meetings.

- Should logging activities be allowed in the area, or part of the area (controlled by the landowners taking part in the meeting)? If yes, in which areas?
- Should agricultural activities be carried out in any part of the area being considered?
- Should water sources be protected? If yes, how?
- Should specific forest resources and/or marine resources be collected for commercial and/or subsistence purposes? Should the use of some of these resources be banned?
- Should some of the resources, considered above, be left for the use of future generations?
- Should a PA be established? What area should it include? What is the term of the PA?
- Are the resources allocated to consumption sufficient for the population (current and future) living near to the area?

Together with the landowners, five areas (of which three comprise both forest and marine ecosystems) were identified and assessed. Detailed management plans for the PAs resulted from the assessment process. The PAs may be described as multiple use areas. They comprise zones dedicated to the conservation of forest resources, zones where agricultural activities are allowed, zones dedicated to the conservation of marine resources. Specific rules developed by the landowners apply to the use of the various resources found in the different zones. For example, they regulate the use of wood and non-timber forest products in forest conservation zones, the collection of shellfish and the protection of marine turtles in marine conservation zones.

During the assessment process, landowners' interest in conservation seemed to be motivated by two main factors:

- they appeared to be interested in protecting the environment in its own right by expressing concern about the impact of logging activities; and
- they appeared to be interested in deriving longer term benefits from the environment than those arising from logging activities.

Landowners' decisions about resource management were also influenced by other landowners' behaviour. On more than one occasion, landowners asked about the decisions made by other landowners in relation to the establishment of PAs. On one occasion, a landowner decided to establish a PA following the example of a nearby community that had taken the initiative to establish a PA. In another case, landowners decided to expand the boundaries of a PA on the basis of the decision made by other landowners.

In order to implement the participatory approach described above, an appropriate institutional structure was devised. Conservation legislation (a by-law) to be adopted by the provincial government was drafted in collaboration with the Attorney General's Office of the Government of Vanuatu. The by-law is aimed at establishing PAs by strengthening traditional customary rights to resources. According to the by-law, the provincial government may declare a PA upon the request of the landowners, who specify the boundaries, resource use rules (eg strict preservation, or multiple use PAs) and the term of the PA. The official declaration of the areas assessed in Malekula will take place when the by-law is enforced.

Discussion about the Theoretical Framework

The ecological economic framework adopted here combines elements that are characteristic of the established ecological economics literature (eg sustainability and intergenerational distribution concerns) with elements taken fom the rural development literature (eg participatory assessment processes). These two fields are brought together on a basis of constructivist methodology. It was shown that the expression and reconciliation of a variety of behaviours and interests (eg self-interested – other-regarding) within and between individuals and communities is facilitated by the integration of participatory decision-making processes and more standard economic tools such as basic cost–benefit analysis. This framework is more suited to the implementation of a strategic approach to the conservation of forests and biodiversity than the neo-classical environmental economic framework. The latter may prove useful in assessing resource allocation issues at *the margin*.

The research took as a given that biodiversity is a critical attribute of renewable natural capital and that conserving biodiversity assists in protecting critical life support functions. Consistent with the Constitution and the National Conservation Strategy, the establishment of a system of PAs in Vanuatu was seen as a measure needed to move towards sustainable resource use, and to achieve minimal intergenerational equity. As a result, the analysis of the specific areas in Erromango and Malekula did not involve an economic analysis (such as cost–benefit analysis) aimed at answering the question whether the PAs should be established or not. Such a question would have been considered if a neo-classical economic approach had been adopted.

The distributional aspects of the conservation initiatives were considered. In the case of Erromango, where the PA proposal was initiated by the government, particular attention was given to the compensation of the monetary benefits forgone by the landowners and to ensuring that their subsistence activities could be carried out within the PA. Note that if a neo-classical economic analysis had been undertaken, and it had found that the PA should be established, then according to the potential Pareto improvement test no actual compensation would have been required. In Erromango, a simple application of cost–benefit analysis was used to inform the landowners about the financial value of the alternative options of logging and land leasing. This also helped the assessment of the appropriate level of compensation.

Several institutional features were considered in the course of the application of the framework. In Erromango, the structure of property and resource use rights was considered and informed the design of the land lease agreement and the compensation package, and the process of participatory decision-making. A further institutional aspect of the work undertaken in Erromango relates to the proposal for the establishment of the Vanuatu Biodiversity Conservation Trust Fund. This initiative was itself informed by the analysis of the local institutions, and can be used to make lease payments and support initiatives across the country.[8] In Malekula, institutional analysis involved the study of the local resource management institutions, the development of resource use rules applying to the proposed PAs, and the design of a provincial by-law aimed at supporting the local customary rights.

The participation process during the work in Vanuatu involved landowners, national government departments and provincial governments. In Erromango, the participation of the landowners was initially limited to involvement in the rapid rural appraisal, when the assessment of the need for government intervention was undertaken. Then, the landowners themselves decided whether they were interested in taking up the offer of a land lease agreement. Once a positive decision was made, they participated in the drafting of the lease agreement, and currently manage the area. In Malekula, the landowners were fully involved in (and in one case initiated) the identification of areas to be protected and the resource use rules to be applied. The provincial government was involved in proposing broad geographical areas to be considered for conservation and in developing the protected area by-law. The Department of Forests supported the work of the project with staff and resources and, once the project was concluded, it took over the task of carrying out conservation work by establishing a Conservation Unit.

Concluding Comments

In recent years, a great deal of attention has been devoted to the establishment of ICDPs. These projects are facing several problems (see Chapter 11) including:

1   often there is only a weak link between income generation activities and conservation;
2   the income generating potential of the projects is often lower than the revenues from activities non-compatible with biodiversity conservation; and
3   income generating projects may take a relatively longer time to bear fruit compared to logging activities.

In some cases a simple attempt to develop income generating activities is not sufficient to convince the local people to opt for the conservation option. Testimony to this is the recent demise of the Lak ICDP in Papua New Guinea, where landowners have opted for the logging option (McCallum and Sekhran, 1997). Therefore, the question of benefits provided to the different stakeholders needs to be addressed in detail by conservation initiatives. The analysis presented in this chapter has relevant implications for ICDPs, and a comparison of relevant aspects of conservation leases and ICDPs is presented in Table 10.6. The adoption of one approach does not exclude the other. Depending on the situation, they may well need to be used jointly. For example, the Department of Forests in Vanuatu, after having established a lease agreement, is attempting to support local development initiatives that are complementary to conservation such as sandalwood cultivation.

In relation to policy implications, the approaches to PA identification, assessment and establishment adopted in Malekula and Erromango have their place in a national approach to conservation, especially in countries where traditional land rights are still significant. The first step towards the implementation of a system of PAs may be carried out by establishing PAs through a process of participatory land use planning. This process may lead to the establishment of PAs that are consistent with local people's needs and wants in relation to development and conservation. The PAs thus established are to be regarded as the first component of a complete PA system. Once these PAs are established, the next step should be a conservation gap assessment. That study would identify ecosystems that should be granted protected status on the basis of ecological criteria, but that have not been covered by the PAs established in

Table 10.6 *Comparing conservation leases with ICDPs*

Characteristics	Leases	ICDPs
Stability of income to community	High	Uncertain
Time to first income for community	Immediate	Medium to long-term
Risk of income failure from community perspective	Nil	Variable, depending on activities, local skills etc
Beneficiaries of funds allocated to the initiative	Resource owners	Consultants, government departments, NGOs, resource owners
Local resources required to maintain project	Nil	Labour, know-how, management skills, natural resources
Assumption about beneficiaries' development	Beneficiaries can manage the income received to forward their development	Beneficiaries need external advice and support to achieve appropriate development.
External inputs required to maintain project	Financial resources	Technical advice, financial resources
Direct contribution to increase in local skills	Nil	Low to high, depending on type of project
Contribution to strengthening conservation relevant institutions	Nil to medium, depending on agreement	Low to high, depending on project characteristics
Impact on nutrition	Indirect through increased purchase of food	Direct through increased food production, and/or indirect
Impact on health	Indirect through increased purchase of health services	Direct through possible provision of health service, and/or indirect
Increase in local commitment to conservation	Unknown	Unknown
Financial sustainability	Dependent on external funding	Dependent on external support/funding in the short-term, may become self-sufficient in the medium to long-term
Economic sustainability	Is a cost to society, but may contribute to increase in future activity if beneficiaries invest the funds	May contribute to increase in future economic activities
Social sustainability	May generate disputes between those receiving rents and those not	Disputes may arise about resource distribution

Characteristics	Leases	ICDPs
Ecological sustainability	Potentially high, if subsistence activities are not a threat	Potentially high, but depends on impacts of income generating activities and subsistence activities
Link between instrument and conservation, from local perspective	Strong	Normally weak
Moral hazard problem[a]	Nil, if payment is not made on a lump-sum basis	High
Enforcement of conservation agreement	Relatively easy, if payment is not made on a lump-sum basis	Complex

Note: a The moral hazard problem is linked to the provision of benefits, such as social services, in exchange for a commitment to conservation. This problem arises when local communities find that threatening the ecosystems or species being conserved brings them benefits. In other words, they may threaten to cause damage unless they are provided with more benefits.

the first phase. If gaps exist, these should be filled through the establishment of other PAs. If the establishment of these latter areas conflicts with the interests of the local people, this process could then follow the approach adopted for the establishment of the EKPA. That is, compensation should be provided to the parties that have been made worse off by the establishment of a PA.

Notes

*   This chapter draws on Tacconi (1995, 1997), Tacconi and Bennett (1995b, 1997).

1   Because of the land tenure system (next section), almost every person in Vanuatu is a landowner, and lack of access to land (at least for food crops) is basically unknown. Control over land resources varies across the country due to cultural differences (eg matrilineal and patrilineal systems) and social and geographic factors (eg population density).

2   Indigenous citizen.

3   It is often argued that insecurity of land tenure and the existence of roads contribute to tropical deforestation (eg Verlome and Moussa, 1999). It is suggested here that deforestation may occur even in the presence of land tenure security, and that the need for roads is actually a driving factor in landowners' decisions to have their areas logged.

4   The respondents could have expressed self-interested behaviour (ie protect the environment because they like it) or purely other-regarding behaviour (ie protect the environment because other species have a right to exist).

5   It could be argued that Group B could also be added as it may refer to benefits for future generations.

6   The need to address this issue was raised by Redclift (1992). Studies regarding natural resources and the attitudes of people living in rural areas of developing countries have considered people's attitudes towards the environment, forests,

protected areas, income generating activities carried out with park areas, resettlement from park areas and wildlife (eg Hackel, 1990; Infield, 1988; Newmark et al 1993; Parry, 1992; Stycos and Duarte, 1994).

7   Maximum duration of a land lease allowed by existing legislation.

8   For details of the Fund see Tacconi and Bennett (1997). The Minister of Forests approved the Fund in 1998 and has approached donors seeking to capitalize it.

11

Negotiating Agendas in Biodiversity Conservation: the India Ecodevelopment Project, Karnataka

Sanghamitra Mahanty

Introduction

The Rajiv Gandhi National Park in Karnataka (referred to here as Nagaraholé) is one of seven parks in India receiving assistance under the India Ecodevelopment Project from the World Bank and Global Environment Facility. Such interventions must negotiate complex relationships from the international to the local scale, between actors, landscape and formal and informal institutions. This chapter examines how these interactions shape the evolution of an intervention and its likely outcomes, and the broader implications for conservation programmes.

I begin with an overview of the Ecodevelopment Project in the context of the ICDP model. An exploratory analytical framework is presented, focusing on the actors in Nagaraholé in relation to their landscape and their institutional context. Finally, emerging issues for the Ecodevelopment Project and the broader relevance of these findings are outlined. The analytical framework used here highlights previously unquestioned assumptions about actors, landscape and institutions in ICDPs, with broader implications for conservation interventions generally.

Integrated Conservation and Development Projects

Current approaches to biodiversity conservation have been shaped by discourses on sustainable development and participatory development over recent decades (Wright, 1994). The ICDP approach is one outcome of the international quest for appropriate conservation models in this vein. The articulation of key concepts by Wells and Brandon (1992) and Brown and Wyckoff-Baird (1992), together with the rise of participatory methodologies have helped ICDPs to rise as a conservation model of choice amongst donor agencies and NGOs. The ICDP symbolizes key issues facing conservation today: a quest for balance between conservation and development, tensions between local and global agendas, and the involvement of actors at many levels.

The India Ecodevelopment Project is one such undertaking, proceeding at Nagaraholé and six other national parks around India, with funding from Central and State Governments (US$14.6 million), credit from the International Development Association/World Bank (US$28 million) and a Global Environment Facility grant (US$20 million). The Project objectives include:

- improved PA management through capacity building and local participation;
- village ecodevelopment to simultaneously reduce negative impacts of local people on PAs and of PAs on local people; and
- developing more support for PA management and ecodevelopment through environmental awareness and research activities.

Project designers note the significant pressures posed by population growth, commercial pressure, and poverty, which cannot all be addressed in the scope of the Ecodevelopment Project. Documentation specifically mentions the need to engender a commitment within government to local participation, and to avoid a blueprint approach to project design and implementation. The use of third party contracts, especially for NGOs, which are able to apply participatory approaches, is another important feature (World Bank, 1996, ppii–iii). In this chapter, the term *Ecodevelopment Project* refers only to project activities in Nagaraholé, while *India Ecodevelopment Project* refers to the national programme.

The Ecodevelopment Project is moving ahead in what might be described as the twilight of the ICDP era. After a decade of enthusiastic promotion of ICDPs, the approach is now being questioned, and in some cases abandoned, by practitioners, donor agencies and NGOs. Some have questioned the capacity of ICDPs to deliver equitable outcomes to local stakeholders (various papers in Ghimire and Pimbert, 1997). Others have found that economic, political and institutional factors beyond the sphere of influence of the project diminish project performance (Wells et al, 1998). A number of project-specific problems in resource management, institutional development and enterprise development have also been identified (World Wildlife Fund (US), 1997; Biodiversity Conservation Network, 1999). Others have suggested that ICDPs are too costly for the limited population reached (United States Agency for International Development: USAID, 1997).

Many such analyses seek regionally, nationally and even internationally relevant lessons and prescriptions from the ICDP experience, to assist practitioners refine and evolve new models. The World Wildlife Fund (US), for instance, concludes that its new post-ICDP direction should be *ecoregional planning*, targeting larger and more biologically coherent areas than ICDPs with broader ranging strategies (1997, p43). This kind of landscape or regional approach has also been favoured by USAID and other conservation agencies (USAID, 1997; Hannah et al, 1998). These new approaches are unlikely to improve equity in negotiations amongst actors at various scales since their founding analyses have not examined the nature of this negotiation process. An exploratory analysis of how actors engage with the intervention process could thus highlight important issues for future conservation programmes.

Analytical Framework and Methods for the Nagaraholé Study

A Post-positivist Paradigm

In contrast with the direction of global efforts towards building models and blueprints for conservation, post-positivist theorists highlight the problems in developing generalized prescriptions or predictive models, and instead direct attention to understanding relationships and perspectives contextually (Guba, 1990). The research paradigm for the Nagaraholé study is post-positivist in this broad sense, exploring the evolution of the project contextually, rather than testing a generalizable hypothesis from which models or prescriptions might be developed. The study is also based on an assumption that the researcher's values and experience have shaped the focus and approach to the inquiry, and aims to understand the differing realities of various actors.

Moving from localized understanding to broader comparison, as is proposed here, pushes the boundaries of post-positivist inquiry, where prediction and generalization are often not amongst the aims (Lincoln and Guba, 1985). This study undertakes a comparison between ICDPs, not to draw broad generalizations, but rather to check whether the issues identified in Nagaraholé resonate in specific cases elsewhere. The resulting analysis highlights issues for other researchers and practitioners to assess in a context and case specific light.

Undertaking exploratory, qualitative research of this kind is in itself a process of negotiation. To professionals and academics trained in a positivist mode within comfortable disciplinary boundaries, qualitative data collection methods might appear unfamiliar, unreliable and biased. Being exploratory rather than prescriptive, the approach may also be regarded as less directly relevant to the policy realm. For the researcher, these factors contribute to a fundamental tension: how to maintain dialogue with the actors operating in a positivist mould, while maintaining the essence and spirit of their inquiry. One outcome of this dialogue could be to sensitize professionals to the value of reflective research, and to the range of methods available to improve the credibility of data, such as triangulation, peer debriefing and member checks.

Actors, Landscape and Institutions

The term *actor* is defined here as a locus of decision and action; a functional notion, which focuses on what actors do, rather than attributes such as class or gender (Hindess, 1988). In Hindess' definition, actors might be either *individuals* or social groupings and organizations that exhibit the capacity for decision-making and action as an entity. Social groupings based on class or gender would not be regarded as actors unless they were organized to take joint action in some way.

The actor-oriented approach advocated by Norman Long (1992) suggests that institutions are realized and changed through the agency of actors, and in fact that macro phenomena are only intelligible in situated micro contexts. Rather than see an intervention as a means to a predictable, pre-specified end, it is viewed as a process of transformation, in which actors engage and negotiate (Long, 1992; Uphoff, 1992). A key objective of research is to understand the differing realities of actors, the interactions amongst actors, and between actors and institutions. In addition to these elements, the Nagaraholé study adds the actor–landscape interaction to the analysis – a necessity in dealing with a resource-oriented intervention. The analytical focus is on:

- interactions between actors at various scales,
- interactions between actors and landscape over time, and
- interactions between actors and their institutional context.

I consider how these interactions influence the Ecodevelopment Project, and reflect on similarities and differences with other ICDPs (Figure 11.1).

Field Methods

The Nagaraholé case was selected because it exemplifies key elements of the debate around people and parks in India, which revolve around human use and habitation of PAs. As an ICDP, the Ecodevelopment Project has faced delays and conflict, and might be regarded as a problematic rather than best-case example. The conflict between actors in Nagaraholé contributes to its interest as a case study for the purpose of examining the negotiation process in an intervention. Conflict highlights the values and views of actors in an explicit and legible way, as they engage in debate, try to promote their perspectives and eagerly seek out listeners to persuade. On the other hand the researcher also needs to be sensitive to quieter actors with a softer voice, and be alert to the danger of receiving and projecting a caricatured picture of relationships and issues.

The views of various actors were explored through semi-structured interviews conducted with individuals and groups involved in the Ecodevelopment

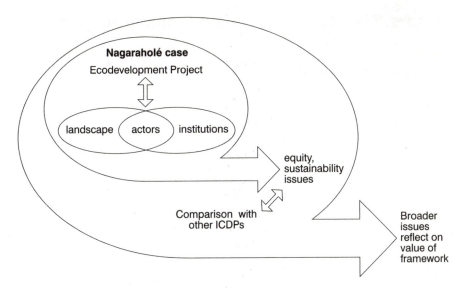

Figure 11.1 *Analytical framework for the Nagarahólé study*

Project and the Nagarahólé area. Informal discussion and participant observation, for instance accompanying NGO and Forest Department staff on village visits, complemented interviews. Historical documentation in the form of working plans, annual reports and gazetteers, and more recent park management plans, provided important historical background on the people–landscape relationship. A revisit to key actor organizations and the Nagarahólé area after initial data analysis enabled dialogue with actors on emerging themes and a check on the researchers' perceptions and analysis of the initial data, a process referred to as member checking (Lincoln and Guba, 1985).

Fieldwork was undertaken with the help of an interpreter because of time constraints and my lack of familiarity with the local language (Kannada). While this inhibited the spontaneity of discussion to some extent, it was an asset in other respects. The interpreter's presence actually accelerated my knowledge of local systems and conditions, and our discussions provided a constant check on my evolving ideas, assumptions and methods, which could then be documented. Important factors that enabled constructive collaboration with an interpreter included selection of an interpreter who was external to Nagarahólé and sensitized to the nature of my inquiry, and the evolution of an open and collaborative relationship between interpreter and researcher.

Interview data and observations were analysed using the qualitative data analysis software NUD*IST-Vivo (Qualitative Solutions and Research, 1999).

Actors, Landscape and Institutions in Nagarahólé

The actor-oriented framework for exploring the Ecodevelopment Project in Nagarahólé encompasses an historical overview of the actor–landscape relationship, analysis of the relationships among actors, and the interaction between institutions and actors.

Actors and their Relationships

The focus here is on actors rather than broad social groupings like tribals and villagers. Table 11.1 sets out some key actors in Nagarahólé, and highlights the different levels at which they operate.

The absence of tribals and villagers as categories deserves explanation, and relates both to the analytical framework and constraints of the study. The analytical framework adopted focuses on actors as organizations, subgroups and individuals. The views of villagers and tribals are therefore examined in the context of tribal organizations and village ecodevelopment committees, in terms of actor relationships, and in the later section on people and landscape. Secondly, a trade-off in attempting to understand the views of a broad range of actors is the limited time available to spend in particular villages or tribal settlements.

The stakeholder/actor picture in Nagarahólé is complex, and cannot be considered in detail here. However some emerging issues, particularly those of interest from a methodological perspective, are highlighted.

First, it is important to consider actors at various levels: individuals, subgroups, organizations and coalitions between organizations. Although organizations were the starting point in the exploration of actors in Nagarahólé, individuals within the organizations emerged as key players in the debate. Informants more often referred to organizational leaders than the organizations themselves, an indication that in some cases individuals actually are the organization according to the perceptions of other actors. In other cases, subgroups within an organization came into play. For example, a gap in status and background divides higher ranking and lower ranking forest officials, reflected in differing networks of communication and extent of knowledge about the Ecodevelopment Project, and in attitudes towards park management issues. For instance, some (but not all) forest watchers of tribal background were against the resettlement of tribal people, while non-tribal staff, at both lower and higher levels, were resolutely pro-resettlement.

Leaders are influential and provide insight into their organizations' strategies and objectives. However, a more complex picture of these organizations can emerge through discussion with a broader range of informants, which is particularly important in considering relations between those organizations and their client groups. Discussion with a range of levels was attempted in the various NGOs active in the Nagarahólé area, and more particularly in the Forest Department. The perceptions of organizational objectives and principles were not uniform across an organization. For instance, staff involved only

Table 11.1 *Actors in Nagarahólé*

Actors in Nagarahólé and India Ecodevelopment Project (organizations/coalitions)	Role in park management and Ecodevelopment Project	Level of operation
Village Ecodevelopment Committees	Formed under the project to plan and coordinate IEP implementation	Local
Tribal organizations	Speak for tribal interests	Local/district/state
Tribal rights NGOs (anti-relocation)	Trying to influence policy/legislation and the IEP	Local/district/state
Pro-tribal resettlement NGOs	Working for tribal resettlement	Local/district
Rural development NGOs (BAIF, MYRADA)	IEP implementers	District/state/national
Conservation/wildlife NGOs	Collaborate with KFD to strengthen park management; pro-resettlement	District/state/national
Karnataka Forest Department	Park managers by legislation	State with regional bases
State Government	Forestry and rural development policies; influence day-to-day management, transfers	State
Ministry of Environment and Forests/Project Tiger	Managers of the IEP	National
World Bank	Donor agency for IEP	International

Source: Interviews, World Bank (1996).

in programme implementation often held less flexible and more simplified pictures of what the programme was trying to achieve – this was found both in discussions on the Ecodevelopment Project within the Forest Department, and on the issue of tribal self-rule within tribal rights organizations. This points to a need for sensitivity to the roles of leaders and organizational sub-groupings, and associated differences in objectives and perspectives, rather than viewing organizations as a cohesive whole.

Second, by examining alliances and variance between actors, insights may be gained into their strategies, interests and perspectives. An actor-oriented analysis allows us to look behind traditional, broad-brush classifications of state and civil society, class and ethnicity to examine sometimes unusual alliances and stances. Two examples are the overlap in the role of vocal actors, and the strategic alliance of conservation organizations and pro-relocation organizations.

Conflict between actors like the Forest Department and tribal rights NGOs is based, amongst other things, around differing agendas and values. But within this difference, these two actors share a common role. Both are involved in defining tribals, their culture and their relationship with nature, as well as defining agendas, debate, which groups constitute legitimate stakeholders and what is in their best interests. This relationship between relatively passive stakeholders (tribal communities, villagers) and vocal actors (Forest Department, tribal rights NGOs) that speak for them deserves further study.

Strategic alliances in Nagaraholé might differ from alliances elsewhere. Western conservation NGOs have formed strong to sometimes shaky alliances with indigenous people, based on an assumption of the indigenous capacity to live in harmony with nature, and therefore to manage the landscape soundly (Dwyer, 1994). However, in the Nagaraholé case, the perspectives of actors favouring nature conservation and those supporting indigenous self-determination are diametrically opposed. In fact, there is a strategic alliance between conservationists and pro-resettlement groups, which share an integrationist perspective on tribal development, and support relocation.

Finally, in gaining an understanding of the differing realities of various actors, we need to be sensitive to the political context. Do some realities hold more sway than others? The following is a very brief overview of interview responses on this question, and the picture of influence varied for different groups of informants. Actors like the World Bank and the Forest Department were both generally seen as being very influential in park management, the former as a donor agency for the Ecodevelopment Project, and the latter through its statutory role. Other influential actors from a Forest Department perspective included elected members of government and the National Project Tiger Office. Actors who were attempting to influence government policies and activities, such as conservation NGOs and tribal rights NGOs, regarded themselves as influential in certain respects. Groups such as tribals and villagers were broadly seen as dependent on park resources, but not influential in park matters. There was also a sense, particularly amongst forest officials, that the condition of the park ultimately depended on whether or not people actually followed the rules established for managing the park; therefore *the public* also influenced the state of the park.

Powerful actors were sustained by a formally agreed or legislated role (in the case of government, Forest Department, World Bank), or strategic capacity (in the case of various NGOs). However, there was also a sense that the powerful can only rule if the less powerful submit to their power, as in the case of villagers, tribals and the public.

The Significance of the People and Landscape Relationship

Biodiversity interventions confront a historical web of interaction between people and landscape, often overlooked in project design. The Ecodevelopment Project appraisals and concept documents focus on the current scene (Indian Institute of Public Administration, 1994; World Bank, 1996). By studying historical and contemporary documentation, a picture can be compiled of people in their landscape, and mutual influences between people and place, referred to by cultural geographers as the cultural landscape (Anderson and Gale, 1992). The temporal scale in this analysis starts from early British intervention in the Nagaraholé forests from the late 1800s to the present.

The reservation of forests under British colonial government is widely recognized as a turning point in the management of Indian forests (Rangarajan, 1996; Buchy, 1996; Gadgil and Guha, 1992). In the case of the forests currently included in the Nagaraholé, this process occurred between 1894 and 1901 (Alva, 1978). The reservation process altered the access rights of local residents to the forest and forest products, and imposed new objectives and imperatives in forest management, such as timber extraction and plantation establishment under the rubric of *scientific* forestry.

Management priorities in the Nagaraholé area included timber and sandalwood production, controlling and capturing revenue from collection of non-timber forest products such as fodder and forest fruits, and the establishment of teak plantations to secure an ongoing timber supply (Tireman, 1914). Controlled burning was conducted to varying extents in the plantations, with numerous documented cases of fires burning out of control: sometimes from controlled burns, and frequently as the result of carelessness or 'wicked acts of incendiarism' on the part of villagers and tribals, which is discussed in more detail shortly (eg Dickinson, 1883). Such management processes altered the species composition and density of the Nagaraholé forests, although the nature and extent of this impact has not been studied.

Areas around the Nagaraholé forests have also undergone radical change. The western side of the park saw the growth of coffee plantations and cardamom leases starting from the mid-1800s. The expansion of agricultural lands on the east sustained food crops as well as commercial crops like tobacco and cotton (Rice, 1876). The areas around what now constitutes the National Park have gradually increased in population density and the conversion of forest for agriculture continues today. Many of the neighbouring villages were established only in the last few decades, for instance as a result of the flooding of the Kabini Irrigation Dam on the southeast of the park. In the 1970s, a Tibetan refugee settlement was established on the previously forested eastern boundary of the Park.

What were the implications of reservation for the relationship between the forest and people living in and around it? Two key social groupings today in this regard are settled farmers (villagers), and indigenous people (tribals).

The initial reservation process involved settlement of rights for farmers, allowing them rights of passage through the forest, and limited rights to graze and water cattle. The use of such non-timber forest products, which previously was unrestricted, now involved payments to the Forest Department by villagers (Tireman, 1914). Strains in the relationship between the Forest Department and villagers flowing from these changes are noted in a letter from the Chief Superintendent of Coorg in 1881, who writes '...it is no easy task to induce the people to cooperate heartily in measures the advantage of which to them is not apparent' (Dickinson, 1881).

Between the tribals and the Forest Department, the relationship seems more mixed. According to historical accounts, Jenu Kurubas and Betta Kurubas, two major tribal groups of the area, lived in the forested Western Ghats and Nilgiri area, subsisting on kumri (shifting) cultivation and various forest produce (Thurston and Rangachari, 1909). After reservation, the Forest Department came to rely on tribals as a labour force for forest operations like felling, weeding and maintaining plantations and roads, to the extent that tribals were actively recruited from outside the immediate Nagaraholé area. From 1892, the tribals were actually allowed to practise a form of kumri cultivation in teak plantation areas, planting food crops alongside teak trees (Proust, 1894), partly as an incentive for tribals to remain in the reserved forest areas as a labour force (Lowrie, 1897).

The tribal role in forest management under the British meant that they were able to maintain an ongoing relationship with the forest areas, even though certain practices such as swidden cultivation, which the British saw as wasteful, were severely restricted. The current perspective of the Forest Department on this relationship is that tribal inhabitation of the forests and conservation are completely incompatible, a view shared by conservation NGOs. Tribal rights organizations, on the other hand, believe that indigenous people live in harmony with nature. The Ecodevelopment Project is based on a premise of breaking the dependency of people on forests, by providing alternative resource options and income sources. The dominant perspective on the people–landscape relationship thus has important implications for project design and equity in terms of maintaining or reducing access to resource-based livelihoods.

The forests of Nagaraholé today are not a relic wilderness so much as an outcome of a long history of interaction amongst people, and between people and place. This process continues. The transition from reserve forest to a Wildlife Sanctuary in 1955 placed further restrictions on activities like hunting. These restrictions were again strengthened with the declaration of a national park in 1975, and expansion of the park area in 1983 and 1992 (Lal et al, 1994). The Wildlife Protection Act 1972 also makes illegal the existence of tribal settlements within the Park. This has been the basis for resettlement of tribals to neighbouring farmlands, and is a key bone of contention in park management today.

In summary, there are numerous ways in which the British attempts to reserve and manage forests in Karnataka were a major turning point for the relationships amongst groups of people, for the people–forest relationship, and the nature of the forests themselves. Restrictions on access and use of the forest were a major consequence, which have been further strengthened with the enactment of the Wildlife Protection Act in 1972, and the establishment and expansion of the national park at Nagaraholé. These institutional changes have not altered behaviour entirely (people still reside within the park, graze cattle, and gather fuelwood) but have imposed formal constraints on use rights.

The relationship between the Forest Department and people living in and around Nagaraholé has varied over time from strained, in the case of villagers, to sometimes collaborative, in the case of tribals. Ironically, the British management regime and production focus enabled tribal groups to maintain access to the park, albeit restricted, whereas the more recent national park model and the Ecodevelopment Project try to break this link.

This historical cultural landscape context helps to understand the stormy passage of a specific project intervention like the India Ecodevelopment Project. The project does not commence on a clean slate, but encounters the struggle between actors for control of resources, and to promote their perspective on the rightful relationship between people and landscape. Such existing patterns of conflict have been undermining the intervention, particularly as they were not examined and therefore not addressed in the process of project design and implementation.

Actors in their Institutional Context

Institutional analysts have observed that the interactions and decisions of actors take place within a web of institutions – rules, enforcement systems and norms of behaviour that structure repeated human interaction (North, 1990). This has evolved in a number of biodiversity studies into a view of institutions as unidirectional determinants of behaviour (Barbier et al, 1994; Swanson, 1997). Studies in other fields are taking a more interactive view of institutions, where actors have agency and choice; institutions pose certain constraints, but they are reified, challenged and potentially changed by actors (Jackson, 1997; Long, 1992). The nature of this interaction between actors and institutions is examined below.

Before commencing this discussion of actors and institutions in Nagaraholé, it is important to note that the socio-political context in rural India, as elsewhere, is extremely complex. This exploration of institution–actor linkages is not intended to provide a global picture of power relations (such as class-based analyses, for instance, may attempt), or explain the rise of social movements dealing with tribal autonomy and with conservation. It aims, rather, to look through an institutional window at the Nagaraholé situation, and see what sorts of insights might be gained.

The kinds of institutions raised by actors in Nagaraholé include:

- international agreements, such as the Convention on Biological Diversity and the International Declaration of Human Rights;
- legislation and policy, including the Wildlife Protection Act, the key PA legislation at the national level; informants from tribal rights organizations are also attuned to policies on tribal development at the state and regional level;
- property rights, particularly access to forests and forest produce, and land in areas neighbouring the forest; and
- systems of governance and decision-making, for instance the establishment of ecodevelopment committees by the Ecodevelopment Project, and the movement towards tribal autonomy for predominantly tribal areas of India (Government of India, 1995).

In Nagaraholé, there was a complex relationship between actors, institutions and level. The Convention on Biological Diversity was not raised by local NGOs or lower level forest officials, but was mentioned by senior officials, national level staff, and in World Bank documentation. On the other hand, the Wildlife Protection Act received comment across every level, by every category of actor. It appears to have cross-level significance, as national legislation, which is implemented by state and regional officials at a local level. This may be attributed to the remoteness of international institutions from day-to-day life, compared with statutory restrictions.

Actors had differing views on the nature of institutions. Forest Department officials regarded the Wildlife Protection Act as sacrosanct, literally referring to it as their *Bible*, while tribal rights leaders were quite emphatic that this legislation arose from human agency, and therefore should be subject to question and revision. This difference in perception shapes whether actors advocate solutions within existing institutional frameworks, as with the Forest Department, or promote institutional change to accommodate more radical solutions, as with the tribal rights NGOs.

Some actors perceived contradictions between co-existing state institutions, and were highlighting these contradictions to promote their own objectives. For example, tribal rights organizations emphasized national human rights policies to challenge the proposed relocation of tribals under the Wildlife Protection Act.

Incongruities in the application of rules were also used strategically by actors. A striking example was the Forest Department's approval for a luxury hotel development inside the park, while simultaneously attempting to resettle park residents. The Forest Department was successfully challenged in court over their inconsistent application of the Wildlife Protection Act. The appeal by tribal rights NGOs to the World Bank Inspection Panel is another example, where the Panel was brought in to investigate inconsistencies in the application of World Bank Operational Directives on indigenous people and community participation.

Through these strategies, actors create a space from which they can challenge existing institutions, and both promote and use institutional change.

The link between institutions and power was noted earlier. In Nagaraholé, state ownership of the forest and the Wildlife Protection Act sustain the Forest Department's power. The World Bank has power in the project context as a donor agency, which helps design, supervise, guide and hold the implementers accountable for project implementation. One forest official noted that the Village Microplans, developed from consultations with the villagers, had already been changed several times on instruction from World Bank staff. Another official commented, 'I think it is too hard to do both policing, which requires terrorizing villagers, and Ecodevelopment Project, which requires being friendly.' These kinds of power relationships evade the application of participatory techniques. Institutional bases for power might take longer to erode, if at all; and a participatory project does not necessarily challenge this. However, it may introduce individuals to new ways of operating and thinking, as a number of Forest Department staff have noted in relation to their communication with villagers.

The institutional dimension is thus important to the relations between actors in Nagaraholé. The analysis highlights how institutions are brought to life by actors with differing perceptions and objectives, who can use perceived tensions in the institutional landscape to promote their own objectives. Power sustained by institutions is not necessarily challenged by a project that promotes a participatory approach, although it may introduce some individuals to different modes of operating.

From Understanding Specifics to Policy Implications

One issue from the Nagaraholé case with potentially broader significance for other conservation programmes is the role of actors in the intervention process. In Nagaraholé, the Ecodevelopment Project has been a venue for negotiation between various actors. Intra-organizational relationships, for instance within the Forest Department, and inter-organization relations both shape the intervention, and are affected by the intervention. Inter-organizational relationships and communication have also emerged as an important factor in the evolution of other ICDPs (Gezon, 1998). Alliances and differences occur for many reasons, including strategic interests, inter-personal conflicts, and differences in the values and needs of constituent groups. Most studies of ICDPs concentrate on actors with an immediate involvement in resource management and development issues (direct stakeholders), but considering a broader constellation of actors, as discussed here, can contribute to a richer picture of factors influencing the project environment.

Interventions take varying stances in relation to the existing institutional landscape. For instance, securing or strengthening tenure has been a critical focus in many of the projects funded by the Biodiversity Conservation Network (Mahanty et al, 1999). This does not necessarily entail securing local ownership of resource areas. For instance, the Arnavon Marine Conservation Area in the Solomon Islands limits local resource rights to a recognition of people's rights to use and manage those resources, as a basis for community involvement in managing the marine conservation area. The stance of the Ecodevelopment Project on tenure questions is neutral, which involves an implicit support for the status quo. Either approach therefore has political implications that need to be recognized. Where institutions disenfranchise certain groups, it may be difficult to empower those groups simply by using techniques like participatory rural appraisal.

A key issue in the Ecodevelopment Project at Nagaraholé is the belief by a number of actors – Forest Department, conservation organizations and pro-relocation NGOs – that conservation cannot be achieved alongside forest-based livelihoods. The Ecodevelopment Project starts from a premise of reducing forest dependence, while other ICDPs, such as those assisted by the

Biodiversity Conservation Network, aim to give communities a payback or incentive for using the forest sustainably. This difference in premise highlights that an ICDP is not just an ICDP: some aim to integrate conservation and development, while others aim to decouple the two processes. The decoupling approach, as adopted in the Ecodevelopment Project, is more likely to place local livelihoods and conservation at odds, and success in reversing resource depletion will depend to a large extent on the viability of the substitutes offered. In the Biodiversity Conservation Network model, effectiveness depends more on finding mechanisms, institutions and products that enable local livelihoods to proceed at a scale and in a way where the resource base is not depleted, and monitoring systems to feed appropriate information back into decision-making.

Conclusion

This chapter has discussed the long history of landscape–people interaction, in which interventions like the Ecodevelopment Project are another event. The intervention is subject to the patterns that exist between people and place, but also tries to manipulate these patterns based on assumptions held by powerful actors about the relationship between people and landscape. For instance, the Ecodevelopment Project attempts to break dependencies between people and landscape, but other ICDPs might take an alternative approach of creating incentives for more sustainable resource use. The core ideas driving an intervention have important ramifications for equity, for instance if a complete transition from resource based livelihoods is neither viable nor successful.

The Nagaraholé case illustrates the value in considering actors at multiple levels: as individuals, sub-groups within organizations, organizations and coalitions. Interventions like the Ecodevelopment Project tend to simplify their analysis of stakeholders in terms of broad-brush categories such as NGOs and Forest Department. However, the study indicates that a different picture of relationships and issues might be found, depending on the unit of analysis. The Ecodevelopment Project is a forum for negotiation between actors with differing degrees of power, but the intervention can also create space for less powerful actors to challenge more powerful ones. In Nagaraholé, the Ecodevelopment Project has created space for tribal rights organizations to question the decisions of the Forest Department on various park management issues.

The analysis of the actor–institution linkage in Nagaraholé highlights further issues impacting on the intervention. The sanctity and appropriateness of statutory institutions, like the Wildlife Protection Act, are viewed differently by various actors. This underlies divergent strategies for resolving issues, for instance whether they promote institutional change like the tribal rights NGOs, or seek solutions within the status quo. In some respects the Ecodevelopment Project has provided a forum for these actors to question current institutional arrangements. Although institutions sustain the power of actors in some respects, the fluidity of the institutional landscape can bring about contradictions between co-existing institutions. The tribal rights NGOs in Nagaraholé were able to use the space created by institutional contradictions to promote their objectives, and gain more influence than they might otherwise have.

Certain issues from Nagaraholé resonate with those emerging in other ICDP studies: the vital role of organizational arrangements and inter-organizational communication patterns in the evolution of a project and the significance of institutions. Most studies of ICDPs have taken a more deterministic view of institutions than the interactive and process-oriented approach to institutions taken here. There are also important differences amongst ICDPs, for instance in the underlying premise about people–landscape interaction and conservation mentioned above.

What does this mean for biodiversity conservation programmes? If the ICDP model passes out of fashion tomorrow, its replacement will still need to understand and work within the complex picture of actors, landscape and institutions unfolding in this study. Although ICDPs may be an improvement on earlier intervention designs, they are still some distance from the non-blueprint, process-oriented approach promised, bearing in mind the diversity in design and process across the ICDP spectrum.

Rather than suggesting variations to the model, the Nagaraholé study highlights some critical issues for conservation interventions and practitioners to consider. The Ecodevelopment Project and many other ICDPs attempt to manipulate relations between actors and landscape to a prespecified end. An actor-oriented framework questions the capacity of any such intervention to ever meet their prespecified objectives. In Nagaraholé, the intervention has been more obviously overtaken by negotiations and politics between actors; this process may be paralleled in less obvious ways elsewhere. This finding points to the need for a more open ended, process-oriented and site specific approach than is embodied in most existing ICDPs and community-based conservation programmes, and for practitioners to critically reflect on their working assumptions.

Acknowledgements
The permission and cooperation of the Karnataka Forest Department and NGOs working in Nagaraholé is greatly appreciated. Field research for this study was financed by the National Centre for Development Studies, The Australian National University.

Conflict Management in Community-Based Natural Resource Projects: Experiences from the Lakekamu Basin Integrated Conservation and Development Project, Papua New Guinea

Michael Warner

Introduction

The word conflict carries negative connotations. It is often thought of as the opposite of cooperation and peace, and is most commonly associated with violence, the threat of violence or disruptive (non-violent) disputes. This view of conflict as negative is not always helpful. In non-violent settings it can often be seen as a force for positive social change, its presence being a visible demonstration of society adapting to a new political, economic or physical environment.

One area of international development currently prone to particularly rapid social change is the management of renewable natural resources. The introduction of new technologies in rural areas, commercialization of common property resources, involvement of rural communities in conservation, privatization of rural public services, growing consumerism, government policies supportive of community-based natural resource management and a general decline in the terms-of-trade for agricultural produce, all exert pressure on individuals and groups in rural areas.

Conflicts and disputes that arise from these external perturbations are not something that can be avoided or suppressed. Development models therefore are needed which acknowledge conflict as a potential obstacle to sustainable development, manage its negative excesses, and transform the residual into a positive force.

Growing conflicts between wildlife conservation interests and local communities over the utilization of natural resources are well-documented, as noted in previous chapters. The dominant response to these disputes has been schemes which raise the value of conservation to local people through the distribution of revenues from tourism or trophy hunting, or through community development designed to compensate for loss of access to conservation-worthy resources. However, the effectiveness and reach of these schemes has been limited, and in many conservation and protected areas, conflicts over resources persist (Metcalf, 1995; IIED, 1994).

This chapter concerns the problem of non-violent conflicts and disputes as a constraint to the sustainability of natural resource management at the community level. First, it provides some background to the role of conflict in natural resource management. Then it presents a methodology designed to contribute to the removal of conflict as an obstacle to sustainability. The methodology was developed to guide a programme of conflict management within NGO-sponsored community-based natural resource projects in the South Pacific. Examples of the outputs of the methodology are described, drawing from conflict management activities undertaken in the Lakekamu Basin ICDP, Papua New Guinea (PNG). The overall benefits of conflict management in community-based natural resource projects are discussed in relation to building social capital and sustaining livelihood security.

Types of Conflicts in Natural Resource Management

Different types of conflicts can be categorized in terms of whether they occur at the *micro–micro* or *micro–macro* levels, that is among community groups or between community groups and outside government, private or civil society organizations. *Micro–micro* conflicts can be further categorized as taking place either within the group directly involved in a particular resource management regime (eg an eco-tourism association), or between this group and those not directly involved (Conroy et al, 1998). Examples of both intra and inter *micro–micro* conflicts and *micro–macro* conflicts are listed in Box 12.1.

The short-term adverse impact of conflicts can range from a temporary reduction in the efficiency of resource management regimes, to the complete collapse of initiatives or abandonment of government, NGOs or donor-sponsored projects. In extreme cases conflicts over natural resource management can escalate into physical violence.

The causes of non-violent conflicts in community-based natural resource management can be divided into four principal types:

1 demographic change;
2 natural resources competition;

Box 12.1 Types of conflicts arising in natural resource management

Intra micro–micro conflicts

* Disputes over land and resource ownership;
* latent family and relationship disputes;
* disputes due to natural resource projects being captured by élites and/or those who happen to own resources of a higher quality; and
* breaking of common property resource rules.

Inter micro–micro conflicts

* Conflict between indigenous CPR groups, and more recent settlers;
* disputes generated by jealousy related to growing wealth disparities; and
* internal land ownership disputes ignited by the speculation activities of commercial companies.

Micro–macro conflicts

* Contradictory natural resource needs and values, eg between wildlife habitat protection and local livelihood security;
* disputes caused by political influence;
* disputes arising from differences between the aspirations of community groups and expectations of NGOs or commercial companies; and
* off-site environmental impacts affecting unintended third-parties.

---

3   developmental pressures, and
4   structural injustices.

The combination of demographic change and the limits to sustainable harvesting of renewable natural resources are often cited as the underlying cause of conflict over natural resources, both among community groups and between community groups and outside public and private organizations. However, these pressures are complicated by development. These include:

1   growing awareness within rural communities and the private sector that commercial value can be attributed to common property resources;
2   increasing importance of the cash economy to rural people and rising local aspirations for consumer products;
3   lack of incentives for resource users to avoid generating environmental and social impacts which adversely affect third parties;
4   new conservation policies; and
5   government policies providing autonomy to communities to manage state-owned natural resources.

Development pressures may be only a part of the problem. Increased competition and conflict over natural resources is sometimes underpinned by deeper lying, structural causes. These include, for example, the inequalities inherent in legal definitions of land ownership, local and regional economic and political inequalities, and ethnic and cultural differences. These structural factors may lie dormant until reawakened by the onset of a particular set of developmental pressures.

Resolving structural conflicts over the management of natural resources is a fundamentally more difficult task than resolving conflicts directly attributable to developmental pressures. Structural conflicts, by definition, can only be resolved at the national or regional level, through short-term policy or legal reform, or longer term education, wealth creation or peace-building programmes. However, it is not necessarily the case that the structural causes have to be resolved in order to remove conflict as an obstacle to sustainable community-based natural resource management. This is the idea of conflict management, a process which in the above context has two objectives:

1   to transform or mitigate conflicts brought about by developmental, environmental or demographic pressures; and
2   to contain structural conflicts such that they do not impinge on the equitable, efficient and sustainable management of project activities.

The most recent common joint policy statement on conflict from the OECD (1998) supports this approach, asserting that a society's capacity to manage conflict without violence is a foundation for sustainable development.

Conflict Management in the Lakekamu ICPD

The aim of the programme,[1] which includes the case study of the Lakekamu ICDP (Papua New Guinea), is to reduce conflicts and disputes between project stakeholders from acting as obstacles to sustainable natural resource management, and to contribute to wider peace-building and conflict[2] efforts within the project countries.

At the time that the programme was conceived, a wide range of conflicts and disputes were adversely affecting the equity, sustainability and effectiveness of the projects considered by the programme. Some of those recorded are summarized in Box 12.2. The impacts of these conflicts included withdrawal of cooperation by project beneficiaries, negative media publicity, threatened withdrawal of project donors, withdrawal of NGO assistance to project beneficiaries, awakening and fuelling of existing political tensions, resignation of project staff, increased time and costs of project operations, low staff morale, withdrawal of cooperation for other projects in same vicinity, and postponement to scaling up of natural resource programmes and projects.

Box 12.2 Conflicts identified by the NGO group in the South Pacific as constraints to the effective and sustainable management of natural resources

Enterprise-based Biodiversity Conservation

- Lack of involvement of local interested parties in defining strategic livelihood objectives with protected areas;
- conflicts between eco-tour operators and local communities over tourist excursions, including routes, profit distribution, local participation;
- conflicts among community groups over involvement in eco-tourism enterprises, eg crafts, guides;
- land ownership conflicts over rules for revenue sharing;
- conflicts between conservation authorities/environmental NGOs, and private enterprises, eg logging companies; and
- disputes between intermediary NGO and project participants over distribution of enterprise benefits.

Community-Forestry

- Conflict between communal owners over profit distribution from forestry resource;
- imbalance of knowledge in forestry creating imbalance of power and mistrust;
- dominance of commercial interests over fodder and fuelwood needs of women, exclusion of local people from access to forest resources;
- social tensions consequent on arrival of portable sawmills;
- misuse and mismanagement of profits from timber resources; and
- corruption of custom chiefs and traditional protectors of land influenced by cash value of timber resources.

Coastal/Marine Planning and Management

- Tensions between communities unaware of forestry practices that create environmental degradation and those who are recipients of downstream pollution of streams; and
- erosion of power of traditional leaders to impose bans to regenerate forestry stock.

General

- Land tenure laws not clear, creating land disputes with no expedient legal method to clarify ownership;
- tensions from rapid socio-economic changes due to shift from subsistence to cash economy;
- political and religious tensions creating family and community divisions;
- growing pressures to find alternative income or subsistence where resources are depleted;
- fear, tension and mistrust over custom beliefs; and
- tensions caused by breakdown of traditional leadership structures and systems, ie respect for and power of leaders, without new systems to replace leadership.

Conflict management methodology

The methodology developed for the programme was informed by a scoping mission to Fiji and PNG in 1998. During the mission, the implementing NGO identified the need for a basket of conflict management strategies, rather than one single approach, and for skills training in conflict analysis and multi-stakeholder workshop facilitation. Subsequently, staff from both affiliated NGOs underwent two weeks of dedicated training in conflict management and consensus building. A guidance manual was also prepared detailing principles, processes and tools for managing conflict in the context of community-based natural resource management projects (UKFSP and ODI, 1998). As the conflict management programme unfolded, some modifications to the overall methodology were made. These changes have been incorporated into the operations of the affiliates and in a revised version of the manual (Warner, 1999).

One of the key strategies promoted by the methodology is consensus building. This is an alternative to the inequalities inherent in confrontational/ adversarial forms of stakeholder negotiation. Consensus building seeks to build the capacity of people to develop a dialogue with each other, either directly or indirectly, to find a way forward based on consensus which generates mutual gains for all parties with the minimum of compromise and trade-off. Other terms of processes of negotiation based on the same principles of mutual gain win–win include: alternative dispute resolution, alternative conflict management and conflict transformation.

Over the last 15 years, developed countries (in particular the USA, Canada and Australia) have experienced an increase in the use of conflict management based on consensus building to resolve disputes over the allocation of scarce environmental resources (Conroy et al, 1998; ICIMOD, 1996; Resolve, 1994). The standard (North American) model used comprises a process of consensual stakeholder negotiation, facilitated by an impartial third-party mediator.

At the same time, the increasing threat of violence in many developed nations has led to the growing use of community-based consensus building and mediation processes to prevent disputes escalating into armed violence, and to promote the reconciliation and reconstruction of society in post-conflict situations (Ndelu, 1998; O'Reilly, 1998; OECD, 1998; International Alert, 1996; Bush, 1998).

The scoping mission to PNG and Fiji concluded that though an approach to conflict management based on multi-stakeholder consensus building has much to merit it, the process – particularly the North American third-party impartial mediator model – is unlikely to become a workable panacea. We found three justifications for this conclusion.

First, the North American model is but one approach to consensus building. Other models include non-facilitated face-to-face consensual negotiation, and partial third-party facilitation. In the latter the mediator has a vested interest in the conflict situation but has permission from the conflicting parties to facilitate proceedings.

Second, consensus building is but one of a range of conflict management strategies. There is no perfect strategy for managing conflict in community-based natural resource management. The strategy adopted needs to be that which is most practicable given the available resources and capabilities of the conflicting parties and local implementing agencies, issues of safety and security, and the availability of viable conflict mitigation options. Figure 12.1 summarizes the key strategies of conflict management. In this diagram the approaches differ depending upon the extent to which a conflicting party values the continuance of good relations with other parties, and the importance each party places on achieving its own goals. Conflict can be managed through *force*, where one party has the means and inclination to win regardless of whether the other party loses, and whether or not the process of winning causes damage to personal relationships. *Withdrawal* is an approach to conflict management suited to those parties whose desire to avoid confrontation outweighs the goals they are trying to achieve. There are occasions when one party in a conflict situation values a strong and continuing relationship with one or more of the other parties above the attainment of its own specific goals. In these cases a party may elect to *accommodate* the other parties' goals, conceding to all or most of their demands. *Compromise* is often confused with *consensus*. To compromise in a negotiation may sound positive, but it means that at least one of the parties perceives that it has had to forgo something. Although processes of consensus building sometimes contain elements of compromise within the final agreement, there are some key differences between the two approaches. Consensus building explicitly sets out to avoid trade-offs altogether, seeking instead to achieve a win–win outcome. In contrast, a compromise approach seeks to minimize what are considered inevitable trade-offs.[3]

Although consensus building between multiple stakeholders can lead to mutually acceptable, and therefore more sustainable, outcomes, such an approach may not always be the most viable (Chupp, 1991). Even where it is, it may not be effective on its own, but require support either concurrently or sequentially from one or more other strategies. The methodology for conflict management presented in this chapter therefore centres on the concept of the most practicable strategy, that is the most desirable and feasible strategy or mix of strategies for managing a particular conflict situation. We found that determining this strategy requires consideration of a range of factors (Box 12.3).

Third, whereas in most developed nations the use of multi-stakeholder consensus building to environmental disputes is still largely experimental, in many developing countries, particularly in rural areas, customary forms of consensus building have a long history. Customary approaches to consensus building primarily target family, labour and civil disputes, with environmental disputes the new growth area (for examples, see Moore, 1996).

Customary forms of consensus building fail when new development pressures generate or reawaken conflicts which overwhelm the capability of these mechanisms to cope. In such situations the conflicting parties themselves may try to modify the customary approach or develop completely new dispute management mechanisms. For example, Conroy et al (1998) recently recorded how groups involved in participatory forest management in India have established new institutions to manage conflicts over forest protection and

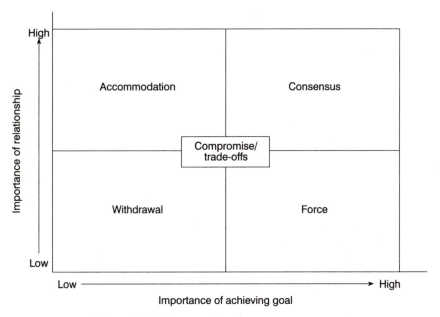

Figure 12.1 *Five conflict management strategies*

mismanagement. But there are many cases when this is not possible (or at least not possible within the time scale of the natural resource project in question). It is in the cases of conflict which overwhelm both the immediate and adaptive capability of community groups to readjust that modern processes of multi-stakeholder consensus building may have a potential role to play.

The Conflict Management Process

There are certain components that tend to comprise processes of conflict management in community-based natural resource management. This is so whether the goal is to manage live conflicts arising within existing projects, or to integrate conflict prevention strategies into a project design.

Although the linkages between the components are not strictly linear, there is a broad sequence to the process of conflict management. It is appropriate for Conflict Analysis to be undertaken first and in two stages. First, to analyse the conflict *in the office* on the basis of existing or readily accessed information.[4] Second, to analyse the conflict in participation with the relevant stakeholder groups.[5] These two activities will need to continue iteratively until a Conflict Management Plan can be agreed as to the way that the conflict will be managed. The process will often include some form of Capacity Building (eg mutual understanding of each parties' objectives, training in negotiation skills, awareness raising of the long-term benefits of sustainable resource management). With all three activities complete, implementation of the Conflict Management Plan can commence.

BOX 12.3 FACTORS TO CONSIDER IN IDENTIFYING THE MOST PRACTICABLE STRATEGY FOR CONFLICT MANAGEMENT

Whether doing nothing is likely to result in the conflict resolving itself without violence, eg because some customary processes of conflict management are effective, or because the parties lose or divert their interest.

The time and resources available to those parties interested in coordinating the process of conflict management.

The extent to which structural conflicts are likely to magnify the immediate dispute, and are able to be resolved or managed.

The power of the different parties, eg to force through their agenda, or to be manipulated during a process of mediation.

The strength of feeling between the conflicting parties towards each other, and towards achieving their own goals.

The importance of building or maintaining good relationships between the parties.

The consequences if the conflict continues, such as its escalation towards violence.

The effectiveness of the existing customary, institutional and legal approaches to conflict management.

Those components within the existing customary, institutional or legal approaches that could be readily strengthened using one or more conflict management strategies (force, withdrawal, compromise, accommodation).

If consensus building approaches are to be used, the principal is Best Alternative to a Negotiated Agreement (ie the fall-back position if consensual negotiation is not effective).

Each building block is described in more detail below, accompanied by examples of relevant conflict analysis and other outputs. The examples are drawn from conflict management work undertaken by the Foundation for People and Community Development (FPCD) in the case study area.

Office-based Conflict Analysis

Office-based Conflict Analysis involves mapping existing or potential conflicts. This mapping draws on any strategic level conflict analysis already completed, as well as locally-sourced information able to be gathered with a minimum of intrusion into the conflict situation. The initial analysis is stressed as office-based in that it aims to inform the design of a subsequent process of stakeholder dialogue without raising false expectations, exacerbating tensions or placing project staff at personal risk of harm.

In cases where an existing project is enmeshed in an open conflict or dispute, or where a planned project is to be introduced into a situation of open conflict or tension, this initial Conflict Analysis should centre on known conflicts. In cases where a project is to be introduced to a situation of latent

Method:
- current and potential conflicts brainstormed (potential = dotted lines);
- related conflicts clustered;
- conflicts differentiated by scale (represented by size of circle); and
- Venn diagram compiled with inter-related conflicts overlapping.

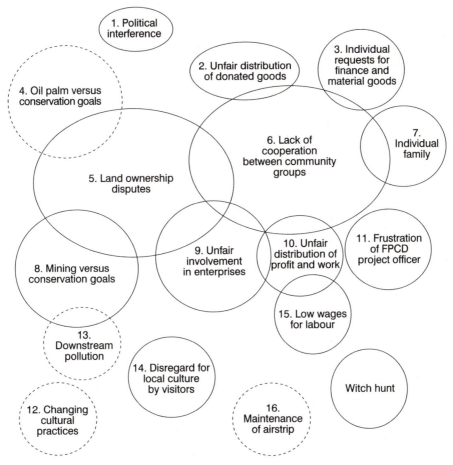

Figure 12.2 *Office-based conflict analysis: Initial conflict mapping*

conflict, the analysis will try to predict conflicts, in the same way as one might predict environmental, social or gender impacts.

In either open or latent conflict situations, it is also more useful to think not of project stakeholders but of conflict stakeholders. Thus in the methodology of Conflict Management, conventional stakeholder identification is extended to include groups who might undermine or assist in conflict management.

Possible outputs from a process of office-based Conflict Analysis are listed below, and particular examples are given in the case study:

Table 12.1 *Office-based conflict analysis: Conflict prioritization in the case study (most important conflicts indicated by **bold** text)*

Conflict	Urgent	Significant
1 Political interference		
– local level		*
– provincial level	*	**
– national	*	***
2 Unfair distribution of donated goods	***	*
3 Individual requests for finance and material		
goods from FPCD	***	**
4 Oil palm versus conservation goals	***	***
5 Land ownership disputes		
– Tekadu research station	**	***
– eco-tourism project land		**
– Tekadu Guest House		*
6 Lack of cooperation between community groups		
– community work	***	***
– project related activities	***	**
7 Individual family disputes	*	***
8 Mining vs. conservation goals	*	**
9 Unfair involvement in enterprises	**	***
10 Unfair distribution of profit and work		
– Kakoro Guest House	***	**
– Ivimka Guest House	***	***
– Tekadu Guest House	*	**
– Okavai Guest House		***
– Butterfly farming		*
11 Frustration of FPCD project officer		
12 Changing cultural practices	*	***
13 Downstream pollution	*	**
14 Disregard for local culture by visitors		***
15 Low wages for labour	***	**
16 Maintenance of airstrip	***	*

- initial mapping of the known or predicted conflict or disputes, including their type, scale and any cause–effect relationships (Figure 12.2);
- the historical context of the conflicts including the past and predicted escalation of the conflicts, the underlying structural causes, the part played by local economic grievances, other contributing factors (eg demographics), and past efforts at conflict management and why these were ineffective;
- any conflict management initiatives currently ongoing or planned;
- the impacts of the conflict on the project schedule, activities, outputs, assets, staff time, beneficiaries;
- the geographical distribution of known or predicted conflicts or disputes (in the form of a sketch map);

Table 12.2 *Office-based conflict analysis: Stakeholder identification of conflicts for the dispute over unfair distribution of profit from the Kakoro Tourist Guest House*

Causing/blamed	Affected	Assist	Undermine
Community Women's Group	FCPD Conservation	Community leaders	Husbands of women
Guest House Women's Group	International Government officers	Church leaders	Biodiversity Conservation Network (BCN)
	Kakoro Guest House owners		
	Remainder of Kakoro population		
	Biodiversity Conservation Network		

- the temporal distribution of the conflicts, such as seasonality;
- prioritization of the conflicts in terms of the urgency of the need to prevent, manage, resolve or transform the conflicts, and significance of the conflict/s in undermining the goal of the project (Table 12.1);
- for the prioritized conflicts, the key stakeholder groups and their prospective representatives;
- initial estimation of the immediate positions and demands of the different stakeholder groups, and their deeper underlying values, interests, needs and concerns (Table 12.2); and
- initial identification of conflict management opportunities.

The conflicts between oil palm and conservation and the dispute over unfair distribution of profit from the Kakoro Tourist Guest House have been addressed through the conflict management programme discussed in this chapter. Because of space limitations and due to the fact that the whole conflict management process has been carried out, only the conflict management activities related to the tourist guest house are presented.

In relation to the guest house, it was constructed in late 1997 by community groups living within the Kakoro region of the Lakekamu Basin ICDP, with financial and technical assistance from FPCD. As tourists and scientists began to arrive, a dispute broke out between two local women's groups over the distribution of profits from the provision of cooking and cleaning services to the guest house. By mid-1998 the influx of tourists had ceased, along with the flow of income into the community. The dispute caused FPCD to consider withdrawing from the project. An evaluation report by the project sponsors cited the dispute as evidence that the Lakekamu Basin enterprise-based conservation initiative, of which the guest house was a part, was looking increasingly untenable. Effective management of the dispute was viewed by FPCD as a matter of urgency.

Table 12.3 *Office-based conflict analysis: Underlying fears and needs of stakeholders for the dispute over unfair distribution of profit and services in Kakoro Tourist Guest House*

Stakeholder group	Underlying needs	Underlying fears
FPCD/Conservation International	Enterprise to provide sustainable income to community; promote equal distribution of work and profit within community; resolve current conflicts; meet conservation objectives	Local stakeholders lose interest in enterprise; Conservation objectives fail; Loss of local jobs; Reputation of FPCD damaged
Donors	Accurate project monitoring data; meeting of conservation/ biodiversity goals	Funds not wasted; Negative results of testing BCN hypothesis that community-based enterprise supports conservation
Local government officers	Peaceful, cooperative community; Peace Corp volunteers continue; skills training for community cooperatives	Increased disharmony in community; Collapse of cooperatives
Community and church leaders	Promote income generating opportunities; prevent emigration; help meet basic needs	Time wasted trying to resolve marital conflicts; Disharmony and hostility in the community; Violence erupting
Kakoro Guest House owners	Cash income; improve standard of living; higher status within community; promote conservation	Guest house fails to generate income; Project discontinued by FPCD; Unable to meet maintenance costs with profit;
Remainder of Kakoro population	Share of income from Guest House; their voices acknowledged by landowners; privacy respected; basic services provided	Being excluded from project (in terms of income and learning new skills); Influence of outsiders on local culture
Community Women's Group	Cash income; put craft-making skills learnt into practice; be recognized and respected by their husbands; opportunities to meet people (especially men)	Not learning new skills; Guest House Women's Group looking down at them

Stakeholder group	Underlying needs	Underlying fears
Guest House Women's Group	Cash income; put cooking and cleaning skills learnt into practice; be recognized and respected by their husbands	Guest House services taken over by Community Women's Group
Husbands of women	Honesty of wives to their husbands; wives to be acknowledged as part of guest house project; transparency of women's involvement	Women's status increasing to the point where it undermines the husbands' position in community; Promiscuity of wives; Their wife in particular being excluded from involvement in project

Participatory Conflict Analysis

The outputs of the office-based analysis inform entry into a process of participatory analysis based on engaging stakeholders in dialogue. This subsequent analysis is as much about beginning to develop trust and understanding between the conflicting parties as it is about verifying the accuracy results of the office-based analysis. The dialogue may take many weeks or months, and may be based on one-to-one interviews (ie facilitator-to-stakeholder) or undertaken in groups. It is generally not something that can be completed in a single workshop.

Towards the end of the process, when sufficient trust and rapport have developed, it may be possible to begin to share the different underlying needs and fears of the various stakeholders with each other. Not only is this important in building an understanding of each other's viewpoint, but it encourages an initial exploration of areas of common – or mutually exclusive – ground.

Some of the outputs of a process of Participatory Conflict Analysis are as follows:

- verification/modifications to the information used in the office-based analysis and of the initial findings;
- development of effective forms of communication between stakeholders;
- shared knowledge between stakeholders about each other's underlying motivations, needs, fears, cultures and values;
- clarification of detail concerning the conflict situation, eg locations, timing, gains, losses and resource requirements;
- stakeholder involvement in refinement of the initial office-based ideas for conflict management;
- identification of new conflict management options.

Conflict Management Plan

The Conflict Management Plan describes the overall strategy for managing the conflict, combined with the proposed process of consensus building and an

Table 12.4 *Conflict management plan for the Kakoro Guest House*

1 Most Practicable Strategy: Consensus	2 Participatory Conflict Analysis
Customary conflict management practices mean that an internal negotiation model is preferred to an external, third-party, mediator model, therefore the strategy is to involve strengthening the facilitation and consensual negotiation skills of local groups so that they are able to manage the conflict themselves; as project sponsor, FPCD to remain a party to the consensus building process, acting as facilitator if the process begins to stagnate; BATNA – if consensus not reached, FPCD to resort to the threat of withdrawing financial and logistical support for the guest house.	Completed

3 Capacity Building	4 Conflict Management Actions/Process*
PEACE Foundation (local NGO) contracted to train stakeholders in: • people's skills training (1 week workshop) in Tekadu, with aim of improving the negotiation skills of the key stakeholder representatives; • conflict resolution training (2 week workshop) in Kakoro, with aim of imparting skills to enable self-management of guest house dispute. Assuming immediate dispute is settled, FPCD to bolster agreement by providing: • training in 'book keeping' skills for relevant groups; and • training in Guest House hospitality	Informal community-based discussions to: • introduce idea of local stakeholders managing the conflict without outside mediation; and • clarify some misconceptions that local people have over the role of FPCD in the development of the local economy. Delivery of training in people skills and consensual negotiation. All parties to be invited to train together to: • begin to build relationships and reduce suspicion; and • analyse the conflict situation together Community groups manage own dispute (with FPCD as *ad hoc* facilitator)

initial set of conflict mitigation or prevention options. In the case study, an initial Conflict Management Plan was prepared at the end of the office-based conflict analysis. The plan was subsequently revised after a process of Participatory Conflict Analysis.

The components of a Conflict Management Plan will vary with each situation. They are, however, likely to share the same broad components, as follows:

- the most practicable conflict management strategy (or combination of strategies);
- a description of the proposed process of Participatory Conflict Analysis (if the plan is being prepared at the office stage);

Table 12.5 *Some capacity building options for promoting more equitable processes of consensual negotiation*

| | Stakeholders | | | |
Capacity building	Community leaders (formal and informal)	Project staff	Government extension staff and regulators	Legal representatives (eg village magistrates, land mediators)
Conflict analysis skills		✔	✔	
Communication skills	✔	✔	✔	
Negotiation skills	✔	✔	✔	
Facilitation skills	✔	✔	✔	✔
Mediation skills	✔	✔	✔	✔

- a description of the capacity building measures (communication skills, leadership training, awareness raising about the process of consensus building etc) required to implement the process of consensus building or to action conflict mitigation/ prevention options; and
- the conflict mitigation or prevention options proposed.

The example of a Conflict Management Plan is presented in Table 12.4. It is designed to manage the dispute between two women's groups over profit and work distribution in the Kakoro Guest House, and is the result of both earlier office-based analysis and a subsequent process of participatory analysis.

Capacity Building

Capacity building is integral to developing a level playing field for less powerful stakeholders to participate equitably in a process of consensual negotiation. Increasingly in the future, community-based natural resource management projects introduced into conflict prone areas are likely to include training in negotiation, facilitation and mediation for both project staff and the project's primary and secondary stakeholders. Some capacity building options for consensual negotiation are described in Table 12.5.

One example of capacity building is that undertaken in the Lakekamu Basin ICDP to enable conflicting community groups to resolve the dispute over the Kakoro Guest House. The format for the training is described in the conflict management plan in Table 12.4. Some of the benefits of this type of training are alluded to in the monitoring report prepared by FPCD following the training sessions (Box 12.4).

Implementation

As the extract in Box 12.4 shows, capacity building in the form of training in consensus building can sometimes begin to mitigate a conflict ahead of a formal process of consensual negotiation. Arguably, conflict mitigation can

---

BOX 12.4 EXTRACT FROM FPCD MONITORING REPORT
OF CONSENSUS BUILDING TRAINING

The Conflict Resolution Training helped a lot in bringing together traditional enemies to participate together in what they are beginning to see as a community project. This training was a major ice-breaking point. The main characters fuelling the conflicts (elderly men) did not turn up but those who came included the majority of the young people, who were very eager to learn from us. Due to the absence of those important elders we were not able to get direct agreement on the Research [station] boundaries. However, with us assisting them they identified ways to solve the lack of community cooperation within each respective village [over the Kakoro Tourist Guest House] .

A learning point from the workshops is that the people's self-esteem was boosted when we assisted them to actually analyse their own conflict and find their own solutions. Most participants expressed their concern that they are learning very essential tools to use in their own clan circle. They left with the task of conveying this message to their elders for a future meeting on Research boundaries negotiation.

Source: Conflict Management Project, Monitoring Report, January 1999

---

start even earlier. For example, during a process of Participatory Conflict Analysis the conflicting parties often begin to understand each other's interests and try to identify areas of possible common ground.

However, there will be many components of a conflict mitigation or prevention strategy that will not be able to be identified at the time that an initial Conflict Management Plan is prepared. These are the ideas and actions that arise during a process of multi-stakeholder consensus building. The settlement agreed by all parties to manage the dispute over the distribution of profit at the Kakoro Guest House is summarized in Box 12.5. Most of the actions proposed could not have been foreseen at the time that the initial Conflict Management Plan was prepared.

Impact of Conflict Management in the Lakekamu Basin ICDP

In the Lakekamu Basin ICDP, the most immediate impact of applying the conflict management methodology has been the cessation of local hostilities over the Kakoro Guest House. In terms of local development, this cessation has allowed tourists to return to the area and income to be generated. With regard to conservation, the generation of local income from eco-tourism increases the likelihood that local people will view conservation as an economically viable activity. Thus it can be argued that management of the Kakoro Guest House dispute has contributed to the goal of effective enterprise-based conservation.

There has also been an observable link between the above process of conflict management and the future of the oil palm proposal. Providing a

---

BOX 12.5 SETTLEMENT OF THE DISPUTE OVER DISTRIBUTION OF PROFITS AND WORK IN THE KAKORO GUEST HOUSE

The Process

Using simple office-based analytical tools, staff from FPCD mapped out the causes of the dispute, the stakeholders involved, each stakeholder's immediate concerns and their underlying motivations. The information was then verified with the stakeholders. This month-long process also served to build the degree of trust necessary for FPCD to act as a broker/facilitator in settling the dispute. Following a series of focus group discussions, a joint meeting was held at which a settlement was negotiated. The meeting format of the final negotiations was designed to be familiar to the participants in terms of its location, eligibility to contribute ideas, style of dialogue and type of decision-making.

The Settlement

By creating awareness of their own and each other's underlying motivations, focusing discussion on areas of common interest, and soliciting fresh ideas, FPCD was able to facilitate a settlement. The process revealed that both sides shared a strong desire to see the dispute resolved such that tourists would return and income would once again flow to individuals and the community. It also became clear that the parties' true motivations had less to do with access to profits from the guest house *per se*, and more with being involved in some way in earning income from the presence of the tourists. Through free and open discussion, and with FPCD clarifying the economic and technical viability of the various ideas, it was agreed that one of the groups, the Community Women's Group, would voluntarily leave the guest house services to the other, the Guest House Women's Group. In return the former group would provide portaging services for the guest house, and make and sell handicrafts. The Community Women's Group would also assume responsibility for collecting and selling Kunai grasses to help construct a proposed FPCD field staff accommodation unit, and develop a small kerosene trading business from earlier guest house profits. Lastly, the Community Women's Group was granted sole responsibility for providing cooking and cleaning services to the field staff accommodation once completed. The overall settlement was tested for its social acceptability with the men and leaders of the communities. Six weeks later field observations suggest that the settlement is holding.

---

non-conflictual environment within which community-based eco-tourism has been shown to be viable has reduced the likelihood that landowners will accede to the oil palm proposals. We wait to see whether FPCD's conflict management plan for managing the oil palm threat works. In the meantime, that part of the plan which involved settling disputes over land ownership and profits in relation to eco-tourism guest houses and scientific research stations continues.

The above impacts form part of the outputs of the wider conflict management programme directed at seven community-based natural resource management projects in Fiji and Papua New Guinea. Given that a conflict cannot operate outside its social context, the analytical framework chosen is not one used to frame the impacts of conservation projects, but to formulate and measure the impact of community development projects. This is a sustainable livelihoods framework.

Conflict Management and Sustainable Livelihoods

A sustainable rural livelihoods approach is about removing constraints and exploiting opportunities to realize positive livelihood outcomes at the community level. It aims to both protect and build critical material and social assets, and strengthen the capabilities of individuals, groups and institutions to cope with vulnerability and transform assets into benefits. A livelihood is sustainable when it can cope with and recover from stresses and shocks and maintain or enhance its capabilities and assets both now and in the future, while not undermining the natural resource base (Carney, 1998).

Operationalizing the concept of sustainable livelihoods will require a range of conflict management and consensus building skills, both to exploit opportunities and overcome constraints. Applications include:

1   the exploitation of opportunities for protecting and building the natural, financial, physical, social and human capital assets (particularly the latter two types) and renegotiating the role of government and private structures in transforming livelihood assets into benefits; and
2   reducing constraints by managing contested processes of stakeholder participation within civil society, and between civil society and external actors.

The effectiveness of the results of the conflict management programme in Fiji and Papua New Guinea can be measured by the extent to which it contributes to these objectives. Each is discussed separately below.

Protecting and Building Capital Assets

In themselves, conflict management and consensus building skills are a form of human capital. For example, skills that enable local leaders to negotiate with conservation authorities, NGOs, public water authorities or private logging companies are empowering in their own right. Yet conflict management and consensus building skills provide far more than this. They offer a rapid and cost-effective means to protect and enhance social capital,[6] and it is human and social capital which *together* provide the capacity for protecting and enhancing natural, physical and financial assets.

For example, the experiences in the Lakekamu Basin ICDP demonstrate the role of conflict management in protecting natural capital. First, by managing the threat of clear-felling from a commercial company. Second, the case shows how even minor disputes in conservation-worthy areas, if not properly managed, can escalate to the point where international conservation interests withdraw their funding and support.

Outside of conservation areas, we know that productive common property resource regimes require robust institutions, and that robust institutions will not emerge without appropriate human skills. Nor will roads (physical capital) or credit (financial capital) be accessible without the capacity of local groups or representative NGOs to negotiate access to transportation services or to affordable terms of loan repayments.

A consensus building approach to conflict management has a particular role to play in protecting and enhancing social and human capital, both within rural populations and between community groups and external actors. Given that jealousies, tensions, disputes and violence can undermine coordination and cooperation between parties at both the *micro–micro* and *macro–micro* levels, it is tenable that conflict management capacities (in particular skills to build consensus between parties) are a means to protect and build this coordination and cooperation.

Table 12.6 shows some of the ways in which a consensus approach to conflict management can contribute to building different types of social and human capital.

Renegotiating the Transformational Role of External Actors

A sustainable livelihoods approach attempts to separate the ubiquitous link between rural and agriculture, and to widen the scope of rural development to other sectors – health, education, training, infrastructure, financial services

Table 12.6 *Role of consensus building in strengthening the social capital component of livelihoods*

Form of social capital	Examples
Family and kinship connections	NGO mediation of family disputes such as domestic violence, drunkenness and attempted rape.
Horizontal social networks, associational life, networks of civic engagement	Training of village chiefs and landowners in facilitation skills for use in building consensus between stakeholders over rules for harvesting forest resources, profit distribution and project membership.
Horizontal trust, norms and rules independent of linkages between civil society organizations	Third-party facilitation by an NGO over tourist revenue distribution. Agreement reached on separating out responsibilities for different service activities. No new associations were created, but horizontal social capital was built in that the parties cooperated in new, mutually beneficial, arrangements for engaging with tourists.

etc. It involves new associations between the intended project beneficiaries and external structures (government regulators, local authorities, policies, laws, cultures and policy, private companies and non-target local stakeholders).

Recent thinking on social capital argues that vertical, *macro–micro* associations are a prerequisite to strong horizontal associations in civil society, in that the former facilitate effective local representation, participation and institutional accountability at the local level (Harris and de Renzio, 1997).

Evidence from the South Pacific conflict management programme suggests that the need to depend on *macro* level social capital to provide the enabling environment for a stronger civil society may be overstated, ie that a one-dimensional focus on civil society may not be as misplaced as current thinking would suggest. This is because in community-based natural resource management, many of the disputes, tensions – and even some violent conflicts – are underpinned as much by localized competition over power, resource distribution and access to limited economic opportunities, as by structural injustices, such as land ownership. In short, it may not always be necessary to address structural injustices in society in order to strengthen civil society. In practice, processes of consensus building which emphasize new and creative, medium term, solutions can help to build cooperation and capital assets, and reduce tensions within civil society, without assistance from government institutions and without prior resolution of the dispute's root cause (see examples in Table 12.6).

Furthermore, the South Pacific programme provides evidence that some locally initiated processes of consensus building (those aimed at the *macro–micro* conflicts), can actually contribute to stronger coordination and cooperation between civil society and transformational structures (private companies, central and local government and the regulatory institutions). Table 12.7 shows how consensus building skills at the local level can help renegotiate the role of *macro*-level institutions in transforming livelihood assets into sustainable benefits.

Managing Contested Processes of Participation

A sustainable livelihoods framework provides a basis for identifying desirable and feasible projects and interventions that reduce rural poverty. However, a focus on reducing poverty raises the possibility of new tensions between project beneficiaries and excluded groups. The concept of civil society as a contested space runs counter to the earlier notion of civil society as a single entity, with the different organizations working towards common objectives of democratic governance. This point is forcibly put by McIlwaine (1998, p656) in the context of El Salvador, where she argues that 'civil society and the social relations that underpin it are not, by their nature, inherently democratic or participatory. Not does strengthening civil society organizations automatically engender democratization. Indeed, it may actually undermine it'.

Conflict management methodology offers a set of principles and tools for managing the evolution of civil society and for defusing the inevitable disputes that arise between various parties and individuals. In the first instance the

Table 12.7 *Role of local level consensus building in renegotiating the transformational roles of macro-level institutions*

Form of social capital	Examples
Cross sectoral (vertical) linkages, eg partnerships between private sector, government agencies and civil society	Training of NGOs to be able to better negotiate with private companies, for example, removing the threat of large scale clear felling by a private oil palm company in the Lakekamu Basin, and agreeing profit distribution and tourist trail routes between community leaders and tour operators.
Macro-level social capital (those constitutions, regulations, laws, statutory institutions and policies which define the formal relationships between state and civil society)	Strengthening formal institutional processes of conflict management at the local level so that they are better able to mediate disputes. For example, the training of local land mediators, village magistrates and local officers from the Government Lands Department, the aim in each case being to facilitate the resolution of land ownership disputes.

methodology can be used to identify the need to strengthen customary approaches to conflict management within and between groups in civil society. Where customary approaches are demonstrably failing, the methodology provides a pathway to develop new or hybrid (customary and modern) approaches to managing conflict.

Conclusion

Analysing the Lakekamu Basin ICDP from a sustainable livelihoods perspective provides evidence of a link between the process of conflict management and the protection and creation of social capital. The theory of social capital, and its application to natural resource management in developing countries, is now well advanced. Less developed are the tools of the trade, ways in which horizontal and vertical social capital can be protected from external perturbations, reinstated when lost, or built when none currently exists.

Tables 12.6 and 12.7 show how a consensual approach to conflict management can build social capital. For example, with regard to external perturbations, a conflict analysis exercise undertaken by a local NGO working in the Lakekamu Basin identified a process by which NGOs, government agencies and the private sector might negotiate to remove the threat to biodiversity conservation from a proposed oil palm project. With regard to social capital being reinstated or built, conflict management training conducted with groups competing over profit distribution from a tourist guest house led to renewed trust between the conflicting parties and new forms of cooperation over the available income earning opportunities.

The conflict management methodology adopted in the Lakekamu Basin adheres to a principle of most practicable strategy. For example, in the case of the oil palm threat, as well as entering into consensual negotiation with the company and government agencies, the local NGO proposed two further strategies. First, to begin political lobbying of the Department of Environment and Conservation. Second, to identify a best alternative to a negotiated agreement, in this case, to engage the media and threaten withdrawal from the Lakekamu Basin if the combined negotiation and lobbying strategy were to fail.

Evidence of the positive effect of consensual approaches to conflict management in community-based natural resource projects are increasing and a new discipline is slowly taking shape.[7] At present, the principles and methods of this emerging discipline draw heavily on the North American model of dispute resolution, a model founded in consensus building through impartial, third-party, mediation. The model overlooks some essential differences between dispute management in North America and that associated with community-based natural resource projects. The latter is often characterized by extreme power imbalances between the disputing parties, widely different cultural values, and different perceptions of what constitutes an acceptable process of dialogue or settlement. Given this context, a monocultural, impartial third-party mediator model of conflict management is limiting (Chupp,1991; Lederach, 1996). In addition, although the North American model embraces the concept of a best alternative to a negotiated agreement, it overlooks the possible benefits of concurrently combining different types of conflict management strategy, some based on consensual negotiation, others based on compromise, non-violent force or withdrawal.

Another difference is the importance in many rural areas of developing countries of customary approaches to conflict management. In the discussed conflict management programme in PNG, impartial third-party mediation was proposed only when two prior conditions were met:

1   the available customary approaches to conflict management had demonstrably failed; and
2   it was impracticable to try to strengthen the customary approaches within the required time frame.

Tangentially, this process of adaptation is raising questions over the conventional wisdom on social capital. For example, recent experiences in the Lakekamu Basin seem to run counter to both the following popular assertions: (a) that building social capital within civil society will be ineffective in the absence of strong political structures; and (b) that a necessary prerequisite to effective local dispute management is to resolve the root causes of the conflict. The advantage of adopting a consensual approach to address disputes in community-based natural resource management is that the process seems to offer medium term, independent, solutions.

Acknowledgements

Thanks to the Coordinators of the FSP South Pacific Conflict Management Programme in Papua New Guinea, Katherine Yuave, and the Fiji Islands, Roshni Chand; Dr Scott Jones of the Centre for Rural Development Training, University of Wolverhampton, United Kingdom; Dorothy MacIntosh, Director of the UK Foundation for the Peoples of the South Pacific (UKFSP); Kathy Fry, Regional Coordinator for FSP International in Vanuatu; and Robert Walker of the Conflict and Humanitarian Assistance Department of the Department for International Development (DFID), United Kingdom. DFID have provided funding for the FSP South Pacific Conflict Management Programme over two years.

Notes

1   See Acknowledgements for details.
2   The Lakekamu-Kunimaipa Basin is a 2500 km^2 area of unbroken humid forest in the southern watershed of peninsular Papua New Guinea. The area contains healthy populations of wildlife and plants. The objective of this ICDP is to develop community-owned and operated scientific field research and adventure tourism enterprises. The idea is to provide a substantial incentive for the conservation of the area's biological diversity and to demonstrate to policy makers at the national level that community management of eco-tourism is an alternative to logging and mining.
3   See Warner and Jones (1999) for a more detailed analysis of these strategies.
4   From this, a provisional *Conflict Management Plan* is prepared. It outlines the Most Practicable Strategy of conflict management, safe steps to take next, and what *Capacity Building* to deliver.
5   This participatory analysis is used to revise the *Conflict Management Plan*.
6   Social capital can be defined as 'features of social organization, such as networks, norms and trust, that facilitate coordination and cooperation for mutual benefit'. It is argued that 'working together is easier in a community blessed with a substantial stock of social capital' and that social capital provides the basis for effective government and economic development (Putman, 1993).
7   See for example the forthcoming book by Buckles (ed), dedicated to exploring the role of conflict management in community-based natural resource projects: http://www.idrc.ca/minga/conflict/cases_e.html

References

Abel, N and Blaikie, P (1986) 'Elephants, people, parks and development: the case of the Luangwa Valley, Zambia', *Environmental Management*, 10(6): 735–751

Agrawal, A and Gibson, CC (1999) 'Enchantment and disenchantment: the role of community in natural resource conservation', *World Development*, 27(4): 629–649

Allen, JC and Barnes, DF (1985) 'The causes of deforestation in developing countries', *Annals of the Association of American Geographers*, 75(2): 163–184

Althaus, C (1999) 'How the social sciences turned the forests debate', in Bureau of Resource Sciences, *Country Matters Conference Programme*, Canberra, 20–21 May. http://www.brs.gov.au/events/country/program/

Alva, UT (1978) *Working Plan of Hunsur Forest Division 1978–79 to 2002–03.* Karnataka Forest Department, Government of Karnataka, Bangalore

Anderson, K and Gale, F (1992) *Inventing Places: Studies in Cultural Geography.* Longman Cheshire, Melbourne

Andreoni, J (1990) 'Impure altruism and donations to public goods: a theory of warm-glow giving', *Economic Journal*, 100(401): 464–477

Angelsen, A (1997) 'The poverty-environment thesis: was Brundtland wrong?', *Forum for Development Studies*, 1: 135–154

ANZECC TFMPA (1998) *Guidelines for Establishing the National Representative System of Marine Protected Areas.* Australia and New Zealand Environment and Conservation Council Task Force on Marine Protected Areas. Environment Australia, Canberra

ANZECC TFMPA (1999) *Strategic Plan of Action for the National Representative System of Marine Protected Areas: A Guide for Action by Australian Governments.* Australia and New Zealand Environment and Conservation Council Task Force on Marine Protected Areas. Environment Australia, Canberra.

Apel, KO (1973) 'Das apriori der kommunikationsgemeinschaft und die grundlagen der ethik', in *Transformation der Philosophie*. Bd. 2, Frankfurt am Main, pp358–435

Apel, KO (1980) *Toward a Transformation of Philosophy.* (Translated by G Adey and D Frisby) Routledge & Kegan Paul, London

Arnstein, SR (1969) 'A ladder of citizen participation', *Journal of the American Institute of Planners*, 35(4): 216–224

Arrow, KJ (1986) 'Rationality of self and others in an economic system', *Journal of Business*, 59(4): S385–S399

Auty, RM and Brown, K (eds) (1997) *Approaches to Sustainable Development.* Pinter, London

Babo, S (1997) Wildlife Management Areas in a broader perspective. Paper presented at the Integrated Conservation and Development Conference, Mutupore Island, University of Papua New Guinea, 1–5 September

Barber, CV, Johnson, NC and Hafild, E (1994) *Breaking the Logjam: Obstacles to Forest Policy Reform in Indonesia and the United States.* World Resources Institute, Washington, DC

Barber, CV, Afif, S and Purnomo, A (1995) *Tigers by the Tail? Reorienting Biodiversity Conservation and Development in Indonesia.* World Resources Institute, Washington, DC

Barbier, EB, Burgess, JC and Folke, C (1994) *Paradise Lost? The Ecological Economics of Biodiversity.* Earthscan Publications, London

Barrett, CB and Arcese, P (1995) 'Are integrated conservation-development projects (ICDPs) sustainable? On the conservation of large mammals in Sub-Saharan Africa', *World Development,* 23(7): 1073–1084

Barry, B (1977) 'Justice between generations', in PMS Hacker and J Raz (eds) *Law, Morality and Society.* Oxford University Press, Oxford, pp268–284

Barry, J and Proops, J (1999) 'Seeking sustainability discourses with Q methodology', *Ecological Economics,* 28(3): 337–345

Batagoda, S and Turner, RK (1997) Towards policy relevant ecosystem services and natural capital values: rainforest non-timber forest products. Mimeo. Centre for Social and Economic Research on the Global Environment. University of East Anglia

Bateman, IJ and Turner, RK (1993) 'Valuation of the environment, methods and techniques: the contingent valuaiton method', in Turner, RK (ed) *Sustainable Environmental Economics and Management: Principles and Practice.* Belhave Press, London, pp120–191

Bates, RH (ed) (1988) *Toward a Political Economy of Development: A Rational Choice Perspective.* University of California Press, Berkeley

Bawa, K, Schaal, B, Solbrig, OT, Sterns, S, Templeton, A and Vida, G (1991) 'Biodiversity: from genes to species', in OT Solbrig (ed) *From Genes to Ecosystems: A Research Agenda for Biodiversity.* IUBS, SCOPE, UNESCO, Cambridge, Mass., pp15–36

Becker, GS (1976) *The Economic Approach to Human Behavior.* University of Chicago Press, Chicago

Beed, C (1992) 'Do value judgements affect testing economic theory?', *International Journal of Social Economics,* 19(2): 6–24

Bentham, J (1970) *An Introduction to the Principles of Morals and Legislation.* Hafner, Darien, CT

Berkes, F and Folke, C (1994) 'Investing in cultural capital for sustainable use of natural capital', in AM Jansson, M Hammer, C Folke and R Costanza (eds) *Investing in Natural Capital: The Ecological Economics Approach to Sustainability.* Island Press, Washington, DC, pp128–149

Berman, M (1981) *The Reenchantment of the World.* Cornell University Press, Ithaca, NY

Binswanger, HP (1991) 'Brazilian policies that encourage deforestation in the Amazon', *World Development,* 19(7): 821–829

Biodiversity Conservation Network (1999) *Evaluating Linkages Between Business, the Environment and Local Communities.* World Wildlife Fund (US), Washington, DC

Bishop, RC (1978) 'Endangered species and uncertainty: the economics of a safe minimum standard', *American Journal of Agricultural Economics,* 60(1): 10–18

Bishop, RC (1979) 'Endangered species, irreversibility and uncertainty: a reply', *American Journal of Agricultural Economics,* 61(2): 376–379

Bishop, RC (1993) 'Economic efficiency, sustainability and biodiversity', *Ambio,* 22(2–3): 69–73

Blaikie, P and H Brookfield (1987) *Land Degradation and Society.* Routledge, London

Blaikie, P and S Jeanrenaud (1997) 'Biodiversity and human welfare', in KB Ghimire and MP Pimbert (eds) *Social Change and Conservation*. Earthscan Publications, London, pp46–70

Blaug, M (1992) *The Methodology of Economics: Or How Economists Explain*. Second edition. Cambridge University Press, Cambridge

Boehmer-Christiansen, S (1994) 'The precautionary principle in Germany – enabling government', in T O'Riordan and J Cameron (eds) *Interpreting the Precautionary Principle*. Earthscan, London, pp31–60

Bonnemaison, J (1984) 'Social and cultural aspects of land tenure', in P Larmour (ed) *Land Tenure in Vanuatu*. The University of the South Pacific, Suva, pp1–5

Borrini-Feyerabend, G (1996) *Collaborative Management of Protected Areas: Tailoring the Approach to the Context*. IUCN, Gland

Braatz, S, Davis, G, Shen, S and Rees, C (1992) *Conserving Biological Diversity: A Strategy for Protected Areas in the Asia-Pacific Region*. World Bank Technical Paper Number 193. World Bank, Washington

Brinkman, R (1994) 'Recent developments in land use planning, with special reference to FAO', in LO Fresco, L Stroosnijder, J Bouma and H van Keulen (eds) *The Future of the Land: Mobilising and Integrating Knowledge for Land Use Options*. John Wiley & Sons, Chichester, pp11–21

Bromley, DW (1991) *Environment and Economy: Property Rights and Public Policy*. Basil Blackwell, Oxford

Bromley, DW and Cernea, MM (1989) *The Management of Common Property Resources: Some Conceptual and Operational Fallacies*. World Bank Discussion Paper No. 57. The World Bank, Washington, DC

Bromley, DW and Chapagain, DP (1984) 'The village against the center: resource depletion in South Asia', *American Journal of Agricultural Economics*, 66: 868–873

Brookfield, H and Stocking, M (1999) 'Agrodiversity: definition, description and design', *Global Environmental Change*, 9: 77–80

Brooks, KN, Gregersen, HM, Ffolliot, PF and Tejwani, KG (1992) 'Watershed management: a key to sustainability', in NP Sharma (ed) *Managing the World's Forests: Looking for Balance Between Conservation and Development*. Kendall/Hunt Publishing Co, Dubuque, Iowa, pp455–487

Browder, JO (1992) 'The limits of extractivism: tropical forest strategies beyond extractive reserves', *BioScience*, 42(3): 174–182

Brown, E (1985) *The Forest Preserve of New York State*. Adirondack Mountain Club, New York

Brown, M and Wyckoff-Baird, B (1992) *Designing Integrated Conservation and Development Projects*. The Biodiversity Support Programme, Washington, DC

Brown, P (1998) *Climate, Biodiversity, and Forests: Issues and Opportunities Emerging from the Kyoto Protocol*. WRI, Washington, IUCN, Geneva

Bryant, CGA (1985) *Positivism in Social Theory and Research*. St Martin's Press, New York

Buchy, M (1996) *Teak and Arecanut: Colonial State, Forest and People in the Western Ghats (South India) 1800–1947*. Institute Francais de Pondicherry and Indira Gandhi National Centre for the Arts, Pondicherry, India

Buchy, M and Hoverman, S, with Averil, C (1999) *Understanding public participation in forest planning in Australia: How can we learn from each other?* Department of Forestry, The Australian National University, Canberra

Burgess, JC (1993) 'Timber production, timber trade and tropical deforestation', *Ambio*, 22(2–3): 136–143

Bush, K (1998) *A Measure of Peace: Peace and Conflict Impact Assessment of Development Projects in Conflict Zones.* Working Paper No 1, The Peacebuilding and Reconstruction Program Initiative, IDRC, Ottawa

Byron, RN (1991) 'Cost benefit analysis and community forestry projects', in DA Gilmour and RJ Fisher, *Villagers, Forests and Foresters: The Philosophy, Process and Practice of Community Forestry in Nepal.* Sahayogi Press, Kathmandu, pp163–180

Caldecott, J (1996) 'Indonesia', in E Lutz and J Caldecott (eds) *Decentralizationn and Biodiversity Conservation.* The World Bank, Washington, DC, pp43–53

Caldecott, J (1996) *Designing Conservation Projects.* Cambridge University Press, Cambridge

Calder, IR (1998) *Water-Resource and Land-Use Issues.* SWIM Paper 3. International Water Management Institute, Colombo

Caldwell, B (1982) *Beyond Positivism: Economic Methodology in the Twentieth Century.* George Allen & Unwin, London

Cameron, J (1994) 'The status of the precautionary principle in international law', in T O'Riordan and J Cameron (eds) *Interpreting the Precautionary Principle.* Earthscan, London, pp262–289

Caporael, L, Dawes, R, Orbell, J and and Van de Kragt, A (1989) 'Selfishness examined: cooperation in the absence of egoistic incentives', *Behavioral and Brain Sciences,* 12: 683–739

Carlsson, B and Stankiewicz, R (1991) 'On the nature, function and composition of technological systems', *Journal of Evolutionary Economics,* 1: 93–118

Carney, D (1998) *Sustainable Rural Livelihoods: What Contributions Can We Make?* Department for International Development and Overseas Development Institute, London

Cernea, MM (1987) 'Farmer organisations and institution-building for sustainable development', *Regional Development Dialogue,* 8: 1–24

Cernea, MM (ed) (1991) *Putting People First: Sociological Variables in Rural Development.* Second edition. The World Bank, Washington, DC

Chambers, R (1997) *Whose Reality Counts?* Intermediate Technology Publications, London

Checkland, P and Scholes, J (1990) *Soft System Methodology in Action.* John Wiley & Sons, Chicester

Chupp, M (1991) 'When Mediation is Not Enough', *MCS Conciliation Quarterly*

Ciriacy-Wantrup, SV (1963) *Resource Conservation: Economics and Policies.* University of California, Division of Agricultural Sciences, Berkeley

Cities International (1996) Volume VIII, No. III, Third Quarter. http://www.icma.org/cities

Clay, DC, Giozlo, M and Wallace, S (1994) *Population and Land Degradation.* EPAT/MUCIA Working Paper No. 14. University of Wisconsin, Madison

Coakes, S (1998) 'Valuing the social dimension: social assessment in the Regional Forest Agreement process', *Australian Journal of Environmental Management* 5: 47–54

Cocks, D (1999) *Future Makers, Future Takers: Life in Australia 2050.* University of New South Wales Press, Sydney

Cocks, KD, Ive, JR and Clark, JL (1995) *Forest Issues: Processes and Tools for Inventory, Evaluation, Mediation and Allocation.* Commonwealth Scientific and Industrial Research Organisation, Canberra

Cohen, J M, Uphoff, N T (1980) 'Participation's place in rural development: seeking clarity through specificity', *World Development* 8: 213–235

Colchester, M (1994) 'Sustaining the forests: the community-based approach in South and South-East Asia', *Development and Change*, 25(1): 69–100

Collins, J (1994) 'The Adirondack Park: How a Green Line Approach Works', in CM Klyza and SC Trombulak (eds) *The Future of the Northern Forest*. Middlebury College Press, Vermont

Collins, NM, Sayer, JA and Whitmore, TC (eds) (1991) *The Conservation Atlas of Tropical Forests: Asia and the Pacific*. Macmillan Press, London; IUCN, Gland

Commission on Sustainable Development (1999) Issues that need further clarification: forest conservation and protected areas. Intergovernmental Forum on Forests, Third Session. http://www.un.org/esa/sustdev/docsiff3.htm

Commission on the Adirondacks in the Twenty-First Century (1990) *The Adirondack Park in the Twenty-First Century*. State of New York, Albany

Common, M (1988) *Environmental and Resource Economics: An Introduction*. Longman, London

Common, MS, Blamey, RK and Norton, TW (1993) 'Sustainability and environmental valuation', *Environmental Values*, 2(4): 299–334

Commonwealth of Australia (1992a) *National Forest Policy Statement: A New Focus for Australia's Forests*. Australian Government Printing Service, Canberra

Commonwealth of Australia (1992b) *National Strategy for Ecologically Sustainable Development*. Australian Government Publishing Service, Canberra

Commonwealth of Australia (1992c) *Inter-governmental Agreement on the Environment*. Department of the Arts, Environment, Sport and Territories. Australian Government Publishing Service, Canberra

Commonwealth of Australia (1996) *National Strategy for the Conservation of Australia's Biological Diversity*. Department of the Environment, Sport and Territories, Canberra

Commonwealth of Australia (1997) *Nationally Agreed Criteria for the Establishment of a Comprehensive, Adequate and Representative System of Forests in Australia*. Australian Government Publishing Service, Canberra

Commonwealth of Australia (1998) *Australia's Oceans Policy*. Environment Australia, Canberra

Commonwealth of Australia (1999) *International Forest Conservation: Protected Areas and Beyond*. A Discussion paper for the Intergovernmental Forum on Forests, Commonwealth of Australia, Canberra

Conroy, C, Rai, A, Singh, N and Chan, MK (1998) *Conflicts Affecting Participatory Forest Management: Some Experiences from Orissa*. Revised version of a paper presented at the Workshop on Participatory Natural Resource Management in Developing Countries: Mansfield College, Oxford, 6–7 April

Cooter, R and Rappoport, P (1984) 'Were the ordinalists wrong about welfare economics?', *Journal of Economic Literature*, XXII(June): 507–530

Cornwall, A and Jewkes, R (1995) 'What is participatory research?', *Social Science and Medicine*, 41(12): 1667–1676

Costanza, R (1998) 'Beyond the argument culture', *Ecological Economics*, 27(2): 113–114

Costanza, R and Daly, HE (1992) 'Natural capital and sustainable development', *Conservation Biology*, 6(1): 37–46

Costanza, R and Perrings, C (1990) 'A flexible assurance bonding system for improved environmental management', *Ecological Economics*, 2: 57–76

Costanza, R, Daly, HE and Bartholomew, JA (1991) 'Goals, agenda, and policy recommendations for ecological economics ', in R Costanza (ed) *Ecological Economics: The Science and Management of Sustainability*. Columbia University Press, New York, pp1–20

Costanza, R, Cumberland, J, Daly, H, Goodland, R and Norgaard, R (1997a) *An Introduction to Ecological Economics*. St Lucie Press, Boca Raton, FL

Costanza, R, d'Arge, R, de Groot, R, Farber, S, Grasso, M, Hannon, B, Limburg, K, Naeem, S, O'Neill, RV, Paruelo, J, Raskin, RJ, Sutton, P and van den Belt, M (1997b) 'The value of the world's ecosystem services and natural capital', *Nature*, 387(May 15): 253–260. Reprinted in *Ecological Economics*, 1998, 25(1): 3–15

Cox, G (1998) *Protecting the Forest Lands as a Renewable Economic Base for the Adirondack Park*. Masters Thesis, Department of Economics, Rensselaer Polytechnic Institute, Troy, New York

Cribb, R (1988) *The Politics of Environmental Protection in Indonesia*. Working Paper No 48. Centre of Southeast Asian Studies, Monash University, Melbourne

Cronbach, L (1975) 'Beyond the two disciples of scientific psychology', *American Psychologist*, 30:116–127

Cropper, ML and Oates, WE (1992) 'Environmental economics: a survey', *Journal of Economics Literature*, XXX(June): 675–740

Dalal-Clayton, B and Dent, D (1993) *Surveys, Plans and People: A Review of Land Resource Information and its Use in Developing Countries*. IIED, London

Daly, HE (1992) 'Allocation, distribution and scale: towards an economics that is efficient, just and sustainable', *Ecological Economics*, 6: 185–193

Dargavel, J (1995) *Fashioning Australia's Forests*. Oxford University Press, Melbourne

Dasmann, RF (1975/76) 'National parks, nature conservation and future primitive', *Ecologist*, 6(5): 164–167

Dauvergne, P (1993–94) 'The politics of deforestation in Indonesia', *Pacific Affairs*, 66(4): 497–518

Davie, J and Djamaluddin, R (1999) The Need for Care in the Use of Resource Substitution as an Instrument in Integrating Conservation and Development. Paper presented at the International Symposium on Society and Resource Management, July 7–10, University of Queensland, Brisbane

Dawes, R, van de Kragt, A and Orbell, J (1990) 'Cooperation for the benefit of us: not me, or my conscience', in J Mansbridge (ed) *Beyond Self-Interest*. University of Chicago Press, Chicago, Illinois

Day, D (1997) 'Citizen participation in the planning process: an essentially contested concept?', *Journal of Planning Literature*, 11(3): 421–434

de Beer, JH and McDermott, MJ (1989) *The Economic Value of Non-Timber Forest Products in Southeast Asia, with Emphasis on Indonesia, Malaysia and Thailand*. International Union for the Conservation of Nature and Natural Resources, Netherlands Committee

Dent, DL and Goonewardene, LKPA (1993) *Resource Assessment and Land Use Planning in Sri Lanka: A Case Study*. IIED, London

Dey, C (1997) 'Women, forest products and protected areas: a case study of Jaldapara Wildlife Sanctuary, West Bengal, India', in KB Ghimire and MP Pimbert (eds) *Social Change and Conservation*. Earthscan Publications, London, pp131–157

Dickinson, FB (1881) *Progress Report of Forest Administration in Coorg 1881/82*, Forest Department (Coorg), Bangalore

Dickinson, FB (1883) *Progress Report of Forest Administration in Coorg 1881/82*, Forest Department (Coorg), Bangalore

Dietz, FJ and van der Straaten, J (1992) 'Rethinking environmental economics: missing links between economic theory and environmental policy', *Journal of Economics Issues*, XXVI(1): 27–51

Dixon, JA and Sherman, PB (1990) *Economics of Protected Areas*. Island Press, Washington, DC

Dobbs, D and Ober, R (1995) *The Northern Forest*. Chelsea Green Publishing Co., White River Junction, Vermont

Douthwaite, R (1996) *Short Circuit: Strengthening Local Economies for Security in an Unstable World*. Lilliput Press, Dublin, Ireland

Dovers, S (1995) 'Information, sustainability and policy', *Australian Journal of Environmental Management*, 2: 142–156

Dovers, S (1997) 'Sustainability: demands on policy', *Journal of Public Policy*, 16: 303–318

Drèze, J and Sen, A (1989) *Hunger and Public Action*. Clarendon Press, Oxford

Dryzek, J (1997) *The Politics of the Earth: Environmental Discourses*. Oxford University Press, New York

Duraiappah, AK (1998) 'Poverty and environmental degradation: a review and analysis of the nexus', *World Development*, 26(12): 2169–2179

Durning, A (1991) 'Asking how much is enough', in LR Brown et al *State of the World 1991*. W.W. Norton & Co., New York, pp153–169

Dwyer, PD (1994) 'Modern conservation and indigenous peoples: in search of wisdom', *Pacific Conservation Biology*, 1: 91–97

Easlea, B (1973) *Liberation and the Aims of Science: An Essay on the Obstacles to the Building of a Beautiful World*. Published for Sussex University Press by Chatto & Windus Ltd., London

Eckholm, EP (1976) *Losing Ground: Environmental Stress and World Food Prospects*. Norton, New York

Eckholm, EP (1982) *Down to Earth*. Pluto Press, London

Edgerton, RB (1992) *Sick Societies: Challenging Myths of Primitive Harmony*. Cambridge University Press, Cambridge

Ehrenfeld, D (1988) 'Why put a value on biodiversity', in EO Wilson (ed) *Biodiversity*. National Academy Press, Washington, DC, pp212–216

Ehrlich, PR and Daily, GC (1993) 'Population extinction and saving biodiversity', *Ambio*, 22(2–3): 64–68

Ellis, F (1998) 'Household strategies and rural livelihood diversification', *The Journal of Development Studies*, 35(1): 1–38

Ellis, JA (1997) *Race for the Rainforest II: Applying Lessons Learned from Lak to the Bismarck-Ramu Integrated Conservation and Development Initiative in Papua New Guinea*. PNG Biodiversity Conservation and Resource Management Programme, Department of Environment and Conservation – UNDP – GEF, Port Moresby

England, RW (1998) 'Should we pursue measurement of the natural capital stock?', *Ecological Economics*, 27(3): 257–266

Environment Unit (1993) *Vanuatu National Conservation Strategy*. Government of Vanuatu, Port Vila

Erickson, JD (1998) 'Sustainable development and the Adirondack experience', *Adirondack Journal of Environmental Studies*, 5(2)

Erickson, JD, Hubacek, K and Duchin, F (1998) 'Sustainable land use design: an input–output analysis of the Adirondacks of New York State, USA', paper presented at the Fifth Biennial Meeting of the International Society for Ecological Economics. Santiago, Chile, 15–19 November

Etzioni, A (1988) *The Moral Dimension: Towards a New Economics*. The Free Press, New York

FAO (1995) *Forest Resource Assessment 1990: Global Synthesis*. Food and Agricultural Organization, Rome

Farrow, S (1995) 'Extinction and market forces: two case studies', *Ecological Economics*, 13(2): 115–123

Faucheux, S and Froger, G (1995) 'Decision-making under environmental uncertainty', *Ecological Economics*, 15(1): 29–42

Fearnside, PM (1993) 'A response to the theory that tropical forest conservation poses a threat to the poor', *Land Use Policy*, April: 108–121

Feeny, D, Berkes, F, McCay, BJ and Acheson, J (1990) 'The tragedy of the commons: twenty-two years later', *Human Ecology*, 18(1): 1–19

Feldman, AM (1980) *Welfare Economics and Social Choice Theory*. Kluwer, Boston

Feyerabend, PK (1975) *Against Method. Outline of an Anarchistic Theory of Knowledge*. NLB, London

Fisher, AC (1981) *Resource and Environmental Economics*. Cambridge University Press, Cambridge

Fisher, RJ (1995) *Collaborative Management of Forests for Conservation and Development*. IUCN, Gland; WWF, Geneva

Fresco, LO (1994) 'Imaginable futures: a contribution to thinking about land use planning', in LO Fresco, L Stroosnijder, J Bouma and H van Keulen (eds) *The Future of the Land: Mobilising and Integrating Knowledge for Land Use Options*. John Wiley & Sons, Chichester, 1–21

Friedman, M (1973) 'The methodology of positive economics', in M Friedman, *Essays in Positive Economics*. University of Chicago Press, Chicago, pp3–43

Funtowicz, SO and Ravetz, JR (1991) 'A new scientific methodology for global environmental issues', in R Costanza (ed) *Ecological Economics: The Science and Management of Sustainability*. Columbia University Press, New York, pp137–152

Funtowicz, SO and Ravetz, JR (1993a) 'Science for the post-normal age', *Futures*, 5(7): 739–755

Funtowicz, SO and Ravetz, JR (1993b) 'The emergence of post-normal science', in R von Schomberg (ed) *Science, Politics and Morality: Scientific Uncertainty and Decision Making*. Kluwer Academic Publishers, Dordrecht, pp85–123

Funtowicz, SO and Ravetz, JR (1994) 'The worth of a songbird: ecological economics as a post-normal science', *Ecological Economics*, 10(3): 197–207

Gadgil, M (1992) 'Conserving biodiversity as if people matter: a case study from India', *Ambio*, 21(3): 266–70

Gadgil, M and Guha, R (1992) *This Fissured Land: an Ecological History of India*. Oxford University Press, Delhi

Gandy, M (1996) 'Crumbling land: the postmodernity debate and the analysis of environmental problems', *Progress in Human Geography*, 20(1): 23–40

Garcia-Barrios, R and Garcia-Barrios, L (1990) 'Environmental and technology degradation in peasant agriculture: a consequence of development in Mexico', *World Development*, 18(11): 1569–1585

Gee, JMA (1991) 'The neoclassical school', in D Mair and AG Miller (eds) *A Modern Guide to Economic Thought*. Edward Elgar, Aldershot, pp71–108

Geertz, C (1973) *The Interpretation of Cultures*. Basic Books, New York

Gezon, L (1998) 'Institutional Structure and the Effectiveness of Integrated Conservation and Development Projects', *Human Organization*, 56(4): 462–470

Ghimire, KB (1994) 'Parks and people: livelihood issues in national parks management in Thailand and Madagascar', *Development and Change*, 25(1): 195–29

Ghimire, KB and Pimbert, MP (eds) (1997) *Social Change and Conservation*. Earthscan Publications, London

Giesen, W (1991) Hutan Bakau Pantai Timur Nature Reserve, Jambi. PHPA/AWB Sumatra Wetland Project, AWB-Indonesia. Bogor

Goodland, R (1995) 'The concept of environmental sustainability', *Annual Review of Ecological Systems*, 26: 1–24

Gössling, S (1999) 'Ecotourism: a means to safeguard biodiversity and ecosystem functions?', *Ecological Economics*, 29(2): 303–320

Government of India (1995) *Report of the Committee of Members of Parliament and Experts Constituted to Make Recommendations on Law Concerning Extension of Provisions of the Constitution (seventy-third amendment)Act, 1992 to Scheduled Areas*. Ministry of Rural Development, New Delhi

Grimes, A, Loomis, S, Jahnige, P, Burnham, M, Onthank, K, Alancón, R, Cuenca, WP, Martinez, CC, Neill, D, Balik, M, Bennett, B and Mendelsohn, R (1994) 'Valuing the Rain Forest: the economic value of nontimber forest products in Ecuador', *Ambio*, 23(7): 405–410

Guba, EG (1990) 'The alternative paradigm dialog', in EG Guba (ed) *The Paradigm Dialog*. Sage Publications, London, pp17–27

Guijt, I and Shah, MK (eds) (1998) *The Myth of Community: Gender Issues in Participatory Development*. Intermediate Technology Publications, London

Gunarso, P and Davie, J (1997) Can Indonesian Production Forest Play a Nature Conservation Role? Paper presented at the conference Conservation in Production Environments, 1–5 December, Lake Taupo, New Zealand

Gunarso, P and Davie, J (1999) How Decentralization Can Improve Accountability of Forest Resources Management in Indonesia. Paper presented at the International Symposium on Society and Resource Management, 7–10 July, University of Queensland, Brisbane

Gurung, B (1992) 'Towards sustainable development: a case in Eastern Himalayas', *Futures*, 24(9): 907–16

Habermas, J (1984) *The Theory of Communicative Action, Vol.1, Reason and the Rationalization of Society*. Beacon Press, Boston

Habermas, J (1996) *Justification and Application: Remarks on Discourse Ethics*. (Translated by C Cronin) MIT Press, Cambridge, Mass

Hackel, JD (1990) 'Conservation attitudes in Southern Africa: a comparison between KwaZulu and Swaziland', *Human Ecology*, 18(2): 203–209

Hahnel, R and Albert, M (1990) *Quiet Revolution in Welfare Economics*. Princeton University Press, Princeton

Hall, CM (1989) 'The 'worthless land hypothesis' and Australia's national parks and reserves', in KJ Frawley and N Semple (eds) *Australia's Ever Changing Forests*. Special Publication No. 1. Department of Geography and Oceanography, University College, The University of New South Wales, Canberra

Hannah, L, Rakotosamimanana, B, Ganzhorn, J, Mittermeier, RA, Olivieri, S, Iyer, L, Rajaobelina, S, Hough, J, Andriamialisoa, F, Bowles, I and Tilkin, G (1998) 'Participatory planning, scientific priorities, and landscape conservation in Madagascar', *Environmental Conservation*, 25(1): 30–36

Hannigan, JA (1995) *Environmental Sociology: A Social Constructionist Perspective*. Routledge, London

Harre, R (1972) *The Philosophies of Science: An Introductory Survey*. Oxford University Press, Oxford

Harris, J and de Renzio, P (1997) 'Missing link or analytically missing? The concept of social capital', in J Harris (ed) *Policy Arena: Social Capital*. Development Studies Institute, London School of Economics, London, unpublished

Harvey (1989) *The Conditions of Postmodernity: An Inquiry into the Origins of Cultural Change*. Blackwell, Oxford

Hausman, DM (1992) *The Inexact and Separate Science of Economics*. Cambridge University Press, Cambridge

Hausman, DM and McPherson, MS (1993) 'Taking ethics seriously: economics and contemporary moral philosophy', *Journal of Economic Literature*, XXXI(June): 671–731

Hecht, SB (1985) 'Environment, development and politics: capital accumulation and the livestock sector in eastern Amazonia', *World Development*, 13(6): 663–684

Hennipman, P (1976) 'Pareto optimality: value judgement or analytical tool', in JS Cramer, A Heertjie and P Venekamp (eds) *Relevance and Precision. From Quantitative Analysis to Economic Policy*. North-Holland, Amsterdam, pp39–69

Hesse, M (1980) *Revolutions and Reconstructions in the Philosophy of Science*. Indiana University Press, Bloomington

Hicks, JR (1946) *Value and Capital*. (Second edition) Oxford University Press, Oxford

Hicks, JR and Allen, RGD (1934) 'A reconsideration of the theory of value', *Economica*, February/May, 1: 52–76 and 196–219

Hindess, B (1988) *Choice, Rationality and Social Theory*. Unwin Hyman, London

Hinterberger, F, Luks, F and Schmidt-Bleek, F (1997) 'Material flows vs. 'natural capital': what makes and economy sustainable?', *Ecological Economics*, 23(1):1–14

Hodgson, A (1997) 'The Wolf restoration in the Adirondacks? Question of local residents', *Wildlife Conservation Society Working Paper Series*, 8

Hodgson, GM (1988) *Economics and Institutions: A Manifesto for a Modern Institutional Economics*. Polity Press, Cambridge

Hohl, A and Tisdell, CA (1993) 'How useful are environmental standards in economics? The example of safe minimum standards for the protection of species', *Biodiversity and Conservation*, 2: 168–181

Holling, CS (1986) 'Resilience of ecosystem: local surprise and global change', in EC Clark and RE Munn (eds) *Sustainable Development of the Biosphere*. Cambridge University Press, Cambridge

Hoover, KD (1995) 'Why does methodology matter for economics', *The Economic Journal*, 105(440): 715–734

Hough, JL and Sherpa, MN (1989) 'Bottom up vs. basic needs: integrating conservation and development in the Annapurna and Michiru Mountain Conservation Areas of Nepal and Malawi', *Ambio*, 18(8): 435–41

House of Representatives Standing Committee on Environment, Recreation and the Arts (1993) *Biodiversity: The Role of Protected Areas*. Australian Government Publishing Service, Canberra

Hueting, R and Reijnders, L (1998) 'Sustainability is an objective concept', *Ecological Economics*, 27(2): 139–147

ICIMOD (1996) Seminar on Conflict Resolution in Natural Resources. International Centre for Integrated Mountain Development, Kathmandu

IIED (1994) *Whose Eden? An Overview of Community Approaches to Wildlife Management*. A report by the International Institute for Environment and Development to the UK Overseas Development Administration. International Institute for Environment and Development, London

Indian Institute of Public Administration (1994) *Biodiversity Conservation Through Ecodevelopment: An Indicative Plan*. Sponsored by the United Nations Development Program, and prepared on behalf of the Government of India, Ministry of Environment and Forests, and the concerned state governments, New Delhi

Infield, M (1988) 'Attitudes of a rural community towards conservation and a local conservation area in Natal, South Africa', *Biological Conservation*, 45: 21–46

Interim Marine and Coastal Regionalisation for Australia Technical Group (1998) *Interim Marine and Coastal Regionalisation for Australia: an ecosystem-based classification for marine and coastal environments of Australia*. Version 3.3. Environment Australia, Commonwealth Department of Environment and Heritage, Canberra

International Alert (1996) *Resource Pack*. International Alert, London

IREE (Institute for Research on Environment and Economy) (1996) *Community Empowerment in Ecosystem Management*. University of Ottawa, Ottawa, Ontario

ITTO (1992) *ITTO Guidelines for the Sustainable Management of Natural Tropical Forests. ITTO Policy Development Series 1*. International Timber Trade Organization, Yokohama

IUCN (1993) *Parks and Progress: Protected Areas and Economic Development in Latin America and the Caribbean*. International Union for the Conservation of Nature and Natural Resources, Gland

IUCN (1994) *Guidelines for Protected Area Management Categories*. Commission on National Parks and Protected Areas with the assistance of the World Conservation Monitoring Centre, Gland

IUCN World Commission on Protected Areas (1997) Protected Areas in the Twenty-first Century: from Islands to Networks. Report of the Conference held in Albany, Western Australia, 24–29 November

IUCN-COE, (1984) *Why Conservation?* Commission on Ecology. Working Paper No. 3. IUCN, Gland

Jackson, C (1997) 'Actor orientation and gender relations at a participatory project interface', in A Goetz (ed) *Getting Institutions Right for Women in Development*. Zed Books, London, pp161–175

Jackson, P (1968) *Life in Classrooms*. Holt, Rinehart and Winston, New York

Jacobs, M (1988) *The Tropical Forest: A First Encounter*. Springer-Verlag, Berlin

Jacobs, M (1994) 'The limits to neoclassicism: towards an institutional environmental economics', in M Redclift and T Benton (eds) *Social Theory and the Global Environment*. Routledge, London, pp67–91

Jacobs, M (1996) 'What is socio-ecological economics?' *The Ecological Economics Bulletin*, 1(2): 14–16

Janis, I and Mann, L (1977) *Decision Making: A Psychological Analysis of Conflict, Choice and Commitment*. Free Press, New York

Jenkins, J (1995) 'Notes on the Adirondack Blowdown of July 15th, 1995: Scientific Background, Observations, and Policy Issues', *Wildlife Conservation Society Working Paper Series*, 5

Jepma, CJ (1995) *Tropical Deforestation: A Socio-Economic Approach*. Earthscan Publications, London

Johnson, A (1997) 'Processes for effecting community participation in the establishment of protected areas: a case study of the Crater Mountain Wildlife Management Area', in C Filer (ed) *The Political Economy of Forest Management in Papua New Guinea*. The National Research Institute, Port Moresby; IIED, London, pp391–428

Jørgensen, SE (1990) 'Ecosystem theory, ecological buffer capacity, uncertainty and complexity', *Ecological Modeling*, 41: 117–125

Kahneman, D, Knetsch, JL and Thaler, RH (1986) 'Fairness and the assumptions of economics', *Journal of Business*, 59(4): S285–S300

Kahneman, D, Slovic, P and Tversky, A (1982) *Judgment Under Uncertainty: Heuristic and Biases*. Cambridge University Press, Cambridge

Kane, M, Cox, G and Erickson, JD (1998) 'An application of a multi-criteria decision model to open space conservation choices', paper presented at the Fifth Annual Conference on the Adirondacks. Saranac Lake, New York, 20–22 May

Kavka, G (1978) 'The futurity problem', in RI Sikora and B Barry (eds) *Obligations to Future Generations*. Temple University Press, Philadelphia

Kelleher, G, Bleakley, C and Wells, S (principal eds) (1995) *A Global Representative System of Marine Protected Areas, Vols I–V*. The Great Barrier Reef Marine Park Authority, Canberra; The World Bank, Washington, DC; The World Conservation Union (IUCN), Gland

Kemf, E (ed) (1993) *The Law of the Mother: Protecting Indigenous People in Protected Areas*. Sierra Club Books, San Francisco

Kemmis, S and McTaggart, R (1988) *The Action Research Planner*. Deakin University, Victoria

Kinsley, MJ (1997) *Economic Renewal Guide: a Collaborative Process for Sustainable Community Development*. Rocky Mountain Institute, Snowmass, Colorado

Kirkpatrick, JB (1998) 'Nature conservation and the Regional Forest Agreement process', *Australian Journal of Environmental Management 5*: 31–37

Kneese, AV and Russell, CS (1987) 'Environmental economics', in J Eatwell, M Milgate and P Newman (eds) *The Palgrave Dictionary of Economics*. Macmillan, London, pp159–163

Knight, F (1921) *Risk, Uncertainty and Profit*. Houghton Mifflin, New York

Kompas (23/2/99) Dibabat Hutan Lindung di Kawasan TNBBS (Illegal Logging in Protection Forest of TNBBS) http://www.kompas.com/kompas-cetak/9902/23/Daerah/diba19.htm

Kompas (29/4/99) Penggunaan Lahan di TN Kutai tak Terkendali (The Use of Land in Kutai National Parks is Out of Control) http://www.kompas.com/kompas-cetak/9904/29/daerah/peng08.htm

Kompas (25/8/99a) Menhutbun Harus Hentikan Penebangan Kayu Ilegal (Ministry of Forestry has to Stop Illegal Logging)http://www.kompas.com/kompas-cetak/9908/25/IPTEK/menh08.htm

Kompas (25/8/99b) Kawasan Taman Nasional Rusak Parah (National Park Area Severely Disturbed)http://www.kompas.com/kompas-cetak/9908/25/IPTEK/kawa08.htm

Kornai, J (1979) 'Appraisal of project appraisal', in MJ Boskin (ed) *Economics and Human Welfare: Essays in Honour of Tibor Scitovsky*. Academic Press, New York, pp75–99

Kottak, CP (1991) 'When people don't come first: some sociological lessons from completed projects', in MM Cernea (ed) *Putting People First: Sociological Variables in Rural Development*. Second edition. The World Bank, Washington, DC, pp431–464

Kowald, M and Williams, R (1997) 'Integrating natural and cultural heritage in Queensland', in J Dargavel (ed) *Australia's Ever-changing Forests III: Proceedings of the Third National Conference on Australian Forest History*. Centre for Resource and Environmental Studies, The Australian National University, Canberra, pp327–338

Krishna, A, Uphoff, N and Esman, MJ (1997) *Reasons for Hope: Instructive Experiences in Rural Development*. Kumarian Press, West Hartford, CT

Kuhn, TS (1970) *The Structure of Scientific Revolutions*. Second edition, enlarged. The University of Chicago Press, Chicago

Kukathas, C and Pettit, P (1990) *Rawls: A Theory of Justice and its Critics*. Polity Press, Cambridge

Lal, R, Kothari, A, Pande, P and Singh, S (eds) (1994) *Directory of National Parks and Sanctuaries in Karnataka: Management Status and Profiles*. Centre for Public Policy, Planning and Environmental Studies, Indian Institute of Public Administration, New Delhi

Leach, M, Mearns, R and Scoones, I (eds) (1997) Community-based Sustainable Development: Consensus or Conflict? *IDS Bulletin*, 28(4)

Leader-Williams, N, Harrison, J and Green, MJB (1990) 'Designing protected areas to protect natural resources', *Science Progress*, 74: 189–204

Lederach, JP (1996) 'The Mediator's Cultural Assumptions', *MCS Conciliation Quarterly*

Lele, SM (1991) 'Sustainable development: a critical review', *World Development*, 19(6): 607–621

Lennon, J (1999) 'Artists of south-east Queensland forests', in J Dargavel and B Libbis (eds) *Australia's Ever-changing Forests IV: Proceedings of the Fourth National Conference on Australian Forest History*. Centre for Resource and Environmental Studies, The Australian National University, Canberra, pp355–371

Leopold, A (1970) *A Sand County Almanac: With Essays on Conservation from Round River*. Sierra Club, Ballantine

Lincoln, YS (1990) 'The making of a constructivist: a remembrance of transformations past', in EG Guba (ed) *The Paradigm Dialog*. Sage Publications, London, pp67–87

Lincoln, YS and Guba, EG (1985) *Naturalistic Inquiry*. Sage Publications, London

Lincoln, YS and Guba, EG (1986) 'But is it rigorous? Trustworthiness and authenticity in naturalistic evaluation', in D Williams (ed) *Naturalistic Evaluation*. Jossey-Bass, San Francisco, pp73–84

Little, PD (1994) 'The link between local participation and improved conservation: a review of issues and experiences', in D Western, RM Wright and SC Strum (eds) (1994) *Natural Connections: Perspectives in Community-based Conservation*. Island Press, Washington, DC, pp347–372

Long, N and Long, A (eds) (1992) *Battlefields of Knowledge: the Interlocking of Theory and Practice in Social Research and Development*, Routledge, London

Lowrie, AE (1897) *Progress Report of Forest Administration in Coorg 1895–96*. Forest Department (Coorg), Bangalore

Lucas, PHC (1992) *Protected Landscapes. A Guide for Policy-makers and Planners*. Chapman and Hall, London

Lutz, E and Caldecott, J (eds) (1996) *Decentralization and Biodiversity Conservation*. The World Bank, Washington, DC

Lutz, MA and Lux, K (1988) *Humanistic Economics: The New Challenges*. The Bootstrap Press, New York

MacCallum, R and Sekhran, N (1997) *Race for the Rainforest: Evaluating Lessons from an Integrated Conservation and Development 'Experiment' in New Ireland, Papua New Guinea*. Department of Environment and Conservation, UNDP, GEF, UNOPS-PNG/93/G31

Mahanty, S, Russell, D and Bhatt, S (1999) What's at Stake? Overview paper on Stakeholder Organisations in the Biodiversity Conservation Network. Unpublished report to the Biodiversity Conservation Network, Washington DC

Maisin Integrated Conservation and Development Association, and Conservation Melanesia (1997) Landownership and community participation: the Maisin experience. Paper presented at the Integrated Conservation and Development Conference, Mutupore Island, University of Papua New Guinea, 1–5 September

Margolis, H (1982) *Selfishness, Altruism and Rationality: A Theory of Social Science*. Cambridge University Press, Cambridge

Marshall, A (1910) *Principles of Economics*. Sixth edition. Macmillan, London

Marshall, C (1990) 'Goodness criteria: are they objective or judgement calls?', in EG Guba (ed) *The Paradigm Dialog*. Sage Publications, London, pp188–197

Martinez-Alier, J (with Klaus Schlupmann) (1987) *Ecological Economics*. Basil Blackwell, Oxford

Mathien, T (1988) 'Network analysis and methodological individualism', *Philosophy of the Social Sciences*, 18: 1–20

Matur, HM (1995) 'The role of social actors in promoting participatory development at the local level: a view from India', in H Schneider and MH Libercer (eds) *Participatory Development: From Advocacy to Action*. Organisation for Economic Co-operation and Development, Paris, pp153–170

Maturana, HR, Varela, FJ (1992) *The Tree of Knowledge: The Biological Roots of Human Understanding*. Revised Edition. Shambhala, Boston

Maxwell, S (1990) 'Attitudes to income-earning opportunities: report of a ranking exercise in Ethiopia', in RRA Notes, Number 8. International Institute for Environment and Development, London, pp19–23

McAllister, D (1980) *Evaluation in Environmental Planning*. MIT Press, Cambridge, MA

McCallum, R and Sekhran, N (1997) *Race for the Rainforest: Evaluating Lessons from an Integrated Conservation and Development 'Experiment' in New Ireland, Papua New Guinea*. PNG Biodiversity Conservation and Resource Management Programme, Department of Environment and Conservation – UNDP – GEF, Port Moresby

McCloskey, D (1985) *The Rhetoric of Economics*. University of Wisconsin Press, Madison

McIlwaine, C (1998) 'Contesting civil society: reflections from El Salvador', *Third World Quarterly*, 9(4)

McKibben, B (1995) *Hope, Human and Wild: true stories of living lightly on the earth*. Little, Brown, and Co., Boston, Massachusetts

McKinnon, K and Artha, S (1982) National Conservation Plan for Indonesia, Vol. 1. Introduction, Evaluation, Methods and Overview of National Natural Richness. Report No. Fo/INS/78/GOI(34) FAO, Bogor

McNeely, JA, Miller, KR, Reid, WV, Mittermeier, RA and Werner, TB (1990) *Conserving the World's Biological Diversity*. IUCN, Gland; WRI, CI, and The World Bank, Washington, DC

McNeely, JA and Weatherly, WP (1996) *Investing in Biodiversity Conservation*. IUCN, Gland

Medawar, P (1974) 'Hypothesis and imagination', in PA Schilpp (ed) *The Philosophy of Karl Popper*. Book 1. The Open Court Publishing Co, La Salle, Illinois, pp274–291

Media Indonesia (1999a) Dari Yang Dicabut Hingga Alih Fungsi. http://www.mediaindo.co.id/publik/1999/09/09/sec27.html

Media Indonesia (1999b) Kegiatan Separatis Semakin Meningkat (Separatism Movement Increasing) http://www.mediaindo.co.id/publik/ 1999/07/20/polo1.html

Metcalf, SC (1995) 'Communities, parks, and regional planning: a co-management strategy based on the Zimbabwe experience', in RE Saunier and A Meganck (eds) *Conservation of Biodiversity and the New Regional Planning*. IUCN, Gland

Meyer, O (1993) 'Functional groups of micro-organisms', in ED Schulze and HA Mooney (eds) *Biodiversity and Ecosystem Function*. Springer-Verlag, Berlin

Midmore, P (1996) 'Towards a postmodern agricultural economics', *Journal of Agricultural Economics*, 47(1): 1–17

Miller, K, McNeely, JA, Salim, E and Miranda, M (1997) *Decentralization and the Capacity to Manage Biodiversity*. World Resources Institute, Washington, DC

Miller, KR (1996) *Balancing the Scales: Guidelines for Increasing Biodiversity's Chances through Bioregional Management*. World Resources Institute, Washington, DC

Ministry of Forestry (1997) *Country Brief: Indonesian Forestry Action Programme*. Ministry of Forestry, Jakarta

Ministry of National Development Planning (1993) *Biodiversity Action Plan for Indonesia*. Ministry of National Development Planning/National Development Planning Agency, Jakarta

Mink, SD (1993) *Poverty, Population, and the Environment*. World Bank Discussion Papers No. 189. The World Bank, Washington

Mitchell, RC and Carson, RT (1989) *Using Surveys to Value Public Goods: The Contingent Valuation Method*. Resource for the Future, Washington, DC

Moberg, F and Folke, C (1999) 'Ecological goods and services of coral reef ecosystems', *Ecological Economics*, 29(2): 215–233

Moore, C (1996) *The Mediation Process: Practical Strategies for Resolving Conflict*. Jossey-Bass, San Francisco

Moote, MA and McClaran, MP (1997) 'Implications of participatory democracy for public land planning', *Journal of Range Management*, 50(5): 473–480

Munasinghe, M and Mc Neely, J (eds) (1994) *Protected Area Economics and Policy: Linking Conservation and Sustainable Development*. World Bank, Washington, DC; IUCN, Gland

Murphree, MW (1994) 'The role of institutions in community-based conservation' in D Western, RM Wright and SC Strum, (eds) *Natural Connections: Perspectives in Community-based Conservation*. Island Press, Washington, DC, pp403–427

Myers, N (1980) *Conversion of Tropical Moist Forests*. National Academy of Sciences, Washington, DC

Myers, N (1993) 'Biodiversity and the precautionary principle', *Ambio*, 23(2–3): 74–79

Myrdal, G (1957) *Economic Theory and Underdeveloped Regions*. Duckworth, London

Naess, A (1989) *Ecology, Community and Lifestyle: Outline of an Ecosophy*. (Translated and edited by D Rothenberg) Cambridge University Press, Cambridge

Narayan, D (1996) 'The contribution of people's participation: evidence from 121 rural water supply projects', in J Rietbergen-McCracken (ed) *Participation in*

Practice: The Experience of the World Bank and Other Stakeholders. World Bank Discussion Paper No. 333. The World Bank, Washington, DC

Narokobi, B (1981) 'Land in the Vanuatu Constitution', in P Larmour, R Crocombe and A Taungenga (eds) *Land, People and Government: Public Lands Policy in the South Pacific*. The University of the South Pacific, Suva, pp149–156

Ndelu, T (1998) 'Conflict management and peace building through community development', *Community Development Journal*, 33(2): pp109–116

Nelson, JA (1996) *Feminism, Objectivity and Economics*. Routledge, London

Newmark, WD, Leonard, NL, Sariko, HI and Gamassa, DM (1993) 'Conservation attitudes of local people living adjacent to five protected areas in Tanzania', *Biological Conservation*, 63: 177–183

Nilsson, C and Götmark, F (1992) 'Protected areas in Sweden: is natural variety adequately represented?', *Conservation Biology*, 6(2): 232–242

Nisbett, R and Lee, R (1980) *Human Inference: Strategies and Shortcomings of Social Judgment*. Prentice-Hall, Englewood Cliffs, NJ

Norgaard, RB (1984) 'Coevolutionary development potential', *Land Economics*, 60(2): 160–173

Norgaard, RB (1985) 'Environmental economics: an evolutionary critique and a plea for pluralism', *Journal of Environmental Economics and Management*, 12: 382–394

Norgaard, RB (1988) 'The rise of the global exchange economy and the loss of biological diversity', in EO Wilson (ed) *Biodiversity*. National Academy Press, Washington, DC, pp206–211

Norgaard, RB (1989) 'The case for methodological pluralism', *Ecological Economics*, 1: 37–57

Norgaard, RB (1995) 'Metaphors we might survive by', *Ecological Economics*, 15(2): 129–131

Norse, EA (ed) (1993) *Global Marine Biodiversity: A Strategy for Building Conservation into Decision Making*. Island Press, Washington, DC

Norse, EA, Rosenbaum, KL, Wilcove, DS, Wilcox, BA, Romme, WH, Johnston, DW and Stout, ML (1986) *Conserving Biological Diversity in Our National Forests*. The Wilderness Society, Washington, DC

North, DC (1990) *Institutions, Institutional Change and Economic Performance*. Cambridge University Press, Cambridge

Norton, BG (1987) *Why Preserve Natural Variety?* Princeton University Press, Princeton

Norton, GB and Ulanowicz, RE (1992) 'Scale and biodiversity policy: a hierarchical approach', *Ambio*, 21(3): 244–249

Noss, RF and Harris, LD (1986) 'Nodes, networks, and MUMs: preserving diversity at all scales', *Environmental Management*, 10(3): 299–309

O'Hara, S (1996), 'Discursive ethics in ecosystems valuation and environmental policy', *Ecological Economics*, 16: 95–107

O'Hara, S (forthcoming) 'Economics, ecology, and quality of life: who evaluates?', *Feminist Economics*

O'Hara, S and Vazquez, J (1998) 'Economic diversity and regional sustainability: the case of the Lake George region in Upstate New York', paper presented at the *Fifth Biennial Meeting of the International Society for Ecological Economics*. Santiago, Chile, 15–19 November

O'Hara, S, Shandas, V and Vazquez, J (forthcoming) 'Communicating sustainable development options: who evaluates the trade-offs?', in I Ring, B Klauer, F

Waetzold and B Mansson (eds) *Regional Sustainability: Applied Ecological Economics Bridging the Gap between Natural and Social Sciences*. Physica Verlag, Heidelberg

O'Reilly, S (1988) *The Contribution of Community Development to Peace-Building: World Vision's Area Development Programmes*. Final Report. World Vision, London

Oakley, P (1991) 'The concept of participation in development', *Landscape and Urban Planning*, 20: 115–122

OECD (1998) *Conflict, Peace and Development Co-operation on the Threshold of the 21st Century*. Development Cooperation Guidelines Series. Organisation for Economic Development and Cooperation, Paris

Olembo, RJ (1994) 'Can land use planning contribute to sustainability?', in LO Fresco, L Stroosnijder, J Bouma and H van Keulen (eds) *The Future of the Land: Mobilising and Integrating Knowledge for Land Use Options*. John Wiley & Sons, Chichester, pp369–376

Opschoor, H (1994) *Sustainable Development and Paradigms in Economics*. Research Memorandum 1994–30, Faculteit der Economische Wetenschappen en Econometrie, Vrije Universiteit, Amesterdam

Page, T (1977) *Conservation and Economic Efficiency: An Approach to Materials Policy*. The Johns Hopkins University Press, Baltimore

Page, T (1991) 'Sustainability and the problem of valuation', in R Costanza (ed) *Ecological Economics: The Science and Management of Sustainability*. Columbia University Press, New York, pp58–72

Paine, JR (1997) *Status, Trends, and Future Scenarios for Forest Conservation Including Protected Areas in the Asia-Pacific Area*. Asia-Pacific Forest Sector Outlook Study, Working Paper APFSOS/WP/4. FAO, Rome

Palo, M and Mery, G (eds) (1996) *Sustainable Forestry Challenges for Developing Countries*. Kluwer Academic Publications, Dordrecht

Panel of the Board on Science and Technology for International Development (1992) *Conserving Biodiversity: A Research Agenda for Development Agencies*. National Academy Press, Washington

Pannel, S (1997) 'Managing the discourse of resource management: the case of sasi from Southeast Maluku, Indonesia', *Oceania*, 67(4): 289–308

Parry, D (1992) 'Attitudes of rural communities to animal wildlife and its utilization in the Chobe enclave and Matabe Depression, Botswana', *Environmental Conservation*, 19(3): 245–252

Pasek, J (1992) 'Obligations to future generations: a philosophical note', *World Development*, 20(4): 513–521

Paul, S (1987) 'Poverty alleviation and participation: the case for government-grassroots agency collaboration', *Economic and Political Weekly*, 14(January): 100–106

Pearce, DW (1988) 'Economics, equity and sustainable development', *Futures*, 20(6): 598–605

Pearce, DW (1990) *An Economic Approach to Saving the Tropical Forests*. LEEC Paper 90–06. London Environmental Economics Centre, London

Pearce, DW and Moran, D (1994) *The Economic Value of Biodiversity*. Earthscan, London; IUCN, Gland

Pearce, DW, Markandya, A and Barbier, EB (1989) *Blueprint for a Green Economy*. Earthscan, London

Perrings, C, Folke, C and Mäler, KG (1992) 'The ecology and economics of biodiversity loss: the research agenda', *Ambio*, 21(3): 201–211

Perrings, C, Maler, KG, Folke, C, Holling, CS and Jansson, BO (eds) (1995) *Biodiversity Loss: Economic and Ecological Issues.* Cambridge University Press, Cambridge

Peters, RH (1991) *A Critique for Ecology.* Cambridge University Press, Cambridge

Phelps, ES (1985) *Political Economy.* W.W. Norton, New York

Pimentel, D, Stachow, U and Tackacs, DA (1992) 'Conserving biological diversity in agricultural/forestry systems', *BioScience*, 42, May: 354–362

Pinedo-Vasquez, M, Zarin, D and Jipp, P (1992) 'Economic returns from forest conversion in the Peruvian Amazon', *Ecological Economics*, 6: 163–173

Pingali, PL, Hossain, M and Gerpacio, RV (1997) *Asian Rice Bowl. The Returning Crisis?* CAB International, Oxon

Pohl, G and Mihaljek, D (1992) 'Project evaluation and uncertainty in practice: a statistical analysis of rate-of-return divergences of 1,065 World Bank projects', *The World Bank Economic Review*, 6(2): 255–277

Polanyi, M (1969) *Personal Knowledge: Towards a Post Critical Philosophy.* Routledge, London

Ponting, C (1991) *A Green History of the World.* Sinclair Stevenson, London

Popper, K (1959) *The Logic of Scientific Discovery.* Basic Books, New York

Popper, K (1974) 'Reply to Medawar on hypothesis and imagination', in PA Schilpp (ed) *The Philosophy of Karl Popper.* Book 1. The Open Court Publishing Co, La Salle, Illinois, pp1030–1037

Porter, D, Allen, B and Thompson, G (1991) *Development in Practice: Paved with Good Intentions.* Routledge, London

Porter, D and Onyach-Olaa, M (1999) 'Inclusive planning and allocation of rural services', *Development in Practice*, 9(1/2): 56–67

Pratt, AC (1995) 'Putting critical realism at work: the practical implications for geographical research', *Progress in Human Geography*, 19(1): 61–74

Press, D, Doak, DF and Steinberg, P (1996) 'The role of local government in conservation of rare species', *Conservation Biology*, 10(6): 1538–1548

Pressey, RL and Tully, SL (1994) 'The cost of ad hoc reservation: a case study of western New South Wales', *Australian Journal of Ecology*, 19: 375–384

Pretty, J (1995) *Regenerating Agriculture: Policies and Practice for Sustainability and Self-Reliance.* Earthscan, London

Pretty, JN (1994) 'Alternative systems of inquiry for a sustainable agriculture', *IDS Bulletin*, 25(2): 37–48

Proust, J (1894) *Progress Report of Forest Administration in Coorg 1892–93.* Forest Department (Coorg), Bangalore

Przeworski, A (1985) 'Marxism and rational choice', *Politics and Society*, 14(4): 379–409

Putman, R (1993) *Making Democracy Work: Civic Traditions in Modern Italy.* Princeton University Press, Princeton, NJ

Qualitative Solutions and Research (1999) *NUD*IST Vivo (Nvivo): Software for Data Analysis.* QSR Pty Ltd Melbourne

Ramsay, J (1999) 'It soothes my soul: Assessing aesthetic values of forests', in J Dargavel and B Libbis (eds) *Australia's Ever-changing Forests IV: Proceedings of the Fourth National Conference on Australian Forest History.* Centre for Resource and Environmental Studies, The Australian National University, Canberra, pp342–355

Ramstad, Y (1989) '"Reasonable value" versus "instrumental value": competing paradigms in institutional economics', *Journal of Economic Issues*, XXIII(3): 761–777

Randall, A (1984) 'Benefit cost analysis as an information system', in GL Peterson and A Randall (eds) *Valuation of Wildland Resource Benefits*. Westview Press, Boulder, pp65–75

Randall, A (1986) 'Human preferences, economics and the preservation of species', in BG Norton (ed) *The Preservation of Species: The Value of Biological Diversity*. Princeton University Press, Princeton, pp79–109

Randall, A (1987) *Resource Economics*. Second edition. John Wiley & Son, New York

Randall, A (1988) 'What mainstream economists have to say about the value of biodiversity', in EO Wilson (ed) *Biodiversity*. National Academy Press, Washington, DC, pp217–230

Randall, A (1991) 'The value of biodiversity', *Ambio*, 20(2): 64–68

Randall, A and Farmer, MC (1995) 'Benefits, costs, and the safe minimum standard of conservation', in DW Bromley (ed) *Handbook of Environmental Economics*. Blackwell, Oxford, pp26–44

Randall, A and Peterson, GL (1984) 'The valuation of wildland benefits: an overview', in GL Peterson and A Randall (eds) *Valuation of Wildland Resource Benefits*. Westview Press, Boulder, pp1–52

Rangarajan, M (1996) *Fencing the Forest: Conservation and Ecological Change in India's Central Provinces 1860–1914*. Oxford University Press, New Delhi

Rawls, J (1972) *A Theory of Justice*. Oxford University Press, Oxford

Raymond, K (1996) 'The long-term future of the Great Barrier Reef', *Futures*, 28(10): 947–970

Reardon, T and Vosti, SA (1995) 'Links between rural poverty and the environment in developing countries: asset categories and investment poverty', *World Development*, 23(9): 1495–1506

Redclift, M (1987) *Sustainable Development: Exploring the Contradictions*. Methuen, London

Redclift, M (1988) 'Sustainable development and the market', *Future*, 20(6): 635–650

Redclift, MR (1992) 'A framework for improving environmental management: beyond the market mechanism', *World Development*, 20(2): 255–259

Reid, WV (1992) 'How many species will there be?', in TC Whitmore and JA Sayer (eds) *Tropical Deforestation and Species Extinction*. Chapman & Hall, London, pp55–73

Reid, WV and Miller, KR (1989) *Keeping Options Alive: The Scientific Basis for Conserving Biodiversity*. WRI, Washington

Renn, O, Webler, T and Wiedemann, P (1995) *Fairness and Competence in Citizen Participation: Evaluating Models for Environmental Discourse*. Kluwer, Dordrecht, Netherlands

Repetto, R (ed) (1988) *The Forest for the Trees? Government Policies and the Misuse of Forest Resources*. World Resource Institute, Washington, DC

Resolve Inc (1994) *The Role of Consensus-building in Community Forestry*. Resolve, Washington DC, FAO, Rome

Resource Assessment Commission (1992) *Forest and Timber Inquiry, Final Report*. 2 Vols. Australian Government Publishing Service, Canberra

Reti, I (1993) 'South Pacific Biodiversity Conservation Programme: its concept and scope'. Working Paper No. 7, South Pacific Conference on Nature Conservation And Protected Areas, Tonga, 4–8 October

Rice, L (1876) *Mysore and Coorg: a Gazetteer Compiled for the Government of India. Volume II – Mysore by District*. Mysore Government Press, Bangalore

Richards, M, Kanel, K, Maharajan, M and Davies, J (1999) *Towards Participatory Economic Analysis by Forest Groups in Nepal*. Department for International Development, London

Robbins, L (1952) *An Essay on the Nature and Significance of Economic Science*. Second edition. Macmillan, London

Robin, L (1998) *Defending the Little Desert: The Rise of Ecological Consciousness in Australia*. Melbourne University Press, Melbourne

Rock, MT (1996) 'The stork, the plow, rural social structure and tropical deforestation in poor countries?', *Ecological Economics*, 18(2): 113–131

Rodman, MC (1987) *Masters of Tradition: Consequences of Customary Land Tenure in Longana, Vanuatu*. University of British Columbia, Vancouver

Rondinelli, DA, McCullough, JS and Johnson, RW (1989) 'Analysing decentralization policies in developing countries: a political-economy framework', *Development and Change*, 20: 57–87

Rowe, R, Sharma, N and Browder, J (1992) 'Deforestation: problems, causes, and concerns', in NP Sharma (ed) *Managing the World's Forests: Looking for Balance Between Conservation and Development*. Kendall/Hunt Publishing Co, Dubuque, Iowa, pp33–45

RRA Notes (1991) Proceedings of the Local Level Adaptive Planning Workshop, London. RRA Notes No 11. London: International Institute for Environment and Development

Runge, CF (1984) 'Strategic interdependence in models of property rights', *American Journal of Agricultural Economics*, 66(5): 807–813

Rydin, Y (1995) 'Sustainable development and the role of land use planning', *Area*, 27 (4): 369–377

Sachs, I (1992) 'Transition strategies for the 21st century', *Nature and Resources*, 28(1): 4–17

Sagoff, M (1988) *The Economy of the Earth*. Cambridge University Press, Cambridge

Sagoff, M (1998) 'Aggregation and deliberation in valuing environmental public goods: a look beyond contingent pricing', *Ecological Economics* 24 (2/3): 213–230

Sahu, NC and Nayak, B (1994) 'Niche diversification in environmental/ecological economics', *Ecological Economics*, 11(1): 9–19

Sainsbury, K, Haward, M, Kriwoken, L, Tsamenyi, M and Ward, T (1997) *Multiple Use Management in the Australian Marine Environment: Principles, definitions and elements*. Oceans Policy Issues Paper 1. Department of the Environment, Canberra

Samoff, J (1990) 'Decentralization: the politics of intervensionism', *Development and Change*, 21: 513–530

Samuelson, PA (1950) 'Evaluation of real national income', *Oxford Economic Papers*, 2(1): 1–29

Sanjayan, MA, Shen, S and Jansen, M (1997) *Experiences with Integrated-Conservation Development Projects in Asia*. World Bank Technical Paper No 388. World Bank, Washington, DC

Sayer, JA and Wegge, P (1992) 'Biological conservation issues in forest management', in IUCN (1992) *Conserving Biological Diversity in Managed Tropical Forests*. International Union for the Conservation of Nature and Natural Resources, Gland, pp1–4

Sayer, JA, Harcourt, CS and Collins, NM (eds) (1992) *The Conservation Atlas of Tropical Forests: Africa*. Macmillan Press, London, in collaboration with IUCN, Gland

Schaeffer, P (1989) *Defending the Wilderness: the Adirondack Writings of Paul Schaefer*. Syracuse University Press, Syracuse, New York

Schneider, P (1997) *The Adirondacks: A History of America's First Wilderness*. Henry Hold and Co., Inc, New York, NY

Schwandt, TR (1990) 'Path to inquiry in the social disciplines: scientific, constructivist, and critical theory methodologies', in EG Guba (ed) *The Paradigm Dialog*. Sage Publications, London, pp258–276

Scoones, I, Thompson, J (1994) *Beyond Farmer First*. Intermediate Technology Publications, London

Self, P (1975) *Econocrats and the Policy Process: the Politics and Philosophy of Cost–Benefit Analysis*. Macmillan, London

Selman, P (1996) *Local Sustainability: Managing and Planning Ecologically Sound Places*. St. Martin's Press, New York, NY

Sen, A (1987) *On Ethics and Economics*. Basil Blackwell, Oxford

SESRTCIC (1999) Basic Indicators for Islamic Countries – Total Arable Land Data. Statistical, Economic and Social Research and Training Centre for Islamic Countries. http://www.sesrtcic.org/subfiles/subrqara.htm

Sharma, NP, Rowe, R, Openshaw, K and Jacobson, M (1992) 'World forests in perspective', in NP Sharma (ed) *Managing the World's Forests: Looking for Balance Between Conservation and Development*. Kendall/Hunt Publishing Co, Dubuque, Iowa, pp17–31

Sharma, UR (1990) 'An overview of park–people interactions in Royal Chitwan National Park, Nepal', *Landscape and Urban Planning*, 19: 133–44

Shepherd, G (1991) 'The communal management of forests in the semi-arid and sub-humid regions of Africa: past practice and prospects for the future', *Development Policy Review*, 9: 151–176

Simon, HA (1957) *Models of Man: Social and Rational*. Wiley, New York

Simon, HA (1982) *Models of Bounded Rationality*. Two volumes. MIT Press, Cambridge, Mass

Simon, HA (1986) 'Rationality in psychology and economics', *Journal of Business*, 59(4): S209–S224

Simpson, G (1997) '"Get what you can while you can": the landowner–government relationship in West New Britain', in C Filer (ed) *The Political Economy of Forest Management in Papua New Guinea*. The National Research Institute, Port Moresby; IIED, London, pp17–34

Sjöstrand, SE (1992) 'On the rational behind "irrational" institutions', *Journal of Economic Issues*, XXVI(4): 1007–1040

Smith, JK (1990) 'Alternative research paradigms and the problem of criteria', in EG Guba (ed) *The Paradigm Dialog*. Sage Publications, London, pp167–187

Smith, PGR and Theberge, JB (1986) 'A review of criteria for evaluating natural areas', *Environmental Management*, 10(6): 715–734

Söderbaum, P (1987) 'Environmental management: a non-traditional approach', *Journal of Economic Issues*, XXI(1): 139–165

Söderbaum, P (1992) 'Neoclassical and institutional approaches to development and the environment', *Ecological Economics*, 5: 127–144

Söderbaum, P (1993) 'Values, markets, and environmental policy: an actor-network approach', *Journal of Economic Issues*, XXVII(2): 387–408

Söderbaum, P (1994) 'Reformulating the valuation issue: positional analysis as an alternative approach', paper presented at the 3rd Biennial Meeting of the International Society for Ecological Economics, October 24–28, 1994, San José, Costa Rica

Solbrig, OT (ed) (1991) *From Genes to Ecosystems: A Research Agenda for Biodiversity.* IUBS, SCOPE, UNESCO, Cambridge, Mass

Soulé, ME (1991) 'Conservation: tactics for a constant crisis', *Science,* 253: 744–750

Squire, L (1988) 'Project evaluation in theory and practice', in H Chenery and TN Srinivasan (eds) *Handbook of Development Economics, Volume 2.* Elsevier North Holland, Amsterdam, pp1093–1137

State Ministry of Environment (1993) *National Strategy on Management of Biological Diversity.* State Ministry of Environment, Jakarta

Stevens, S (ed) (1997) *Conservation through Cultural Survival: Indigenous People and Protected Areas.* Island Press, Washington, DC

Stewart, F (1975) 'A note in social cost–benefit analysis and class conflict in LDCs', *World Development,* 3(1): 31–39

Stewen, M (1998) 'The interdependence of allocation, distribution, scale and stability – A comment on Herman E Daly's vision of an economics that is efficient, just and sustainable', *Ecological Economics,* 27(2): 119–130

Stiefel, M and Wolfe, M (1994) *A Voice for the Excluded – Popular Participation in Development: Utopia or Necessity?* Zed Books, London

Stonich, SC (1989) 'The dynamics of social processes and environmental destruction: a central American case study', *Population and Development Review,* 15(2): 269–295

Stycos, JM and Duarte, I (1994) *Parks, Population and Resettlement in the Dominican Republic.* Working Paper No. 16. EPAT/MUCIA, Natural Resources Policy and Training Project, University of Wisconsin, Madison

Suara Pembaruan Daily (1999) Otonomi Daerah Tak bisa Ditunda Lagi (No Delay on Regional Autonomy) http://www.suarapembaruan.com/news/1999/06/220699/headline/h108/h108.html

Suppe, F (ed) (1974) *The Structure of Scientific Theories.* University of Illinois Press, Urbana

Swaney, JA (1987a) 'Building instrumental environmental control institutions', *Journal of Economic Issues,* XXI(1): 295–308

Swaney, JA (1987b) 'Elements of a neoinstitutional environmental economics', *Journal of Economic Issues,* XXI(4): 1739–1779

Swanson, T (1997) *Global Action for Biodiversity.* IUCN/WWF/Earthscan, London

Swanson, TM (1994) *The International Regulation of Extinction.* Macmillan, London

Tacconi, L (1994) *Review of the Forest Revenue System of Vanuatu.* Vanuatu Forest Conservation Research Reports No. 8, Department of Economics and Management, University College, The University of New South Wales, Canberra

Tacconi, L (1995) The Process of Forest Conservation in Vanuatu: A Study in Ecological Economics. PhD dissertation, University College, The University of New South Wales, Canberra

Tacconi, L (1997) 'An ecological economic approach to forest and biodiversity conservation in Vanuatu', *World Development,* 25(12): 1995–2008

Tacconi, L and Bennett, J (1995a) 'Economic implications of intergenerational equity for biodiversity conservation', *Ecological Economics,* 12(3): 209–23

Tacconi, L and Bennett, J (1995b) 'Biodiversity conservation: the process of economic assessment and establishment of a protected area in Vanuatu', *Development and Change,* 26(1): 89–110

Tacconi, L and Bennett, J (1997) *Protected Area Assessment and Establishment in Vanuatu: A Socioeconomic Approach.* Australian Center for International Agricultural Research, Canberra

Tacconi, L and Tisdell, C (1992) 'Rural development projects in LDCs: appraisal, participation and sustainability', *Public Administration and Development*, 12(3): 267–278

Taylor, CR (1995) 'The right of participation in development projects', in K Ginther, E Denters and PJIM de Wart (eds) *Sustainable Development and Good Governance*. Martinus Nijhoff Publishers, Dordrecht, pp205–229

Terrie, PG (1994) *Forever Wild: A Cultural History of Wilderness in the Adirondacks*. Syracuse University Press, Syracuse, New York

Terrie, PG (1997) *Contested Terrain: A New History of Nature and People in the Adirondacks*. The Adirondack Museum/Syracuse University Press, Syracuse, New York

Thapa, GP and Weber, KE (1990) 'Actors and factors of deforestation in Tropical Asia', *Environmental Conservation*, 17(1): 19–27

Thompson, H (1993) 'Malaysian forestry policy in Borneo', *Journal of Contemporary Asia*, 23(4): 503–514

Thorne-Miller, B and Catena, J (1991) *The Living Ocean: Understanding and Protecting Marine Biodiversity*. Islands Press, Washington, DC

Thrupp, LA (1998) *Agricultural Biodiversity and Food Security: Predicaments, Policies and Practices*. World Resources Institute, Washington, DC

Thrupp, LA, Cabarle, B and Zazueta, A (1994) 'Participatory methods in planning & political processes: linking the grassroots & policies for sustainable development', *Agriculture and Human Values*, 11(2/3): 77–84

Thurston, E and Rangachari, K (1909, reprinted 1987) *Castes and Tribes of Southern India. Volume IV: K to M*. Asian Educational Services, New Delhi

Tietenberg, T (1988) *Environmental and Natural Resource Economics*. Second Edition. Scott, Foresman and Company, Glenview

Tiffen, M, Mortimore, MJ and Gichuki, F (1994) *More People Less Erosion: Environmental Recovery in Kenya*. John Wiley, New York

Tireman, H (1914) *Working Plan for the Eastern Forests of Coorg*. Forest Department (Coorg), Bangalore

Tisdell, CA (1983) 'Dissent from Value, Preference and Choice Theory in Economics', *International Journal of Social Economics*, 10(2): 32–43

Tisdell, CA (1990) *Natural Resources, Growth, and Development: Economics, Ecology, and Resource-Scarcity*. Praeger, New York

Tool, MR (1986) *Essays in Social Value Theory: A Neoinstitutionalist Contribution*. M.E. Sharpe, Armonk

UKFSP, ODI (1998) *Manual on Alternative Conflict Management in Community-based Natural Resource Projects*. Overseas Development Institute, London

Ulrich, P (1989), 'Lassen sich Oekonomie und Oekologie wirtschaftsethisch versoehnen?', in E Seifert and R Pfriem (eds) *Wirtschaftsethik und ökologische Wirtschaftsforschung*. Paul Haupt Verlag, Bern, Stuttgart, pp165–72

UNEP (1994) *Convention on Biological Diversity*. United Nations Environment Programme, Geneva

UNEP (United Nations Environment Programme) (1992) *Biodiversity Country Studies: Synthesis Report*. UNEP, Nairobi

UNEP (United Nations Environment Programme) (1993) *Guidelines for Country Studies on Biological Diversity*. UNEP, Nairobi

UNEP (United Nations Environment Programme) (1995) *Global Biodiversity Assessment*. Cambridge University Press, Cambridge

Uphoff, N (1986) *Local Institutional Development: An Analytical Sourcebook with Cases*. Kumarian Press, West Hartford

Uphoff, N (1998) 'Learning about and for participation: from theoretical and empirical studies to practical experience, and back to theory', *Canadian Journal of Development Studies*, XIX(3): 439–460

Uphoff, NT (1992) *Learning from Gal Oya: Possibilities for Participatory Development and Post-Newtonian Social Science*. Cornell University Press, Ithaca

Uphoff, NT, Wickramanasinghe, C and Wijayaratna, MLM (1990) '"Optimum" participation in irrigation management: issues and evidence from Sri Lanka', *Human Organization*, 49(1): 26–40

USAID (1997) *Strategic Agreement Objective: Annex 1. Amplified Description*, USAID, Washington DC. http://www.info.usaid.gov/countries/mg/sntzsoag.htm

Utting, P (1994) 'Social and political dimensions of environmental protection in Central America', *Development and Change*, 25(1): 231–259

van Helden, F (1997) Kampani bilong environment: community motivation for biodiversity conservation in the Bismarck-Ramu. Paper presented at the Integrated Conservation and Development Conference, Mutupore Island, University of Papua New Guinea, 1–5 September

van Lier, HN (1994) 'Land use planning in perspective of sustainability', in HN van Lier, CF Jaarsma, CR Jurgens and AJ de Buck (eds) *Sustainable Land Use Planning*. Elsevier, Amsterdam, pp1–11

van Trease, HN (1987) *The Politics of Land in Vanuatu*. The University of the South Pacific, Suva

Vanclay, JK (1993) 'Saving the tropical forests: needs and prognosis', *Ambio*, 22(4): 225–31

Vatn, A and Bromley, DW (1994) 'Choices without prices without apologies', *Journal of Environmental Economics and Management*, 26: 129–148

Verlome, HJH and Moussa, J (1999) *Addressing the Underlying Causes of Deforestation and Forest Degradation: Case Studies, Analysis and Policy Recommendations*. Biodiversity Action Network, Washington, DC

Wainwright, C and Wehrmeyer, W (1998) 'Success in integrating conservation and development? A study from Zambia', *World Development*, 26(6): 933–944

Walters, JF, Maragos, J, Siar, S and White, AT (1998) *Participatory Coastal Resource Assessment*. Silliman University, Cebu

Wardhana, D (1998) Nature Conservation and Neighbouring Communities: Resource Use and Management Options for Gunung Halimun National Park, Indonesia. Masters Thesis. Gatton College, School of Natural and Rural Systems Management The University of Queensland, Lawes

Warner, M (1997) 'Consensus participation: an example for protected areas planning', *Public Administration and Development*, 17: 413–432

Warner, M (1999) *Conflict Management and Consensus-Building in Community-based Natural Resource Projects: Context, Principles, Tools and Training*. Overseas Development Institute, London

Warner, M and Jones, P (1999) Assessing the Need to Manage Conflict in Community-Based Natural Resource Projects, *Natural Resources Perspective Paper*, 35, Overseas Development Institute, London

WCMC (1999) http://www.wmcm.org.uk/protected_areas/data/summstat_html

WCMC (World Conservation Monitoring Center) (1992) *Global Biodiversity: Status of the Earth's Living Resources*. Chapman and Hall, London

Weber, M (1968) *Economy and Society*. Bedminster, New York

Weizsäcker, CC (1971) 'Notes on endogenous change of tastes', *Journal of Economic Theory*, 3: 345–372

Wells, M (1992) 'Biodiversity conservation, affluence and poverty: mismatched costs and benefits and efforts to remedy them', *Ambio*, 21(3): 237–243

Wells, M and Brandon, K (1992) *People and Parks: Linking Protected Area Management with Local Communities*. The World Bank, Washington, DC

Wells, M, Guggenheim, S, Khan, A, Wardojo, W and Jepson, P (1998) *Investing in Biodiversity: A Review of Indonesia's Integrated Conservation and Development Projects*. The World Bank, East Asia Region, Washington, DC

Western, D and Wright, RM (1994) 'The background to community-based conservation', in D Western, RM Wright and SC Strum, (eds) *Natural Connections: Perspectives in Community-based Conservation*. Island Press, Washington, DC, pp1–10

Western, D, Wright, RM and Strum, SC (eds) (1994) *Natural Connections: Perspectives in Community-based Conservation*. Island Press, Washington, DC

Whitmore, TC and Sayer, JA (1992) *Tropical Deforestation and Species Extinction*. Chapman and Hall, London

Whyte, WF (ed) (1991) *Participatory Action Research*. Sage Publications, London

Wibowo, DH, Tisdell, C and Byron, N (1997) *Deforestation and Capital Accumulation: Lessons from Upper Kerinci Region, Indonesia*. Economics, Ecology, and The Environment. Working Paper No. 8. The University of Queensland, Brisbane

Wilson, EO (1988) 'The current state of biological diversity', in EO Wilson (ed) *Biodiversity*. National Academy Press, Washington, DC, pp3–18

Wilson, EO (1992a) *The Diversity of Life*. The Penguin Press, London

Wilson, GA (1992b) 'A survey on attitudes of landholders to native forest on farmland', *Journal of Environmental Management*, 34: 117–136

Wind, J (1990) *Buffer Zone Management for Indonesian National Parks: Inception Report*. World Bank National Park Development Project:DHV/RIN Consultation, Bogor

Winpenny, JT (1991) *Values for the Environment: A Guide to Economic Appraisal*. Overseas Development Institute, HMSO, London

Winter, SG (1986) 'Comments on Arrow, and on Lucas', *Journal of Business*, 59(4): S427–S434

Witte, J (1992) 'Deforestation in Zaire: logging and landless', *The Ecologist*, 22(2): 58–64

Wolf, FA (1981) *Taking the Quantum Leap*. Harper and Row, San Francisco

Wood, M (1997) 'The Makapa timber rights purchase: a case study in project failure in the post-Barnett era', in C Filer (ed) *The Political Economy of Forest Management in Papua New Guinea*. The National Research Institute, Port Moresby; IIED, London, pp84–108

Woodhill, J and Röling, N (1998) 'The second wing of the eagle: the human dimension in learning our way to more sustainable futures', in NG Röling and MAE Wagemakers (eds), *Facilitating Sustainable Agriculture: Participatory Learning, and Adaptive Management in Times of Environment Uncertainty*. Cambridge University Press, Cambridge, pp46–71

World Bank (1992) *World Development Report 1992*. World Bank, Washington, DC

World Bank (1996) *The World Bank Participation Sourcebook*. The World Bank, Washington, DC

World Bank (1996) *India Ecodevelopment Project. Project Document*. South Asia Department, Agriculture and Water Division, The World Bank, Washington DC

World Commission on Environment and Development) (1987) *Our Common Future*. Oxford University Press, Oxford (Brundtland Report)

World Wildlife Fund (US) (1997) *Lessons from the Field: a Review of World Wildlife Fund's Experience with Integrated Conservation and Development Projects*. WWF (US), Washington DC

WRI, IUCN, UNEP (1992) *Global Biodiversity Strategy: Guidelines for Action to Save, Study, and Use Earth's Wealth Sustainably and Equitably*. WRI, IUCN, UNEP, Washington

Wright Mills, C (1959) *The Sociological Imagination*. Oxford University Press, New York

WWF and DEC (1992) Review of the Management and Status of Protected Areas & Action Plan. World Wide Fund for Nature and Department of Environment and Conservation, Port Moresby. Unpublished report

Wynne, B (1992) 'Uncertainty and environmental learning: reconceiving science and policy in the preventive paradigm', *Global Environmental Change*, June: 111–127

Young, MD (1992) *Sustainable Investment and Resource Use: Equity, Environmental Integrity and Economic Efficiency*. UNESCO, Paris; and The Parthenon Publishing Group, Park Ridge

Zukav, G (1979) *The Dancing Wu-Li Masters*. Bantam, New York

Index

Page numbers in *italics* refer to figures, tables and boxes.